D0278556

THE DEMON
& the Lobster

THE
DEMON

& the Lobster

CHARLES KORTRIGHT
AND DIGBY JEPHSON,
REMARKABLE BOWLERS IN
THE GOLDEN AGE

ANTHONY MEREDITH

THE KINGSWOOD PRESS

The Kingswood Press
an imprint of William Heinemann Ltd
10 Upper Grosvenor Street, London W1X 9PA
LONDON   MELBOURNE
JOHANNESBURG   AUCKLAND

First published 1987

ISBN 0 434 98114 1

Typset by Hewer Text Composition Services, Edinburgh
Printed and bound in Great Britain by
Billing & Sons Ltd, Worcester

PARENTIBUS OPTIMIS

Contents

List of illustrations

*All drawings come from newspapers
and periodicals of the 1890s and 1900s.*

Acknowledgements

I am very grateful to Louise Hidalgo and Derek Wyatt of The Kingswood Press for much perceptive advice and friendly encouragement. Stephen Green has been most helpful at Lord's, while the hard-pressed staff at the Newspaper Library, Colindale, have cheerfully met my every request. Much pleasant research has been carried out at the British Library, the Surrey Records Office and the Brighton Public Reference Library and I am most grateful for all the help received there. I am also indebted in varying ways to the late Ronnie Aird, The Revd Chris Barber, Ralph Behrend, Dr Chris Brown, Jean Bullman, Mary Cannell, the late Mrs Enid Citovich, Judy Cowan, Justin Davies, Harry and Margery Dobson, Paul Drayton, Mary English, Elizabeth Fane, Catherine Haw, Frank Hudson, Grenville Jennings, F. R. Jephson, Michael Jephson, Barry Mann, The Revd S. E. Marsden, Dr Pat Nicholl, The Revd R. Orton, Ruth Pearce, Clive Porter, H. D. 'Hopper' Read, Allan Scott, Joan Slater and Alan Smith.

Consulted books are listed in a separate bibliography. Among many delightful volumes, David Kynaston's *Bobby Abel* and Eric Midwinter's *W. G. Grace* were particularly provoking. Charles Sale's

Korty, on which I collaborated for a while, contains all the Demon's statistics.

There remain some special thanks. My wife Heather has played both lobs and bouncers with the straightest of bats. Even at moments of greatest crisis in the creative process (e.g. when the cat got the goldfish) she has remained impressively calm. My brother Michael very kindly proffered many valuable criticisms of the manuscript. My mother likewise has been a great source of encouragement from start to finish, making any number of helpful observations. My father was a life-long cricket enthusiast. Visits with him to The Oval and Lord's laid the foundations of my own enthusiasm. Accordingly, as a small token of thanks, this book is dedicated to my parents.

Chatham House, Stowe   *Anthony Meredith*
March 1987

Fascination

Strange fascination of a wooden bat!
Weird magic hidden in a leathern ball!
Ye clutch the heart as bands of hardened steel
When baby summer calls us once again
To close-trimmed turf; we say we will not go,
  But yet we go.

Strange fascination of those all brave hours
Through which we strive to hold the twin-bailed sticks
Intact! Strange fascination when we hurl
The ball with grim exactitude until
We drop. Some laugh, they cannot understand,
  But yet we do.

Strange fascinations these, that force the feet
Of age to crawl between the triple pegs
Once more! Strange fascination, when the jest
Of tactless youth turns on our bulk, our years,
Our childish joy, they cannot understand,
  But yet we do.

Strange fascinations these, in serried ranks
We see men sit throughout the live-long day
Content! Strange fascinations, that do build
A very world of fellowship, for those
That play. Fools laugh, they cannot understand;
  Are we fools too?

D. L. A. Jephson

THE UPPER CIRCLE. *(Surrey v. Lancashire.)*

Introduction: Parallel lives

The historian Plutarch was famous for writing biographies in parallel lives. He would choose a distinguished Roman and compare him with a distinguished Greek; by adopting this dual approach, he would be able to throw the life of each of his subjects into greater relief. Had Plutarch been living at the turn of the present century and had his interests stretched to cricket, he would have found fascinating material in the parallel lives of Charles Kortright, the Demon of Essex, and Digby Jephson, the Lobster of Surrey. Not only were they most distinguished cricketers in their day, but their lives were full of arresting similarities and contrasts.

Both men were born in the same year, 1871, within weeks of each other. They were also distantly related, Charles Kortright's father having married a Jephson with whom Digby could trace kinship. Both men loved the game of cricket with a rare passion, playing as amateurs and devoting their lives to it. Both captained their counties in troubled times.

On the other hand, the Demon lived man's alloted span and more, untroubled by the need ever to earn a living, whereas the Lobster died in middle age after a life full of struggle. On the cricket field there was an even more striking contrast. Charles Kortright was the fastest bowler of his (and perhaps any) time, the very latest thing in speed and belligerency, while Digby Jephson was the slowest of bowlers, a practitioner of the ancient art of underarm lob bowling at a period when it had already gone right out of fashion and was something of a museum piece. To the historian Plutarch, Charles Kortright would have been the forthright, no-nonsense Roman, Digby Jephson the more subtle, intellectual Greek.

Their parallel lives are interwoven during one of cricket's most colourful and exciting periods, the so-called Golden Age of cricket of late Victorian and Edwardian times. Never before had the game taken such a hold upon the imagination as in the last decade of the nineteenth century and the first decade of the twentieth; never again would county cricket attract such national attention. Where better, then, to start the story of the Demon and the Lobster than on 1 August 1898, August Bank Holiday in the sixty-first year of Victoria's reign?

1
The Golden Age of Digby and Charles

The sun poured down on The Oval as over 20,000 people made their way there. The traditional Bank Holiday fixture of Surrey v. Nottinghamshire was a very big attraction. Fifty police constables, hired specially for the occasion by the Surrey Committee, were casting an avuncular eye over their exuberant charges, blissfully unconcerned about being so heavily outnumbered.

Batting at no. 6 for Surrey on this auspicious summer morning was Digby Jephson, 27 years old and just established in the county team after some phenomenal performances in club cricket. He was a hard-hitting batsman as well as a subtle bowler of underarm lobs. The Ovalites, suspicious at first of this unfashionable mode of bowling, had just begun to take him to their hearts. An extra buzz of anticipation now travelled round the ground whenever he was given the ball. There was much amusement at his bowling action whereby, with a few crab-like steps, body bent double and with knuckles scraping the turf, the ball was sent on its spinning flight. Quick runs or quick wickets would usually result, for Digby's lobs seemed to elicit a belligerent response from the most pacific of batsmen. As the ball was struck, raucous encouragement and laughter would echo round the ring. And if a wicket fell – to a catch on the leg-side boundary or the stumping of a stranded charger – the cheerful abuse would transfer from perspiring bowler to retreating batsman. Digby Jephson was rapidly becoming one of The Oval's great ornaments and pleasures.

Digby was also a journalist, a stockbroker and a poet. He took his poetry very seriously. Tradition relates that he would come in from batting, unbuckle his pads and retire to some solitary spot, to scribble down the poetic inspiration of the moment. Most of his poems were about cricket. He wrote one about The Oval on an August Bank Holiday. The first verses describe the pre-match excitement:

'Tis August Bank Holiday, 10 a.m.,
   And the turnstiles every one
Are galloping round with incessant click
To the hurrying feet that come fast and thick,
The thousands who struggle – they must be quick
   If they wish to see every run!

And the motley throng that goes surging by
   Is a sight to gladden the day,
For on every face is there hope serene,
Their work is behind them, their pleasure's keen;
This one day at least in the year, I ween,
   Will strengthen them on their way.

There are soldiers, sailors, and postmen there,
   There are clerks from their high-backed stools,
There are tinkers, tailors, and booing brats,
And swells of the city in silken hats,
And men from the clubs in immaculate spats,
   But they all of them know the rules.

And all of them push till at last they squeeze
   Through the members' or turnstile gate,
Swells of the city and men of the clubs
Separate now from the folk of the pubs,
A moment when *wealth* against *labour* rubs –
   In pavilion and ring they wait.

The pavilion which he mentions had only just been built. It was one of a number of splendid new structures around the country, buildings which also helped to emphasize the great divide of spectators into

2

'wealth' and 'labour'. Lord's had led the way with a new pavilion in red brick and terracotta, its grandeur in keeping with cricket's growing importance within the life of the nation. Surrey had asked the architect of Old Trafford's new pavilion to design one 'second to none in the country in its internal arrangements'. Two buildings, pavilion and tavern, had accordingly arisen the previous winter at The Oval, costing the very large sum of £38,000.

The comfort which the new pavilion offered the Surrey members – and there were some 4000 of them – contrasted sharply with what was available to the general public, paying sixpence to come through the turnstiles. Such was the attraction of Surrey cricket to the spectator that, if there was no room on the grass, he would cheerfully spend a whole day standing on the terraces. Jephson's poem continues:

> The great green circle of play is curtailed
>   By some stakes and a piece of twine,
> And the people lie on the sun-scorched sward,
> Like an ocean surf held back by a cord,
> The ground is as soft as a three-inch board,
>   But they stretch there line upon line.
>
> The asphalt terraces, tier upon tier,
>   Rise packed with their load of sardines,
> The straw-hatted thousands who wait the play,
> Who have come to stand for the livelong day,
> And swelter and sweat in the same old way;
>   Though some try to lie down by the screens.
>
> And now of a sudden a hush is felt.
>   Then a murmur goes swiftly round
> The Ring, as the players in spotless white
> Emerge at last to prepare for the fight
> By a knock at the nets in the blazing light
>   On a cast-iron August ground.

The matches proceeded in leisurely fashion in the Golden Age. A 12 o'clock start, the usual time, might easily be delayed if a player had been held up *en route* to the ground. There was, however, some entertainment for the crowd before the match began, because it was unthinkable to start a day's play without net practice, which was watched avidly.

The description of the players in 'spotless white' may be misleading to a generation brought up on washing detergent advertisements. Pads tended to be cleaned now and then rather than every day. Socks were often black. Boots, though no longer totally brown, were sometimes two-toned, white and brown. And around many an ample waist in those golden days of plenty were belts or ties in varying hues. A light-blue one sufficed for Digby – he had won a Blue for three years at Cambridge – as he emerged down the central steps of the new pavilion, chatting to Frank Crawford, one of the two other amateurs in the side.

The crowd could readily recognize Digby Jephson by his unusual rolling gait; he had had the misfortune to be born with one leg shorter than the other. He was of medium height and had distinctive features. His dark hair was centrally parted, his full moustache drooped slightly at the edges, and a high brow and Roman nose lent him a scholarly look. It was a handsome, animated face. His friend, Frank Crawford, a tall, powerfully built 19-year-old, was one of Surrey's best hopes for the future, expected to develop into a famous hitter. They crossed the grass together, boon companions, while at the nets, already mustered, were some of the professionals. Bobby Abel, diminutive hero of the Ovalites, was already batting, indulging in much more ambitious shots than he was likely to show when he got to the middle:

> The 'Guv'nor' is there, he is always there,
>   First to come and the last to go;
> And he slogs away like an Albert Trott,
> Till all the bowlers are tied in a knot;
> The critics remark 'What an eye he's got!
>   He ain't always so blooming slow!'
>
> And Lockwood is there, and Tom Hayward too,
>   With Tom Richardson close behind,
> And all of them pile up four after four,
> They raise in the nets a colossal score,
> They'd like to make these in the match, or more,
>   And contented they'd be in their mind!
>
> A quarter to twelve and the bell is rung,
>   And the nets disappear apace,
> The ground is cleared and the players retreat;

The five-ton roller retires from its beat,
Drawn by Apted's men, who sweat in the heat;
  There is pride in Sam's genial face.

And then down the steps both captains come,
  Anxious in mind and slim,
They spin on the grass and the toss is won,
And Surrey should bat till the setting sun
Glides 'into the West' when his work is done,
  Like the youth from the city dim.

'Anxious in mind' both captains probably were, but 'slim' both of them were not! In particular, Sir Kingsmill Key of Surrey had one of the biggest paunches in county cricket, a fact not unremarked upon by

the Ovalites. But Surrey did indeed bat on till nearly the set of the sun, Digby scoring a bright 54 in their total of well over 300. They had time to capture one Notts wicket before the close of play, sending the Bank Holiday crowd home in happy vein. The next day came Digby's chance to bowl. In his first spell he clean bowled John Gunn, a member of the famous bat-making family, and in his second he finished off the Notts tail, taking 3 for 32 in his 12 five-ball overs.

The crowd watched with approval as Notts followed on. An innings victory looked likely, but Notts had two magnificent professional batsmen. One of them, Arthur Shrewsbury, fell cheaply, but William Gunn, uncle of John Gunn, occupied the crease for over eight hours in scoring 236 not out and he saved the match. Digby bowled 23 overs of lobs and was treated with the greatest respect, but failed to take a wicket. Time and again he tempted Gunn, who stood 6 feet 4 inches and had an enormous reach, but he was unable to encourage a lapse of concentration. Perhaps it was this innings of Gunn's which encouraged a young lady to write admiringly that year: 'There is something strong and trustworthy about Gunn. He resembles an apparently immovable rock, as he stands before his wicket, his broad white hat half hiding the keen, kind face.'

Meanwhile, on the same August Bank Holiday, another large crowd was enjoying another sun-blessed match. Leicestershire were playing Essex at Leicester. Both counties were newcomers to first-class cricket, but Essex had already developed into one of the best teams in the country, in just four seasons.

It was no surprise to any but the most partisan of home supporters when Essex made a weak Leicester attack suffer in the Bank Holiday sunshine. Their leading professional batsman, 'Bob' Carpenter, made a hundred, their famous batting 'twins', Perrin and McGahey, each scored fifties and Charles Kortright, batting at no. 7, struck the ball mightily in the late afternoon. By the close Essex were well beyond 400 and on the next day Kortright completed his hundred, 112 out of 515.

The Bank Holiday crowd had probably hoped to see him bowl rather than bat, for in 1898 his name was on everybody's lips as England's leading amateur fast bowler. Less than two weeks before, Kortright had played a memorable part in W. G. Grace's Jubilee match, the fixture between the Gentlemen and Players at Lord's which had been arranged to coincide with the Doctor's fiftieth birthday.

Kortright was now considered faster than England's other fast bowlers, Richardson, Lockwood and Mold. He was also wilder and less predictable. There was much eager speculation as to what he might do to the Australians on their coming tour the following year. Many spectators, therefore, came back the day after the Bank Holiday to see Charles Kortright bowl.

He was a wonderful sight to watch. A long, menacing run, elbows pummelling the air like pistons, strides ever lengthening. Then a flurry of delivery in a strange, baulking action. Finally, a fiery follow-through, right down the wicket, with athletic fielding if needed. The whole procedure was accompanied by the most aggressive of facial expressions. He did not indulge in these deliberately to intimidate the batsman. But a bat at 22 yards was simply like the proverbial red rag to him and, at its sight, a bull-like hatred flared up within him. 'He runs at you, just as if he were jumping a gate,' muttered one batsman expressively.

There was aggression too in Kortright's face when in repose. Smiles did not come easily. The broad chin suggested pugnacity. And there was a startling lack of hair! It was receding early, thinning on top, and this year, for the first time since boyhood, he was without his moustache. Nearly all his Essex team-mates favoured the still-fashionable moustache. There was a stark severity about Charles Kortright.

If the crowd had come to see the Demon bowling at his best, it was not disappointed. Leicester were bowled out twice, to an innings defeat, and Kortright bowled 45 torrid overs, taking 8 wickets. Three dismissals were by courtesy of wicket-keeper Tom Russell, who somehow managed to cling on to searing snicks. The other five wickets were clean bowled. This was Kortright's usual method of removing a batsman, beating him by sheer pace.

The spectators at Leicester, watching the Demon in full cry, were witnessing cricket at its most exciting. The Ovalites too were similarly privileged, as the Lobster plied his art to their delight. The Golden Age of Charles and Digby may therefore seem to have been an idyllic period in cricket's history. So it was, for some participants. But the extent of the idyll depended on one's social and financial position; the same dichotomy between 'wealth' and 'labour' existed for the players as for the Ovalites in Digby Jephson's poem. For the wealthy, amateur cricket offered a stimulating diversion, a most attractive alternative to the humdrum business of the real world outside 'the great green circle of play'. For the amateur of limited means and the poorly paid professional, cricket was no hobby but rather an uncertain means of livelihood of precariously short duration.

It is significant that, from those four county teams playing out their Bank Holiday matches in 1898, one member of each side ended his days in tragedy. 'Timber' Woodcock, Leicestershire's fast bowler, poisoned himself; at 44 he was penniless and out of work. Fred Bull, the Essex slow bowler and assistant secretary, killed himself for similar reasons. Arthur Shrewsbury of Notts, for many years one of England's leading professional batsmen, succumbed to the strain of his own eminence and, at 47, believing himself seriously ill, shot himself. Tom Richardson, one of the most talented fast bowlers ever to play for England, met so mysterious a fate that suicide must remain a distinct possibility. At 41, he was both penniless and ill. The night that he died on a French mountainside, he had crept out of his hotel in slippers and collarless shirt, eluding the watchfulness of his friends. Earlier, he had written the saddest of testimonies (for, of all things, a nerve-tonic advertisement): 'When I retired from cricket, my nervous system was impaired. I began to get upset over trivial matters. My appetite fell off and my memory often failed me. But the most worrying trouble was insomnia.' The deaths of Woodcock, Bull, Shrewsbury and Richardson are not isolated examples. Many other players of the Golden Age lived ill-starred lives. For many of its participants, therefore, the Golden Age of cricket was far from perfect.

The cricket itself, was *that* at least golden? Certainly it was full of drama and rich in personalities. Its chief protagonists, men like Grace, C. B. Fry and Ranjitsinhji, now enshrined in their own legends, have transcended the passage of time. As often as not, the leading players were difficult personalities, possessing, like Homeric heroes, over-large egos and an exaggerated sense of the honour due to them. Indeed crises on and off the field loomed so large throughout the period that one must seriously question whether cricket's Golden Age has not been misnamed. For it mirrors with strange exactitude the constant anxieties that beset the modern game. On that August day in 1898, however, not many of cricket's problems were uppermost in the spectators' minds as they revelled in the sunshine, while the Demon and Lobster contributed richly to their holiday entertainment.

2

*The old
school
patch*

The game I loved when I would scratch
For singles on the old school patch,
    A hopeful imp of ten,
Now ten is multiplied by five
Is just as great, as fine, as live
    To me, as it was then!

D.L.A.J.

1871 was a vintage year for cricketing babies. Two of the finest professionals of the Golden Age, Tom Hayward and George Hirst, opened their innings that year and likewise two of its most elegant amateurs, Archie MacLaren and Richard Palairet. At the top of the batting order, however, came the Demon and the Lobster. Charles Jesse Kortright was born on 7 January 1871 and, six weeks later, Digby Loder Armroid Jephson.

Although their families were related, the two cricketers were born into very different social backgrounds. The Kortrights were land-owners, who dominated the countryside around the village of Fryerning, Essex. It was, and still is, a green, tranquil landscape and

9

relatively hilly for the county. There, a few miles from Chelmsford, the Kortrights took their social responsibilities as the local gentry very seriously, playing a leading role in parish life, dispensing charity to the needy and following all the traditional country pursuits. Charles Kortright, born into such a rural environment, remained a country-man all his life. Digby Jephson, by contrast, was born in Brixton and ever after remained a city dweller. His family was less affluent than the Kortrights, yet comfortably middle class. The Jephsons were recent arrivals in suburban London, offshoots of several generations of churchmen, and it was a Church connection which fortuitously provided the link between the families of the two cricketers. It so happened that a Reverend Jephson came to live among the Kortrights of Fryerning as rector of a nearby church. His pretty daughter, one Mary Jephson, caught the eye of the squire's son, Augustus Kortright, and it was their subsequent union which produced for Essex cricket the Demon bowler.

The Kortrights had originally come from Denmark, but they were well established in Essex by the end of the eighteenth century. In Regency times they were living at Hylands, a large estate on the outskirts of Chelmsford. Here the Demon's great-grandfather, Cornelius Hendrickson Kortright, used to entertain lavishly, often giving supper parties for over 100 guests in his impressive and recently enlarged mansion. Family estates in the West Indies helped pay for his lavish lifestyle, but eventually Cornelius was compelled to sell Hylands (for the very large sum of £40,000) and he moved the few miles to Fryerning.

At Fryerning the family fortunes were augmented by the opportune marriage of the Demon's grandfather, William, to Sarah Coesvelt, a lady of Dutch descent and an heiress to a big fortune. Captain William in time took over St Leonards, the house which his father-in-law had built, and much land and many houses swiftly became Kortright property. The Demon seems to have inherited the qualities of pugnacity and courage as well as opportunism from his grandfather, for Captain William had spent 12 years in the Coldstream Guards, fighting with distinction in several battles of the Peninsular War.

His son, Augustus Kortright, the Demon's father, took his soldiering less seriously. As a very young man he spent one year with a commission bought in the Durham Light Infantry. Later on, he did some weekend soldiering with the Essex Yeomanry. It was the tradition of the time for the local gentry to supply the officers for these reserve units, as they were the only people rich enough to furnish the horses, grooms and food needed for the occasional manoeuvres. Augustus Kortright fought most of his campaigns from the safety of the Army and Navy Club. Around Fryerning he indulged in all the sports appropriate to a country gentleman, taking particular interest in Ingatestone cricket club. Then, at the age of 39, he courted and married the 18-year-old Mary Jephson. Their marriage at nearby Childerditch, where Mary's father was rector, united the families of Demon and Lobster, the Demon's father marrying a distant aunt of the Lobster.

Mary's father was no retiring country parson, but a formidable personality, renowned for his High Church views and his scholarship. A Fellow of the Society of Antiquaries, The Revd John Mounteney Jephson was a devoted lover of Shakespeare, publishing a text of *The Tempest* full of great academic detail. He also published a biography, *Shakspere, His Birthplace, Home and Grave*; for the research he travelled from Essex to Stratford-on-Avon on horseback, accompanied there and back only by his faithful dog. He was as outspoken as he was learned. In an earlier book, *Narrative of a Walking Tour in Brittany*, he had described his parishioners of Childerditch as 'dull of brain and narrow of prejudice'! The family of Mounteney Jephson was well known in the area; indeed, it had lent its name to the nearby village of Mountnessing. The Jephsons claimed that they could trace their family back through several early English kings to Charlemagne and Alfred the Great.

The newly married Augustus and Mary Kortright settled down at Furze Hall, Fryerning, a white, straggly farmhouse with 50 acres attached, which Captain William had improved with a brick frontage, converting the simple farmhouse to an impressive country mansion. It was soon full of children, and to accommodate them, Augustus added a new wing, known today as the Victorian Wing. It was here, at Furze Hall, that the Demon was born, the fifth of seven children who lived beyond infancy. He was christened Charles Jesse. 'Charles' honoured one of his uncles, Her Majesty's Consul of Philadelphia, later knighted for his services to the diplomatic corps. 'Jesse' was after a family friend (and keen cricketer), William Jesse, who had died only days after the baby was born.

The Lobster came into the world in less exalted circumstances at his parents' home, 2 Herne Cottage, Herne Hill Road, Brixton, just a mile down the road from The Oval. His mother, the dominant partner, chose the name Digby in honour of her brother. Herne Cottage has long since disappeared from Herne Hill Road, so it is not possible today to examine the Lobster's birthplace. Perhaps that is just as well, for time has not been kind to houses of that period in this area. In 1871 Brixton was a very rural London suburb with fields surrounding the houses of Herne Hill Road. There was no hint of the heavily populated Brixton of today with its racial tensions and high crime figures. Even so, there would have been a big difference between the country grandeur of Furze Hall, Fryerning, and the suburban, middle-class simplicity of Herne Cottage, Brixton.

Digby's parents, Cuthbert and Emily Jephson, were a young, newly married couple. Cuthbert came from Hinton Waldrist, Berkshire, Emily from Litchfield, Taunton, and both were the children of clergymen. The Church predominated as a family career. Uncle Arthur was the most successful of the clerics, ending up as a canon, and Grandfather William was the most enterprising, moving abroad in his retirement to become English chaplain at Geneva, winning the hand of a local Swiss lady in the process. Many of Digby's other relations were vigorously unconventional. Uncle Hubert gave up his Church ministry, which had taken him to America, and founded the Home of Alpine Plants in Herne Hill, close to Digby's first home. Uncle Oswald became a Doctor of Music and was a composer of many light pieces, one of which, 'The Girl He Left Behind Him', was a popular hit. An ever-expanding empire offered Englishmen of ambition considerable scope, and the Jephsons, like the Kortrights, were active in the colonies. Uncle Alban did much to combat the slave trade at Racoon on the west coast of Africa while serving in the Royal Navy. Despite contracting yellow fever, he lived to become superintendent of Her Majesty's dockyard in Hong Kong, where he ended his days. Uncle Cyril emigrated to New Zealand to farm.

Contrasts between the two families begin to emerge. The Kortrights lived off their inherited wealth and land, acquiring conservative upper-class attitudes. These dictated a public school education and a limited choice of career, in which armed services and diplomatic corps predominated. The Jephsons were less orthodox, more open to risk. They were not poorly off, but their lesser resources may have been the determining factor in their greater enterprise. Not that all the

Kortrights were bereft of enterprise! For example, Charles Kortright's great-uncle, R. Mounteney Jephson, was one of the most widely read authors of the 1870s and 1880s, producing any number of novels 'for railway and seaside reading' with tantalizing titles like *Through The Keyhole* and *Blackmail*. The Jephson link would seem to have added new vigour to the more conventional Kortright side of the family.

Cuthbert Jephson, Digby's father, is a somewhat mysterious figure. He was a mechanical engineer by training and it was no doubt this which had initially brought him and his young wife from the countryside to London. But domesticity does not seem to have been to Cuthbert's liking, for, when Digby was only three months old, his father joined the 3rd London Rifle Volunteers as a junior officer. Cuthbert served in the army for six years, rising to the rank of captain, before resigning his commission at the age of 30 in 1877. Significantly, this was the year in which the British annexed the Transvaal because it was rich in gold. A gold rush to South Africa ensued, first to the Cape and then to the Rand. Cuthbert became a gold miner and his brother Maynard similarly joined the hunt for gold and diamonds, giving up a headmastership in Australia to become Warden at the Kimberley works.

By the 1880s Cuthbert had vanished for good. Emily Jephson, the girl he left behind him, was living in Clapham with her young son at 18 Offerton Road, which lay at the end of a smart terrace of very large, newly built houses. Despite the loss of her husband Digby's mother, at this period of her life, seems to have been comfortably off. She could afford to send Digby to a nearby private school and, later, on to Cambridge, a most expensive undertaking. One can only conjecture how she was able to live in such a style. Her husband might have been supporting her with money from his mining exploits, or she might have found herself a rich benefactor some time before, thus precipitating Cuthbert's forays into foreign fields. More prosaically, she may have taken lodgers.

Emily Jephson often took her son on summer holidays to Broadstairs. Digby later recalled how he played cricket on the sand there, often with two other small boys who subsequently became good sportsmen: 'Jerry' Weigall, the eccentric and outspoken Kent amateur, and Francis Street, a footballer with the Corinthians and an occasional cricketer with Essex.

Despite such holidays and the private schooling, Digby must have suffered much from the loss of his father in his formative years. The loss remained total throughout his life, for, although Cuthbert eventually outlived his son, he was present neither at his son's wedding nor at his funeral. In the continued absence of his father the relationship between Digby, an only son, and his mother became particularly close as he grew up in Clapham.

Clapham was a most select area in the 1880s. It is difficult today to look at the traffic-choked streets with the eyes of a Victorian. A contemporary description is helpful: 'Rural though Clapham be, it is within easy walk from town, and can be reached in half an hour. The air is the finest for the smoke-choked lungs of the jaded Londoner. The good Claphamite claims that there is nothing between him and Brighton on one side; and that, on the other, he is on a plateau, high above the densely crowded streets of the great City.' The inhabitants of Clapham enjoyed an Arcadian simplicity: 'The natives have a kind of rustic indifference to town distractions. They are given to lectures, concerts, readings and pastoral walks.'

The big houses around the common easily converted into private schools. It was something of a growth industry at the time. Emily Jephson chose one such establishment for Digby, Manor House School, situated at 2 Old Town (now a doctor's house and surgery). It was a happy choice, for the headmaster, Frederick Maxwell, was to prove to be a big influence on Digby. A keen cricketer himself, he took the sporting side of school life very seriously. As a Surrey member, he was soon bringing the natural talents of his young protégé to the notice of the county club. He also influenced Digby in other ways. Maxwell ran Manor House School as much on public school lines as possible. Muscular Christianity was the order of the day. Accordingly when Digby later mixed with public school cricketers, he more easily assimilated their distinctive approach to life. Above all, it was Maxwell's influence which persuaded Emily Jephson to send her son to Cambridge, where his cricket education was completed.

Clapham Common was, of course, a marvellous place for the boys to play casual cricket. Digby always treasured one occasion when he was there as a 14-year-old: 'Three or four of us were playing cricket on the wilderness of Clapham Common. A young man watched the game for a little and eventually took a hand. He bowled to us and he batted for us and we learnt something. At the end of half an hour he left. We asked his name. "Lohmann" came the reply. We said "Good

14

morning and thank you."' George Lohmann, 20 years old when Digby met him, went on to become one of England's greatest medium-pace bowlers.

Manor House School played its cricket at a ground at Trouville Road and later, Broomwood, on the west side of the common. The wicket at the latter must have been reasonably true, for in one match a visiting team put on 200 runs in one hour. Digby was the star batsman, bowler and wicket-keeper of his day. He bowled overarm, as much in the manner of Lohmann as the art of imitation allowed, and sometimes, as for instance on one occasion against the London International College, his deliveries proved unplayable. In later life Digby retained happy memories of these times. Even as a busy county player he always tried to be free to captain the Old Boys against the School.

In contrast to Digby's narrow home life, Charles enjoyed the company of three brothers and three sisters in his early days at Fryerning. But their time with governesses was short, for soon came a boarding school education. When Charles was nine and his brother Mounteney eight, their father sent them to Brentwood, his old school. Proximity to Fryerning was a recommendation and so were the low fees of £9 a year! The school buildings were a straggling ribbon of red brick, stretching away from a small recently constructed chapel. The Kortright boys arrived at the same time as a new headmaster, The Revd J. H. Newnum, who firmly believed in the traditional values of a classical education. Newnum most enjoyed discussing the beauty of Greek tragedy, delighting in the difficult chorus speeches and the subtleties of grammar. Later in life Charles could recall Latin and Greek quotations with apparent ease, so perhaps, though never a scholar, he owed something to Newnum.

At the age of 13 Charles played for the Brentwood 1st XI as a slow bowler. There were only 81 boys of all ages in the school, so, unsurprisingly, it was a weak team. The Old Brentwoods, although fielding only six players, beat the school by 275 runs to 31! The scorebooks have long since vanished, so Charles' figures that day will never be known, but it is known that he showed promise as an athlete. In the junior events in one Sports Day he achieved better results than the older boys in the open events. Charles took part eagerly in all sports and any spare moments were occupied with long walks, for Brentwood in his schooldays was a small rural town. On school

15

holidays he and Mounteney could walk the five miles to Fryerning. There was cricket too at the County Ground, for Essex – still a second-class county – had been playing all home matches at Brentwood since the club's formation a few years before.

Charles in later life talked warmly of his days at Brentwood. He recalled creeping out of a dormitory window at four in the morning, to play cricket against the chapel wall until seven o'clock, the official time for rising. 'If discovered, we were in trouble, but I thought the game well worth the risk, and I was always ready for two and a half hours of compulsory cricket when school was over for the day.' At Brentwood Charles practised his throwing assiduously with balls or stones: 'I was forever wanting to project things farther or faster than any of my friends and this, I think, accounted for the pace I was able to develop later as a bowler.'

It is possible that Charles and Mounteney would have completed their education at Brentwood, but for a tragedy which struck the school. Two young boarders died of diphtheria. Panic set in among the parents and it was not just the Kortrights who left; the roll sank fast to just 41. Ironically the Kortright family did not escape a tragedy of its own. Charles' elder brother, Henry, who had been training for a naval career on HMS *Worcester*, contracted double pneumonia and died at the age of 16.

So in 1885 – the year when Gordon was killed at Khartoum, and, a little closer home, George Lohmann began to make his presence felt at The Oval – the two Kortright brothers were sent to Tonbridge School, where Mary Kortright had strong connections. As one of Charles' uncles was teaching there, it was possibly inside information which led to Charles and Mounteney becoming members of Parkside House. Its housemaster, The Revd Arthur Lucas, was as big an influence on Charles as the headmaster of Manor House School was on Digby. Not only was Arthur Lucas a keen cricketer himself, his brother was a Test cricketer! A. P. 'Bunny' Lucas had played in the famous Ashes Test of 1882, when the unthinkable had happened and England had lost at home to Australia. It was not long before the schoolboy Charles met 'Bunny' Lucas himself and listened with rapt attention to stories of Lord Harris' tour of Australia. A friendship, begun at Tonbridge as hero-worship, endured for many years, and later Lucas, 14 years the senior, was to play alongside Charles Kortright for Essex and be his neighbour at Fryerning.

In a Parkside House photograph of 1887, 27 boys faced the camera, all dressed conventionally for the period in black coats and vests, the majority with wing collar and tie. Charles is immaculately turned out, a watch chain across his waistcoat lending him an extra touch of dignity. He looks determined and assured, as well he might, for his four years at Tonbridge were very good ones.

Charles proved a splendid athlete and a useful 1st XV full-back and three-quarter, better at kicking then tackling. He played for the Tonbridge 1st XI for two summers, after doing very well in two junior XIs. In his first season he took 52 wickets, with big hauls against the MCC, Old Boys and Stoics. In his second year he took 53 wickets (for just over 7 runs each), taking 7 against both Marlborough Blues and Brighton College. The latter match was an exciting affair. Brighton ended up needing 4 to win with 3 wickets left. Charles bowled two of them out and Tonbridge won. He always fancied tail-enders. The same fixture the previous year had been made memorable by the inclusion of Sammy Woods in the Brighton College side. The 19-year-old Woods had left school the year before, but nobody seemed to mind at this time whether masters, coaches or Old Boys took part in inter-school matches. Even so, Sammy Woods was rather special, for at the time of the match he had already played for Somerset! He was reckoned to be as fast a bowler at 19 as at any time later. The wicket was perfect, but, with Charles and Sammy Woods bowling on opposite sides, the four innings were quickly completed. 'We finished the match in one day', recalled a member of the Brighton side six years later. 'C. J. Kortright was bowling for Tonbridge. He was fast then, but nothing like as fast as he is now, and did not, I believe, take a particularly long run.'

Quite how fast a bowler Charles was at 16 or 17 it is difficult to judge. The school magazine commented that 'Kortright's bowling hardly needs description. With an exceptionally high delivery and any amount of wrist flick, he was popularly supposed to be two yards faster then any of his contemporaries.' Although Charles later said 'I did not bowl at Tonbridge at the great pace I bowl now,' he also claimed: 'I always did bowl fast, even at Tonbridge.' It seems, then, that he was fast for his years. It was, perhaps, a pointer to the future that, in helping Parkside to win the House Cup by taking 13 wickets in the final, he bowled one batsman off his head!

The Demon ended his schooldays in 1888, the Lobster one year later. At this stage the former was the more mature player, good enough, indeed, to represent a Public Schools XI. Charles had already learnt some of the secrets of fast bowling, helped by Walter Wright, the Notts fast bowler, who as luck would have it, was coaching at Tonbridge while waiting to complete his residential qualifications for Kent, at the very time that Charles reached the 1st XI. Digby's progress, by contrast, was slower. He had not yet thought of bowling underarm.

In Charles' development as a cricketer, both his family and school background played a part. His father and brothers were all keen cricketers and it was at Tonbridge that he enjoyed his first formal coaching. But Charles was too forceful a character, even as a schoolboy, to be coached into a mould. The public schools at the time concentrated on batting at the expense of bowling. And 'Bunny' Lucas, his mentor, was acknowledged as the leading batting stylist of the day. Yet Charles stubbornly resisted the art of batting and concentrated on bowling. Even more unconventionally, he chose *fast* bowling, which was barely considered a gentlemanly occupation in some circles!

Digby Jephson, without the benefit of family help, depended entirely for his cricket development on Frederick Maxwell and Manor House School. While there he began to make a mark in local club cricket and was introduced to influential Surrey Committee members. It is likely, however, that Digby's grounding was haphazard and not technically sound, for immediately on leaving school he experienced problems with both bat and ball, which suggests that he had learnt bad habits. Perhaps it is too fanciful to relate his later adoption of unconventional lob bowling to his school years, spent without a father in an unconventional family of two; but it is certainly true that both Digby and Charles conceived their burning love of the game during their time at school.

3
Golden Blue

I sing thy well-belovèd name
Thou fostering nurse of England's game,
Thou ground whence men have leapt to fame,
    O Fenner's!

D.L.A.J.

Digby went up to Cambridge in 1889. He spent three years at Peterhouse, where he achieved a second-class pass in the General Examination, but did not read for the Tripos. In not taking an honours degree, Digby followed the fashion of many of his contemporaries. A Cambridge education at this period offered the sons of the wealthy and well-born a minimum of study and a maximum of extra-curricular activity. Cambridge, for many, was an expensive finishing school and cricket one of the arts which it efficiently taught.

There was plenty of cricket to be found at Cambridge. By 1890 almost every college had its own ground and own professional. There were wandering sides in plenty, too, such as the Perambulators, the Pilgrims, the Quidnuncs, the Crusaders, and others with ornithological names like the Hawks, the Jackdaws and the Magpies, all with

19

their own distinctive caps and blazers, sufficient to bewilder the unsuspecting freshman. Then there was Fenner's, the university ground, with perhaps the finest wickets in England. So close, smooth and level was the turf that it was claimed that games could be played on the outfield where the bounce would be as true as on the square. Round the boundary ran an athletics track and in Digby's time the practice nets were still in the old orchard. Here 12 professionals, among them some of the finest young cricketers in the country, bowled by the hour to the young gentlemen, each of whom paid one guinea a year for the privilege.

Privilege reigned. The university team was chosen almost exclusively from those who had done well in their public school XIs. Each April, gilded youths, whose reputations had reached Cambridge ahead of them, were watched eagerly as they performed in two freshmen's matches before the university season began. Certain colleges always provided the bulk of the players – Trinity, St John's, Jesus and Caius – because it was to these that the well-coached Etonian, Harrovian or Wykehamist cricketers came. But boys from newer public schools had recently staked their claim: Repton, Malvern, Clifton and Cheltenham were among those that helped to swell the university sides in the 1890s.

To Digby this was a strange world in which he felt he had no place. Here he was, at an unfashionable cricket college, knowing no one and lacking a public school education. True, he was a promising round-arm bowler and had had some success in London cricket, having taken 5 wickets in 8 balls when on tour with the Crystal Palace side at Eastbourne the previous summer. What was that compared to the exploits of those who had already played at Lord's for Eton or Harrow? No one had heard of him and it seemed almost impossible to break into the charmed circle.

That summer fate took a hand, in the venerable figure of Dr James Porter, Master of Peterhouse and treasurer of the university cricket club. He possessed the same sporting and artistic tastes as Digby and he used his influence to recommend the young freshman from his own college for a university trial. Digby found himself included in the first freshmen's match and took 9 wickets in a 14-a-side game. He took another 7 in the second trial, playing for the 1st XII against the Next XVI, and then 80 wickets in college games for Peterhouse. This was enough to win him his first Blue, although the 5 first-class wickets he took for Cambridge that first year cost nearly 60 runs each!

So for three happy years Digby, quickly nicknamed 'Baby' because of his youthful appearance, was one of the young bloods of Fenner's, an exclusive brotherhood whose ties would never be broken by the passage of time:

> I see them yet, a stalwart band,
> I grasp each friendly outstretched hand,
> The pick of those who took their stand,
> On Fenner's!

The Varsity teams exuded a glamour which made them irresistible in the eyes of the public. In part, it was the manner in which they played that made them so compelling. The carefree negligence of the man of means, combined with the impetuosity of youth, resulted in a fresh, dynamic approach to the game. Stepping down the wicket, they gracefully and powerfully plied their bats through elegant arcs, off-driving and cover-driving as never before. There was an inspirational zeal about their fielding and, with rare passion, they bowled their hearts out. Above all, they brought with them to the adult cricket world their own philosophy, a fusion of the public schoolboy's code of good sportsmanship with a deep sense of moral obligation inculcated by patriarchal Victorian headmasters. In their code, cricket was a game of utter purity, played properly only by the pure in heart.

Fenner's proved the most formative influence of Digby's life. He fell in love not only with the ground but also with the Fenner's philosophy. In his later writing he was forever promoting the Varsity view of life:

> Play with a straight bat, sonnie,
> In the game of life or at school.
> You may have bad luck,
> You may make a duck,
> But stick to the golden rule;
> PLAY STRAIGHT!

Many of the Blues did indeed play the game of life in the same way as their cricket. This, too, added to their attraction. They had been schooled to believe that they were a superior class of a superior nation. Understandably in these circumstances there was a confident swagger about them, a self-possession, which other lesser mortals found awesome and oddly attractive. The working-class spectator of the Golden Age looked up to the Varsity Blue with a deep devotion, comparable perhaps with that of the private soldier of 1914 for his platoon commander. The professionals, too, admired the authoritarian leadership of men like Lord Hawke, Lord Harris and F. S. Jackson, men who epitomized the Varsity spirit.

Digby, of course, did not entirely fit this classic mould. Not only had he been to the wrong school, but his mother's private means were very limited, and it was during his time at Cambridge that she moved from her large house in Clapham to a tiny cottage in Union Road, Cambridge. The move was that of a mother straightening her own circumstances to pay for the expensive education of her son. However, Digby was a fine all-round sportsman, as useful with the racket and golf-club as he was with bat and ball. Physically he was strongly built and strikingly handsome. In the world of Golden Age Fenner's, this would have counted for much; it may even have clinched his social acceptability.

Digby's cricket career at Cambridge was not impressive and he was lucky to win his Blue for three consecutive years. In his moderate first season he made useful scores against Yorkshire and the Australian tourists and he began to be considered as an all-rounder. However, in 1891 his bowling skills deserted him and he batted no. 11 for the Cambridge side, with a 45 against Yorkshire as his highest score. He fretted about his bowling and analysed his action so closely that he lost his natural rhythm. His eyes kept catching the crease as he approached the stumps: 'I could do absolutely nothing. There seemed no reason for it at all, for I was quite well and not stale. As I have always enjoyed bowling much more than batting, I was very vexed at having to give it up.' His bowling gone, Digby depended on his batting for his Blue in his third year. Sadly he came bottom of the university averages in 1892. But the importance of Digby's cricket career lay not in the runs he scored or the few wickets he took, but in the friendships he made with the men who were to become his companions and opponents on cricket grounds throughout the country during the next 12 years. In particular, he served under three captains at Cambridge, each of whom, though of very different character, embodied aspects of that Varsity spirit which so pervaded English cricket in the Golden Age.

Sammy Woods, a hard-hitting batsman and tearaway bowler, was

captain in 1890. Much had happened to him since he had appeared for
Brighton College against the Demon in the fixture with Tonbridge.
He had played cricket for Australia against England, had represented
the Gentlemen v. the Players and he had played rugger for England as
a rampaging forward. The 22-year-old Cambridge captain was a
national celebrity and the toast of the undergraduate population.
It was his exceptional sporting prowess which had broken down
any social barriers which might otherwise have impeded him at
Cambridge, for Woods, the son of an Australian merchant, was in
Digby's words 'as rough as rough can be'.

Woods was a big man, over 6 feet and 13 stone. He was admired
everywhere he went. To the British public in 1890 he exemplified
young British manhood. He was like John Bull's son (and no one bore
him any malice for his Antipodean origin). To the average undergraduate he was a god. When, after three unproductive scholastic years,
he was at last told he must pass his 'Little Go' or leave, there was
overwhelming student support for his being given an honorary
degree. Great gloom descended on Cambridge when this was turned
down and Sammy was sent to the Corn Exchange to fight the unequal
battle with the examiners. A fellow examinee wrote: 'Hundreds of
men were proceeding in the same direction to the Exchange – among
them, a great, broad-shouldered figure, with a shock of thick hair and
a lean, sunburnt face. He wore a short and somewhat tattered gown –
an ancient, battered College cap. The friend with whom I was walking
said: "That's Sammy Woods!" It was the first time I had seen him; and
I gazed, in humble admiration, at the towering form stalking moodily
in front of us.'

As a captain he demonstrated the natural, peremptory authority of
the Varsity Blue. His motto in the field was 'The nearer the game, the
greater the knowledge' and, to practise this theory, he would often
stand at silly point (that position so favoured today in Test cricket),
where the proximity of his jutting chin, towering above, must have
intimidated many a batsman. In the hard-hitting Golden Age mid-off
was a vital position and sometimes Woods would go there if the
batting was aggressive enough. 'Come on, you little blighter, out of
it!' shouted Woods to Digby one afternoon. 'I received curt instructions,' wrote Digby, 'to remove myself from mid-off, where for five
or six overs I had been stopping or attempting to stop the fierce
off-punches of J. J. Lyons, the great Australian hitter. So I bolted, like

a rabbit, to mid-on, my forearms puffed and bruised and aching, while Sammy took my place . . .'

Thanks to some friendly, sporting dons, Sammy Woods passed his exams, though he was rumoured only to have been able to write 'S. M. J. Woods. Jesus' on his papers and, even so, to have made one spelling mistake. Part of the condition of his staying up for one more year was handing over the captaincy. His friend, Gregor MacGregor, became captain.

MacGregor, whom Digby hero-worshipped, had a much more correct social background than Woods, being a member of an illustrious Scottish clan. He had been educated at Uppingham and, like Woods, was an all-round sportsman. Keen on rugger, he played full-back for Scotland. He was an accomplished wicket-keeper, unfussy and brave. Already, while still an undergraduate, he had kept for England. His skill in standing up to the bowling of Woods was the talk of Cambridge. 'A machine-like precision – that foreshadowing of the possible – existed between Gregor MacGregor and Sammy Woods', Digby wrote. 'The faster Sam bowled, the nearer the sticks stood Mac, and he took the five and a half ounces of leather, cork and string, as if it were a ping-pong ball! He took it on the off or on the on-side with equal facility, and he would throw the ball back, time in and out, with the suggestion that he was a little tired with it all!'

MacGregor differed greatly from the extrovert Woods in temperament. He was the strong, silent type. His critics might have called him moody and sullen, but to Digby he was 'silent, determined, full of supreme self-confidence'. He was the dourest of Scots, slow of speech, his saturnine features rarely creasing into a smile. On the field of play, he exhibited a grim determination. 'He was always the same', wrote Digby, ' – even-tempered, imperturbable – at times perhaps bordering on the cynical; rarely if ever depressed by fear of disaster, or over-elated with the joy of success. He was a pessimist at the start of the day – he was an optimist all through it!' The total commitment of MacGregor, the steely determination beneath the casual façade, was an important aspect of the Varsity Blue.

Digby's third captain, the Hon. F. S. Jackson, was even more typical of the Varsity Blue than his two predecessors. Stanley Jackson, known to all as 'Jacker', was a born leader and a born winner. He had captained Harrow and he had captained the public schools when, with the Demon in their ranks, they had beaten the touring Indian Parsees. He was later to captain Yorkshire and England. Son of a member of Lord Salisbury's cabinet, he himself subsequently became an MP. In the 1920s, as Governor of Bengal, he survived an assassination attempt, ducking out of the way of five close-range pistol shots, much as a few years earlier he had ducked out of the way of the Demon's worst fire at Leyton.

Jackson was a splendid all-rounder, taken by many to be the perfect example of the Golden Age amateur. Contemporary photographs reveal a front-footed batsman of enormous power, master of the full-faced drive, ever so sweetly timed. He drove with a flowing, superbly controlled freedom. His was perfection in front-foot play. Digby, strangely, rarely wrote of Jackson's batting, and on his bowling he was only luke-warm: 'F. S. Jackson is a confident bowler. He bowls with a confidence born of the past and with an unlimited confidence in the future, and to this self-reliance I attribute a large proportion of his success. Bowling fast-medium, with an occasional off-break and an occasional slower ball, he invariably manages to keep the runs down, and at the same time takes his quota of wickets, and a bowler that can go with Sam Woods through the whole of a Gentlemen v. Players match unchanged must be a really good bowler, even though, as we watch him, we cannot exactly determine *how* he succeeds . . .'

This grudging praise of one of the finest cricketers of his generation is surprising. Perhaps it reveals more about Digby's social insecurity than his cricketing judgment, because he and Stanley Jackson were never close friends. He never felt completely at ease in the Old Harrovian's company; Jackson was too poised and sophisticated and possessed none of those public school eccentricities Digby so much enjoyed. Jackson was a perpetual reminder that university cricket was still a gentleman's game.

Nowhere was this more evident than in the Oxford and Cambridge match at Lord's, which was one of the events of the London season. Fifty thousand came to watch the game in 1892, Digby's last year, and the green turf was barely visible beneath the chattering multitude, promenading before the pavilion during the lunch interval. For the ladies it was a fashion parade; for their well-groomed escorts it was an opportunity to display their social graces; and for the members of the general public, who had not gone, nor would ever go, to either university, it was a time to sit on the grass, sporting a dark or light blue rosette, and admire the cricket and the elegance of the scene.

For the upper classes there were stage-coaches or 'drags' affording the gentlemen a good view of the cricket and the ladies an excellent vantage point from which to be seen. Some of the social implications of a Varsity match find expression in Emily Bardswell's novelette of the 1890s, *Played On*, in which the heroine, Beatrice, untypical of her sex, is a passionate devotee of the game: 'So at last Beatrice found herself really on the way up to the historic ground, passing, as they neared it, long strings of empty hansoms returning from that paradise of cricket lovers. Lady Charlotte insisted on their all waiting in the carriage while the footman went to discover the exact position of the drag to which they were to transfer themselves. But, at last, the man returned and they all left the landau and entered the ground. "Let Beatrice have the box. She wants to see the cricket," said Flora, as they reached the side of the coach. She lost no time in mounting to the coign of vantage offered to her, but here a disappointment awaited her. The coach had two others in front of it; ladies with parasols and gentlemen with tall hats covered them both. It was simply impossible to see the play!'

Digby's own contribution to this glamorous event lay mainly in his fielding, an aspect of the game which was not always taken seriously in the Golden Age, but at which both Demon and Lobster excelled. In 1890 Cambridge won a low-scoring match. Digby was not called upon to bowl. He did, however, score a few runs at no. 7. 1891 saw him demoted to no. 11 and again he didn't bowl. In his last year, when clear favourites, Cambridge lost. Digby was one of several victims of a lob bowler, J. B. Wood, who won the game for Oxford. That dismissal may well have set Digby thinking, for shortly afterwards he was to try lob bowling himself.

The most exciting finish of Digby's Varsity matches was that of 1891. Sam Woods had destroyed the Oxford batting and Cambridge found themselves needing only 90 to win. But the light was drawing in and it was considered unsporting to appeal against it when a match was reaching a conclusion. Wickets began to fall in the gloom. Thirty runs were wanted with 6 wickets left; then 23 with 5 wickets left. It got darker and darker. At 6.30 p.m. MacGregor himself went out to bat, amidst tremendous cheers. He hung on grimly. Twelve to win with 4 wickets left; 2 to win with 3 wickets, and Cambridge men were smiling confidently. Then, with the scores equal, MacGregor fell. There were 2 wickets left, those of Woods and Digby. Out strode the former amidst the darkening gloom. He wore neither gloves nor pads. He had not expected to bat. He had simply seized the first bat he set eyes on. The crowd shouted itself hoarse as he marched to the wicket, hushing quickly to total silence when he reached the pitch and took guard. The bowler approached, Sammy flailed his bat, there was a resounding smack and the ball went scudding to the boundary. Sammy had won the match and the players were engulfed in teeming humanity as they raced back to the new Lord's pavilion.

Almost as exciting as the games on the field were the games off it. Just as Digby learnt much of his cricketing skills from his three university captains, so he also learnt from them some less public, not entirely creditable aspects of the Varsity Blue. The 1890s were a time of college clubs, drinking port, eating oysters, singing lusty ballads . . . In addition Cambridge cricket had a tradition of off-field wildness and extravagance. So Woods and MacGregor, taking their cue from the Wildean tag that nothing succeeds like excess, did their energetic best to foster this Fenner's tradition. Digby, initially diffident and uncertain, soon became a rejoicing acolyte in their revels. His third captain, Stanley Jackson, by contrast brought discipline and respectability to the Cambridge dressing room, qualities which may not entirely have endeared him to Digby. Yet Jackson too revealed another university weakness of the period, the inability to apply the philosophy of fair play to those of a different-coloured skin.

There are many stories of Woods and MacGregor. MacGregor, it was said, one night played a game of 'bounce ball' with a small Jesus College porter, who had foolishly tried to interrupt a midnight revel. The porter was tossed skywards, caught, tossed again in a continuing process until fortunate relief was brought to the poor man, when the waistband of his trousers caught in the spikes of the railings and held him suspended. On another occasion the young MacGregor, bear-fighting with Woods, was pushed by the latter right through a window. Despite badly cut hands, the story runs, the Scot kept wicket as superbly as ever the next morning.

Scene of much carousing were the palatial rooms which Woods and MacGregor shared at Prospect House opposite Jesus Common. Visiting amateurs were lavishly entertained there. Great was the consternation of seven visitors once, when offered a pre-match breakfast of huge lobsters and jugs of college ale. It proved too much for them, so Woods and MacGregor duly ate all the lobsters, swilling them down with all the ale. It proved an efficacious diet: Sammy Woods took 10 wickets. Even older generations of visitors were influenced by the wildness of Prospect House. W. G. Grace, playing at Cambridge with his friend the deep-drinking W. L. Murdoch, responded to the mood: 'I remember W.G. and Billy Murdoch', wrote Woods, 'bumping A. J. L. Hill and myself into the fireplace. I thought Hill was badly injured; the two former were just like a couple of boys – splendid boys those!'

Sammy Woods was for ever getting into scrapes. He was a good billiards player and one afternoon was challenged by a couple of hefty bookmakers in a Bristol hotel. 'He beat them both,' wrote Digby. 'One of them took his defeat badly, and remarked in an undertone to his pal something about billiard sharps. "What, you two beauties call me a billiards sharp, do you?" In a flash he had each of them by the scruff of the neck and hammered their heads together till they fell senseless to the floor. He rang the bell. "Waiter, a syphon of soda, please, and ask the manager if he would kindly step up here." He sprayed the inanimates, who slowly recovered. "Now," he said, "here is the boss; ask him who I am," and, with that, he sauntered out of the hotel.'

Unruliness was coupled with racism. Ranjitsinhji, arguably the finest batsman ever to play at Fenner's, had a terrible time winning acceptance when he first arrived in England, fleeing from political intrigues at home in India. Digby might write later of:

> The Eastern mage, whose every stroke
> His inborn genius loudly spoke

but the sad fact remains that Stanley Jackson and his friends perversely turned their backs on that 'inborn genius' in 1892, preferring to give a regular place in the Cambridge side to the struggling Digby.

In an early Varsity trial Ranji scored a fifty but after that was given no further opportunity. Yet all round Cambridge he was scoring runs prolifically. He is said to have made three centuries in one afternoon in different matches which were going on simultaneously on Parker's Piece. Bill Lockwood, the Surrey professional, did his best to further Ranji's claims. 'I remember bowling to him one day in the orchard,' he later said, 'when Mr Jackson came up and looked on. He asked me what I thought of him and I said, "Well, sir, you are playing two or three worse Blues than he is." Then he asked me, "Can he *really* play?" So I said, "Well, sir, you come and try to bowl him out!" He laughed and went away.'

Ranji's omission from the Cambridge XI of 1892 was a simple case of racial and social prejudice. Even though Ranji was a prince, his high Indian rank to the average, very insular undergraduate of the 1890s was not to be compared with British birth. An Indian at Cambridge was an oddity. Besides, he was known to be quick-tempered, flamboyant and casual. His extravagant lifestyle would have commended him more to Sammy Woods than Stanley Jackson. There were lavish parties with lots of sing-songs and games of poker in his two floors of rooms in Sussex Street. He loved fine clothes and jewellery. He possessed the first motor car ever to be seen at Cambridge. He also acquired a pet parrot, Popsy, which, though totally bald, outlived him. However hard he might try to play the English gentleman, with membership of Hawks, billiards at the Liberal Club, shooting and fishing parties, it took a long time for him to force acceptance.

Eventually, of course, Ranji won through. The year after Digby went down from Cambridge, Jackson, captain a second year, selected Ranji and his talent did the rest. It was probably helpful to Ranji's cause that Stanley Jackson toured India with Lord Hawke's party in the intervening winter of 1892–3, thereby acquiring a new perspective.

Digby's thoughts on Ranji's extravagant lifestyle aren't known. He probably approved. Yet Digby, the most modest of men, must surely have found some aspects of the Varsity ethos very unacceptable. The self-confidence, so much the hallmark of the Golden Age Blue, could so easily degenerate into conceit. There was, for example, much irritating posing at the wicket. Charles Fry, one of Oxford's finest batsmen, is said to have strutted about the wicket insufferably 'his head held contemptuously high and shoulders militarily tense'.

Digby would have contrasted this attitude with those of the professionals, because he was one of the few amateurs who broke the conventions, fraternized with the professionals and numbered them among his friends. Tom Hayward was the first of these, one of the young professionals engaged to bowl in the nets at Fenner's. Tom helped out in his father's sports shop, though his heart was in his batting and he was planning to make a career in first-class cricket. Partly through Digby's help and advice, he established links with Surrey, for whom he made over 1000 runs every season from 1895 to 1914.

A second friendship also had its origins in the Cambridge nets. One day early in the season Digby strolled into Fenner's, thinking that a little practice might be of service to him: 'I journeyed to the nets (as most people know they are not of the best) with the usual equipment of pads and gloves. Out of the pavilion came a thin, lithe form of a man with black curly hair. I took the usual casual guard; he took a run of some seven yards. I believe the ball pitched six inches outside the off stump; at any rate it came back like lightning, and the middle stump disappeared into the net; the next ball, pitching nearly straight, hit me on the chest; the third removed the off stump; the fourth hit me on the arm; the fifth removed the leg stick; the sixth and seventh found my ribs. I said: "Thank you very much, I don't think I'll practise any more today," and walked slowly and painfully back to the "hutch". "Who was that bowling?" I asked. "Oh, a young fellow named Richardson – Surrey, I think," came the answer.' As Digby got to know Tom Richardson better over the years, he disregarded those who told him that, as an amateur, he should keep his distance with professionals, off the field. It mattered not one jot to Digby that Richardson was born in a gipsy caravan. The man loved his cricket and that, to Digby, was the basis for friendship.

In his time at Fenner's Digby met many of the leading professionals. From them he was able to perceive an alternative approach to the game, less flamboyant, more exact and equally effective. As with Tom Hayward and Tom Richardson and so with countless others, there was a real love for the game, the love which was all too commonly claimed to be the sole prerogative of those who played for no financial reward. It was, at the very least, inevitable that a deep affection would develop for a game which had raised many professionals from humble circumstances, perhaps even poverty and slums.

To the end of his days Digby painted a picture of Cambridge cricket and of Fenner's in richest gold. He was rarely critical of anything but his own performances there. It is easy for us today to smile. There is little doubt that the overall standard of first-class cricket was considerably lower in the Golden Age than it is now. Those lovely

Cambridge off-drives may have been easier to play at a time when it was normal practice for bowlers to limit their attack to the off stump and it was considered bad form to bowl short. Swing bowling, too, was then in its infancy. Easier university entrance requirements meant that most of the very best public school cricketers spent time at one of the two universities, where the relaxed atmosphere, the good wickets and the strong competition improved their game.

At the same time it was undoubtedly a peacock world, with narcissistic undertones, embracing a code of purity and good sportsmanship which wasn't always upheld. Digby, although he loved his time at Cambridge, was never fully at ease within it and so he strove harder than most to conform to the mould. At Cambridge he learned to eat well, drink well and to gamble, habits which were to last a lifetime. Free of pride or snobbery himself, he was curiously blind to the emptiness of his friends' style of life and he proclaimed the Fenner's philosophy whenever he could. Shortly before he died, he wrote: 'Cricket is and always has been the whitest game on earth; if occasionally the spirit of selfishness has entered into it for some brief space, the men from the two great universities have immediately cast it into the outer darkness where the followers of self weep and gnash their teeth!'

4
Contests
keen

I sing of the joy of a contest keen,
On a classic ground or a village green,
  Or the shard sown patch
  Where the urchins scratch
With the splintered half of what once has been
  A bat.

D.L.A.J.

For Charles and Digby cricket was not rigidly categorized into
first-class and second-class, for the distinctions between county,
minor county and club cricket were not nearly so precise then as they
are today. Throughout their careers, therefore, Digby and Charles
would consider a game on a 'village green' or even a 'shard sown
patch' just as much worth the playing as one on a 'classic ground'.
Indeed, although they both moved up to the first-class game after
making their reputations in club cricket, they continued to play at club
level whenever their County commitments permitted. In doing this
they were simply following the amateur practice of the period. Gregor
MacGregor, for example, Digby's erstwhile captain at Cambridge,

mixed matches for Middlesex with ones for Hampstead. 'Bunny' Lucas turned out as often for Chelmsford as for Essex. His team-mates, McGahey and Perrin, frequently played for Leyton and Tottenham respectively. Their captain, Hugh Owen, enjoyed making runs for Burnham-on-Crouch. Fred Bull, the Essex spinner, was often to be found bowling at Blackheath or Lee. This cross-fertilization of club and county was one of the great strengths of the Golden Age. Indeed, it could be said that without its flourishing club background cricket's Golden Age could never have been.

Cricket was still a limited pastime at the period of the Demon and Lobster's birth, but, as easier travel and greater leisure became more steadily available, cricket clubs proliferated in the 1880s and, by the late 1890s, the game at all levels of performance had become a masculine obsession. The keeping and publishing of averages and all other manner of cricket records became almost a fetish, both nationally and locally. Newspapers, which a few years before had contained little or no cricket news, now devoted whole pages to the publication of scores and reports of matches which were, in the main, of a most modest nature. Digby, on coming down from Cambridge, and Charles, on leaving school, did not need much persuading before being swept along by the torrent of enthusiasm for cricket at club level.

Although cricket as a whole tended to blur class distinctions, nonetheless Golden Age club cricket reflected the social structure of the day. At the top of the scale were the very smart, socially exclusive clubs, often long established, like I Zingari, public school dominated and purveying much of the philosophy of the Varsity Blues. The Zingari motto – 'Keep your promise. Keep your tongue. Keep your wicket up' – was duly applauded by Digby as 'a splendid motto to live up to'. In similar vein, Kent's Band Of Brothers declared as one of its rules that loss of temper be punished by immediate expulsion. Charles in the course of time became a Zingaro but, wisely, kept clear of the Brothers. Then there were the public school Old Boys. 'Bunny' Lucas and Gregor MacGregor would turn out for Uppingham Rovers, while Charles played for the Old Tonbridgians. Sides of Old Boys were particularly welcome guests at country houses, whose cricket-loving owners raised scratch XIs to play at weekends or even for whole weeks. Such matches were, perhaps, the most perfect expression of Golden Age club cricket.

Next in the social scale came the many excellent town clubs, which tended to be the preserve of the upper middle classes, though containing a comparatively wide social mix. Charles played regularly for the Brentwood town club, while Digby, playing for the Clapham Wanderers, must have visited most town grounds in the south-east of England by the end of his career. Many of these town clubs would employ a professional, who looked after the ground, did some coaching and played in the matches. For this he would receive a pitifully small wage and the occasional modest ground collection. Sometimes an enterprising club fielded an extra professional. Thus the young Jack Hobbs played his first really competitive club game with Royston, while being paid the sum of ten shillings for the occasion. The cost of town club membership was relatively high and so too the cost of equipment.

If lower-paid workers found such clubs prohibitively expensive, there was still much cricket played by the working classes, particularly in parks and recreation grounds, where equipment might be minimal and membership subscriptions non-existent. Employees of large firms often had their employers to thank for their cricket. 'Dick' Lilley, for example, the Warwickshire and England wicket-keeper, met serious cricket for the first time when working at Cadbury's, playing for the Bournville club, started by some Cadbury's foremen. When the club proved popular, George Cadbury paid for the services of an old Warwickshire professional to coach the team in the evenings. Bobby Abel, similarly, started his cricket with a Hops Warehouse XI and then a Leatherworkers' team. He moved on to a higher grade of club cricket only when a discerning member of Southwark Park Club paid his membership subscription. Jack Hobbs, the son of a slater's labourer, had an even more unusual beginning, playing first for a Bible Class XI and then for a team of young Liberals.

With such a club structure it was easier for the amateurs, enjoying a higher standard of play and better facilities, to move into the first-class game than for the would-be professionals, whose club standards were often very low. Accordingly many counties engaged young players on their ground staff, for the lowest of retainers, and this enabled the talented, but unpolished, youngsters to play against the better club sides for the County Club & Ground XIs (in which leading amateurs mingled with young or out-of-favour professionals). It could not have been much fun being a young professional in such matches. For example, when the Kent Club & Ground XI was playing against the Band Of Brothers, the captain of the Brethren, the autocratic Lord Harris, took exception to a young professional who had bowled him a no-ball and ordered him out of the ground! Harris is said to have explained his action later to the poor professional in these words: 'Humphreys, I only did this for your own good. There may be an excuse for a fast bowler to be no-balled, but never a slow bowler; it is sheer laziness in his case. Never forget that.'

Charles Kortright, however, never had any such fears of being ordered out of the ground. Nor had he experienced any of the early problems of Hobbs or Abel. From the moment that he decided, on leaving school, to devote himself to cricket, the doors of any club were open to him. He chose Brentwood partly for its proximity to Fryerning (15 minutes away by pony and trap) and partly for its good facilities. He made a spectacularly impressive club début in 1889. Bowling at a very brisk pace, the 18-year-old Charles took 89 wickets for Brentwood at a cost of only 6 runs each! Essex took note and he played his first game for the county that year and also impressed when playing the Essex Club & Ground XI. In the first three balls of the Club & Ground match with the Colchester Garrison, he took 3 wickets, all clean bowled.

His father, Augustus, however, was unimpressed. Charles' younger brother, Mounteney, had by now joined the army and William, the eldest, was helping to run the estate. But Charles himself was showing no inclination to do anything with his life except to play sport and to enjoy chatting about it afterwards in the local. Noting the latter, Augustus adroitly offered his leisure-loving son a share in the Mackeson Brewery, at Hythe, on condition that he took some interest in learning about the running of such a business. Accordingly Charles was sent to Berkshire, as a guest of the Wells family, who ran their own brewery at Wallingford.

Wallingford was no rural backwater, but a thriving market town. What Augustus probably did not know was that it was teeming with cricket clubs, both in the town and surrounding villages. Charles at once joined two clubs, Wallingford Town and Ipsden. Rumours quickly flew around many a Berkshire lane and into many an Oxfordshire pub: a young man had arrived who bowled uncomfortably fast. In just those matches recorded in the local Press, the 19-year-old Charles took 146 wickets. Those which he took for

Wallingford cost only 5 runs each. The Demon bowler had arrived! No quarter was given to his victims, who often remarked upon the ferocity of his visage, his flared nostrils, his antipathy towards anyone holding a bat. Before the Kortright assault the village of Garsington perished for 23. The village of Bradfield perished twice, equally ignobly. The men of High Wycombe crossed the Chilterns, confident in their past performances; they returned with byes as their highest scorer. When the Wallingford cleric, the Revd Farrar, took a team to Littlemore to challenge his friend and rival, the Revd Cummings, he uncharitably invited along the Demon, who shattered the Cummings ranks: all out for 15 and probably very relieved to be so. It was the Thames-side villagers of Dorchester who had the worst of Kortright that year. Four times they had played against him, at home and away at Wallingford and Ipsden. Great had been the number of their fallen: 35 wickets to the unstoppable Demon. One can therefore imagine their feelings of despair when, turning up to play the staff at Moulsford Asylum and quietly fancying their chances, they spotted the dreaded scourge limbering up as a special guest among the ranks of the opposition. Another 12 Dorchester wickets fell to him that day. Charles became a local celebrity. Big crowds came to see him play.

As summer turned to winter and the cricket club turned to football, Charles was just as big a hero, playing at right-back. When Wallingford, for example, played Abingdon on the Kine Croft ground, it was noted: 'The Abingdon backs were not up to the calibre of Kortright, who was sure tackling for all comers and evoked frequent outbursts of applause from the many spectators.'

At Wallingford Charles continued to enjoy the social life of a cricket club, chatting with friends after matches, a pint of Wells ale in their hands. At 19 he displayed more social graces than in his later years, when he was often gruff to the point of rudeness. At one post-match dinner, Charles, who had represented the Singles, proposed the toast of the Marrieds. As guest of another club (for whom he had only played twice) he replied to the toast of Kindred Clubs. 'I have never taken part in two nicer games,' he remarked with consummate tact, 'or games in which the teams played more together or backed their captain better.' He also sang one of the songs which occurred during this convivial evening.

In time Charles went down to Hythe to see the Mackeson Brewery in which he now had a share. Whether Charles had much to do with the production of their bitter beer (a mere 4/6d for 4½ gallons) is doubtful, but George Mackeson was a keen cricketer, the presiding guardian of the local club, so the young Demon was soon enjoying himself. He destroyed Folkestone, took 6 for 3 against Dover Garrison, and knocked down the stumps eight times when playing for Hythe against a scratch XI. He became as feared in Kent as in Essex and Berkshire. South Hampstead, touring in Kent, had the bad luck to meet the Demon playing for Rye. After taking 141 off the South Hampstead attack very quickly, Charles took 9 of their wickets and caught the tenth! He was now bowling very fast indeed and traded on creating an atmosphere of great physical danger. But even he must have paused for thought when a member of a Hythe XI died after ducking into a bouncer from a bowler of lesser pace than himself.

It is probable that his great successes as a bowler at Hythe and Wallingford inhibited his development. Many of the batsmen were as rustic as the surroundings. A score of 60 was often a winning total in Berkshire. When speed was the sole ingredient for success, there was no need for him to explore the subtleties of seam or swing. It was an all-or-nothing technique (and the one which he later took to first-class cricket).

It must have come as no surprise to Augustus when his son announced that business management was not for him. Charles had enjoyed his four years on the brewery circuit, making good friends and taking many, many wickets. Now, at the age of 23, with his father's reluctant consent, he sold his share in the brewery and, by investing the proceeds, was able to live comfortably, a gentleman of leisure, for the rest of his days.

Charles never lost his zest for club cricket. Even when a well-known first-class cricketer, he would take the train to Berkshire, as keen to play at St John's Paddock, Wallingford, as at St John's Wood. The fixture with Magdalen College, Oxford, was his especial favourite. In 1893 he took 7 wickets for 7 runs in eight memorable overs. Five wickets fell to him in consecutive balls. The following year a re-arranged county match forced him to miss the fixture. Such was the general disappointment that later in the year Magdalen were persuaded to bring a scratch XI down on a date when the Demon was free to play. A big crowd gathered and the match did not disappoint. It gave birth to one of the Kortright legends, the bowling of six byes! The Magdalen team was captained by Henry Leveson Gower, the future Surrey captain. Cecil Headlam kept wicket for the visitors. Headlam (who later played for Middlesex under Warner) wrote a first-hand account of the incident: 'The ground was rather small and surrounded by a high hedge; the wicket was not over choice. We observed with amusement not only that the wicket-keeper was standing further back than any ever did, but also that he had a long stop who stood close to the boundary hedge behind him. We were enlightened when the match began. A quite extraordinary fast bowler, running up to the wicket with a terrifying rush, hurled down the ball with a superb action. It pitched rather short, flew straight over the batsman's head, over the far-retired wicket-keeper's head, over long stop, over the hedge behind him and out of the ground! That was my first introduction to C. J. Kortright!' It became one of Charles' favourite stories: 'On a very small ground,' he wrote over 50 years later, 'on a pitch best described as "sporty", I bowled a ball which rose almost straight and went out of the ground, without a second bounce . . . I suggest this made me the first man to bowl a six in byes! The ball pitched right up to the batsman and on the wicket, so that it was undoubtedly within the striker's reach, and there was no question of wides being awarded.' Charles was bowling from the lower end of the ground. A low hawthorn hedge, now removed, marked the town end boundary. The ball had flown approximately 63 yards.

If Charles' early club cricket was dependent on the topography of breweries, Digby's was influenced by the Colman mustard family. Stanley Colman, cousin to the mustard millionaire and Surrey Committee member, Sir Jeremiah Colman, had founded an itinerant club, the Wanderers, known earlier by its place of birth as the Clapham Wanderers, when Digby was still a Manor House school-boy. Stanley Colman had close Surrey connections. He had played some games for them as a young man and afterwards served on their Committee and helped bring on their younger players. With his wide contacts he was able to build the Wanderers, whom he captained for over 50 years, into one of the most formidable London club sides. Digby, nine years his junior, opened the Wanderers' batting with Colman for many years. It became a famous partnership; they were the Hobbs and Hayward of London club cricket. A club captain who had opposed Digby when he was still a boy, remembered many years later his sweet timing: 'When Jephson, a fair, slight, unathletic-looking figure, came out to bat, I noticed a dear old cricketer who was standing at point, edge a bit closer. I warned him not to go too far in. "Oh, that boy can't hurt anyone," came the reply. I said no more but an over or two later Jephson got something like a long hop on the off, and he cut it square. The ball went like a rifle bullet and I thought my point was dead. Fortunately it went between his arm and body. At the end of the over my friend came up and said, "If there is a vacancy anywhere in the long field, I should like to apply for it. This young man is dangerous."'

Although he did not make much impression with his batting at Cambridge, Digby's performances with the Wanderers became better and better. Twice he and Colman put on over 300 together. At Norwood he scored 301 not out in just over three hours. His reputation in club circles grew and grew. One morning Digby turned up for a match looking pale and worn, and a girl, who had heard all about him, asked him how many runs he was going to make. 'I feel absolutely tired out,' he said, 'I'm not worth a dozen runs.' 'Rubbish,' she said. 'Well,' said Digby, ever alive to a bet, 'I'll give you half a crown now and you shall give me a penny for every run I make.' Digby was still not out at tea-time, when someone congratulated him on the bet. 'Heavens!' said Digby, 'I'd forgotten about it. How many have I made?' 'Two hundred and thirty-two,' came the reply.

Manor House School had imbued Digby with a love not only of sport but also of music and literature. He was therefore very much in sympathy with the strong artistic element which was always part of the Wanderers. E. A. Fischer was a well-known artist. George Beldam was an inventor and highly skilled photographer. Reginald Crawford, middle of the three Crawford brothers, was a leading professional singer, whose appearances for Leicestershire were limited by his musical engagements. A. H. Behrend was a song-writer with several great successes to his name – even if Bernard Shaw, music critic at the time, did not appreciate them. '"When Roses Bloom", he wrote, 'is of the drawing room, drawing roomy.' Behrend also wrote operas, cantatas and chamber music. Another famous name was that of Gunby Hadath, soon to become known for his countless boys' stories set in mythical public schools, but already known for his adapting of musical plays and as a lyricist. His great success, 'Down The Vale', was sung in most homes which could afford a piano. Hadath's running between the wickets, however, left something to be desired. 'How not to run', wrote Digby, 'was shown at Horley once by an eminent song-writer, who, evidently trying to evolve another "Down the Vale", never backed up a yard – he was called and ran straight to *cover*! He was not "run out" – he was "walked out"!'

With such an artistic membership it is not surprising to discover that the Wanderers had a fixture with the Thespids, a team of actors, run for many years by C. Aubrey Smith, the Sussex cricketer, who became a Hollywood film star. The fixture nearly came to grief early on. 'Our first ground', wrote Aubrey Smith, 'was at the Grange, Acton – small but good enough till the proprietor got the habit of turning horses in. It couldn't be said that they were good for wet wickets, and a lot of forking was necessary at times. I remember our beating the Wanderers there with Stanley Colman, D. L. A. Jephson, and their usual side. Colman said some raspy things about those wickets . . .'

A Wanderers' dinner, held to mark the departure of a member, a travel-writer, to Java, reveals topics of conversation most dear to Digby: 'The toast of the evening was given by Mr Jephson and right royally received, after which speeches and other toasts occupied the time pleasantly until the early hours of the morn. Everyone had something to say and all branches of music and sport were discussed . . .'

The right social mix made the Wanderers' tours particularly pleasant things for Digby, who went on over 20 of them. It was, he said, the most enjoyable way to spend a holiday 'provided, of course, that you take the right people with you'. The vital ingredient was a good captain, who would 'see that the team plays cricket and not the fool', someone who would 'not allow the game to degenerate into what is so aptly termed "brown sherry cricket" that carries a two-hour lunch and a forty-minute tea and which starts when you like and finishes in the same haphazard manner.' Wives were, for preference, left at home. Digby had pronounced views on this subject: 'If possible, tour with a bachelor team or a side of "grass-widowers" – for ten out of eleven women care very little for cricket for cricket's sake, and though from the goodness of their hearts they insist on coming to the grounds and sitting through the weary hours till at length they grow tired, restless, fretful, it would be kinder to all concerned, and less like cruelty to animals, to leave them quietly at home. Somehow, however, this point of view rarely appeals to them as it should!'

Off the conjugal leash and away from where he was known, the Victorian cricketer on tour was able to revert to a juvenile frame of mind, in which drink and horseplay figured prominently. For Digby it was a wonderful opportunity to pursue one aspect of the Varsity Blue philosophy: 'With a good skipper and a jolly lot of fellows what can beat the splendid hours one spends in a two-days match at the Saffrons, Eastbourne, or the Central ground at Hastings, at St Lawrence, Canterbury, or at Tonbridge – hard work, a fine sweat – a swim, dinner together, and the chit-chat and the chaff of the day's play afterwards; occasionally a harmless practical joke, but all in the truest fellowship? I remember years ago we arrived at Canterbury and stayed at a well-known hostelry in the Main Street. We had the usual merry, heterogeneous crowd, a solicitor, a doctor, a couple of stock-brokers, an Oxford philologist and men of various occupations and men of none. The philologist was an eccentric, he bowled off the wrong foot and at times he bowled wonderfully well, and his only luggage for a ten-day tour was a brown paper parcel which contained his boots and a cheque book! After dinner, it was a birthday night, the professor grew exceedingly festive, so two of us suggested a walk as a slight restorative, but the fresh air only accentuated his festivity. Suddenly, as we were passing a cabbage patch, we heard a "whoop", and in a second we saw our philologist smashing green stuff right and left with the heavy blackthorn that he invariably carried. "That's for you, you consanguinated 'Hiro-oan' – for you, for you – " at each ejaculation a fresh cabbage lay prostrate. We rushed to stop him, but before us rushed the infuriated proprietor. "What the – ?" "It's all right," we said in the latter's ear, "we're his keepers." With difficulty we stayed the slaughter of the innocents, squared the now smiling proprietor and led our "patient" homewards.'

At the stipulated hours, however, there was serious cricket. It was often of a spectacular nature. The Wanderers, for example, met a dashing batsman called Harry Bush (who later played for Surrey under Digby), an army officer, who scorned the use of batting gloves however fast the bowling. 'We were fielding against the strong Eastbourne XI and had done well until no. 8 arrived on the scene. A player in a pink shirt, a black and white cap, and a stiff four-inch white collar; "rabbit" we murmured joyfully, but oh, what a surprise; the "rabbit" proceeded to paste us to every part of the sea-side ground – he drove, he cut, he hit – in an hour and a half he made 176! Crestfallen, footweary, we returned to the pavilion at six o'clock. "Who's that batsman?" "Captain H. S. Bush," came the reply, "arrived from India this morning." We wished he'd stopped there, for in the second innings he made 123 not out in less than an hour.'

As a young man Digby sometimes accompanied the Crystal Palace Club (as did Stanley Colman) on its three-week tour, in which nine two-day matches were played. The club secretary happened to be F. C. Barchard, who had been Charles' captain at Tonbridge. Taking full advantage of the country's flourishing railway system, Barchard devised an itinerary of some grandeur. In 1893, for example, the team travelled to Bath (where Digby took 5 wickets against the Lansdowne Club), thence to Wellington (where Digby scored 77) and on to Exeter (where Digby scored a century and took 6 wickets). They toured in Devon for the next week. At Exmouth Digby scored 70, at Seaton a fifty, and at Sidmouth another fifty. They then travelled to Salisbury (where Digby took 5 South Wilts wickets) and then along the south coast, Digby ending the tour with 64 and 8 wickets against the South Saxons and 7 wickets and a double century (261) at Eastbourne. There was a similar itinerary the next year when Digby was equally successful, scoring three centuries, averaging over 50 and taking 60 wickets. The cricket was played on some of the loveliest grounds in England.

As Digby and Charles became better known, invitations came to play at country houses. A well-tended cricket field in one's grounds had become the status symbol of the 1890s. On some estates the wickets were of a very high quality and leading amateur players were sought to embellish the occasion. The social nature of these gatherings appealed very much to Digby, and Charles too found the matches to his liking. 'In country house cricket', wrote Ranji, 'a captain's chief duty is to let everyone have a bowl and make the match a social success.' Charles would not necessarily have agreed with such sentiments and his competitive instinct might have made his presence an embarrassment to some hosts. But the invitations still flowed. Whilst a regular Essex player, he would, for example, often journey to Nuneham Park, south of Oxford, to play for a Wallingford XI. Charles frequently made a nonsense of these games with overwhelming performances with bat and ball. He and Freddie Fane, the Essex opening bat, were also welcome guests at Hainault Lodge, north of Romford. The Hainault Lodge cricket weeks were not an entirely male preserve, for on one of the days a match took place between 11 ladies and 11 gentlemen. The latter were handicapped by the use of the left hand only and with broomsticks instead of bats.

One of the most vivid pictures of country house cricket has been painted by E. H. D. Sewell, who played some games with Digby for the Wanderers. One of his favourite country houses was Ascott, Buckinghamshire, the home of the Rothschild family. Sewell's introduction there was through Digby: 'My innings was just over for the Wanderers v. Sutton (and that was for years one of the blood matches in London club cricket), when Digby Jephson sang out to me: "Doing anything tomorrow?" It so happened that there was no big match in or near London so, on my replying in the negative, he said: "Read this. Like to go?" handing me a wire he had received from Ernest Beldam, the Middlesex cricketer. "Can you play at Ascott tomorrow for me against Rothschild's XI, if not send substitute, train Euston – Leighton Buzzard, wire Beldam." ' Every August, for one week, the Rothschilds would play strong sides like Harrow Wanderers, I Zingari and the Gentlemen of Bucks. The pitches were excellent and play of a high standard. Generally on such occasions, the male of the species predominated, off the field as well as on: 'Good players used to assemble from all points of the compass, and there were some merry stag parties staying in the long, low, ivy-clad building which was the house. I have no idea how many bedrooms or bathrooms there were on what seemed to me to be the only upper floor, but two XIs were easily put up in the utmost comfort. Everyone did just as he liked, breakfast was the help-yourself function which is so pleasant; then one loafed about, or had a set or two of lawn tennis, or strolled in the lovely gardens.' At the end of the game the serious business of the day began. 'We just doddled off to the House', wrote Sewell, 'and those of us who had got a duck or so, or had not had much bowling or fielding, had some lawn tennis before tubbing and changing for dinner.' Dinner was a full-dress occasion, the first part of the day in which the ladies had much share. I Zingari brightened up such already bright evenings with their sashes of red, black and yellow worn diagonally across their dress shirts and a bow tie of similar colours. Dinner was always 'a joyous occasion in a merry company, enjoyed to the pleasing tune of the subdued, well-bred chink of silver on fine porcelain'. After dinner, when the Zingari would sing their club song, the company split up, some to cards, some to billiards, some to 'a comfy chair and a book'. Sewell himself 'generally anchored in a small armchair, in which one almost sank out of sight, or had a quiet cricket chin-wag'.

In Essex one big supporter of country house cricket was Charles Green, who lived in a large mansion, Theydon Grove, near Epping, from where he devoted himself to his twin passions, Essex cricket and the Essex Hunt. Green was an extremely rich amateur sportsman. His money came from his family's shipping business, the Orient Steam Navigation Company, of which he was a director. As a cricketer, he had captained Cambridge, played a few games for Middlesex and Sussex and had represented the Gentlemen with honour. He was a hard-hitting batsman. In the manner of the 1870s, he would stand firm on his right foot and drive hard in front of the wicket.

In 1882, when he was 35 years old, Green took over the captaincy of Essex and for the next 30 years he became the grand puppet-master of Essex cricket. Green was an idealist. He saw county cricket as an extension of club cricket. He wished Essex to become a first-class county, but, even more fervently, he wished the county to exhibit all the best traits of a top-class amateur club. He conceded that he needed a small band of professionals to do some bowling and keep the ground in good fettle, but Green's Essex was essentially a club of gentlemen cricketers. Accordingly, he gathered around him a nucleus of younger, like-minded Cambridge men. Bunny Lucas, a fellow member of Uppingham Rovers and fellow habitué of the City, moved at once from Surrey to Essex to join Green (the Kortrights finding him a house in Fryerning, the old Rectory, where he lived for many years). Bunny Lucas was a life-long friend of Green, ten years his senior; many years later, Green, when he lay dying, wrote a codicil bequeathing £500 to Lucas, 'my very dear old friend and associate in the cricket field'. Co-partner in Green's early labours, helping him to raise teams to play at Brentwood, was Hugh Owen, freshly down from Cambridge and rescued by Green from schoolmastering. Youngest of Green's Varsity blues was Cyril Buxton, a Harrovian, captain at Cambridge two years before Sammy Woods. Buxton took over the Essex captaincy from Green. It proved a heavy torch to carry, for the Essex XI, strong in social graces, was weak in other, more vital aspects of the game.

After four years in control at Brentwood, Green moved his club to Leyton, acquiring a ground there from the Lyttelton estate. The cost was enormous, £12,000, and the mortgage repayments were a crippling burden for the county over the coming years. But the move itself was a sensible one, for the little market town of Brentwood would not have been able to provide the size of crowds needed to pay the professionals' wages. Leyton, on the other hand, to the east of London, was an expanding town of 30,000 people, the home of commuting city clerks and prosperous local traders. Leyton's vast red-brick Town Hall, recently erected, expressed the current feeling of civic pride and so too, in a less exalted way, did the neat terraced houses of Brewster and Cowley roads, which soon arose around the ground to keep an eye on the cricket. Green equipped his ground with a new pavilion, its pebble-dash and mock-Tudor timber reflecting its suburban locale, its grandeur of design emphasizing Green's determination to achieve first-class status.

Green was now free to develop Essex cricket on club lines. The new pavilion was used for monthly dinners for members and, in the summer, garden parties were inaugurated. One of these took place just after Charles' first county match. On a lovely July evening the pavilion was resplendently adorned with many-coloured Chinese lanterns. So too was the court, set aside for dancing. On the grass, in front of the pavilion, a concert took place, members singing favourite ballads like 'The Bedouin Love Song' and 'My Queen' and humorous items, such as 'See me dance the Polka'. There was banjo playing by some not-so-dusky minstrels, while a string band played wistful melodies into the quietude of a night unadulterated by the noise of anything more raucous than the occasional passing horse and cart. There was a social exclusiveness about the occasion. 'The company which assembled', it was said, 'was large enough to make intercourse pleasant and sufficiently select to prevent over-crowding.'

Among Charles Green's efforts to promote his new ground was the invitation to W. G. Grace to play there, for the first time, in Essex's recently acquired fixture with the MCC. The arrival of W.G. caused great interest and 2000 spectators watched the Saturday's play. Green had known Grace for many years; they were near contemporaries and had played for the Gentlemen together. But they were ill-suited companions temperamentally. Both men were too accustomed to getting their own way for an easy relationship. The Master of the Essex Hunt knew how to crack the whip and stayed agreeable only as long as his will was not crossed. The match turned out to be a triumph for Essex, which would not have pleased Grace, even though he himself scored a well-applauded 71 in the first innings. During the days of the match Green entertained Grace, Lucas and Owen at Theydon Grove, an occasion which he later recalled: 'Of course Bunny Lucas and W.G. had many cricket yarns and reminiscences they were able to recall. I also remember that we had a party of young people in the house, and W.G. was just like a boy, playing games and telling amusing stories.' Grace was royally entertained, his host even mounting him on his favourite grey and bringing up the hounds to the house for him. Then things went wrong. First, Green was not at all pleased when Grace rushed off unexpectedly at the end of the match, when Essex had planned, in his honour, a smoking concert in the new pavilion. It was the first event of its kind and announcements had been made that Grace would preside. His absence caused great disappointment which even sweet renditions of 'Come into the Garden, Maud' and 'The Song of Hybrias the Cretan' would not have lessened. Then, shortly after the visit, Green received a letter from Grace, thanking him warmly, but asking for 20 guineas 'for the advertisement which he had afforded to the new ground'. Green paid up, but was not amused. Such profiteering from the gentlemanly game was not in accord with the Varsity Blue ethos. The two men did not speak to each other for some time and Grace did not play at Leyton for another nine years.

For all his enterprising attempts to develop the club atmosphere at Leyton, Green's dream seemed in danger of collapsing. Poor performances led to low membership and dangerously uncertain finances. As the season of 1892 dawned there were threats that the club might cease. Worse followed. The club suffered the most terrible of blows. Its captain shot himself. Cyril Buxton had been suffering from depression for some time and ended his life when only 25 years old. For Green it must have come as an appalling shock. The Buxtons lived close to him at their home at Knighton, Woodford Wells, and the two men had hunted regularly together for the past two years. The younger man had taken several falls and the inquest considered that this may have affected the balance of his mind. Hunting was mentioned in the hasty, incomprehensible note he scrawled before firing off the double-barrelled gun by the elaborate contrivance of a poker and handkerchief.

Charles would have felt Buxton's death deeply, for he knew him well and often discussed their common interest, brewing. Cyril Buxton's father (a big financial support to Essex cricket) ran the eponymous family brewery, which later merged wth Truman's. Not only were the two young men similarly situated in their careers, they shared the same scepticism about work and the same love of the outdoor life. Cyril Buxton's happiest hours were spent walking through the park of Knighton with his favourite dogs.

All was gloom, therefore, at Leyton. First-class cricket seemed further away than ever. And then the Demon arrived! In 1892 Charles began to play regularly for Green's XI and soon it was clear that the 21-year-old tearaway bowler might well turn the mixture of competent gentlemen and useful professionals into a winning combination. Expectant crowds began to arrive in tram-loads just to see him, for that season he sometimes performed feats which transformed a match. At The Oval he dismissed Kingsmill Key, Billy Brockwell and wicket-keeper Harry Wood in 4 balls. The dismissal of Brockwell was one of his legendary feats. Charles was fond of recalling how the bails flew up into the air on impact, one of them breaking in two over his head and flying past him and over the bowler's wicket. On another occasion Hampshire slumped from 150 for 3 to 150 all out, as 7 wickets fell before his onslaught, Charles clean bowling 6 victims. His 7 wickets against the MCC raised some eyebrows back at Lord's. Essex, with Charles, became a formidable club.

Inevitably, as Essex cricket rapidly improved with the advent of the Demon, the nature of the county club altered. As it became more competitive and strove for first-class status, it necessarily became bigger, less personal. Charles Green was forced to accept that more professionals were as much a necessity as the admittance of greater number of hoi polloi around the ring. Yet, for all its growing commercial success, Green's Essex never entirely lost its unique club atmosphere.

Charles and Digby, too, throughout their first-class careers, never lost their love for the club ethos. Both men cared little for the politics and pressures of county cricket. Both men cared a lot for the simplicity of the club game. Whether it was played on a classic ground, in the grand surroundings of a country house, on a village green or even a 'shard sown patch', the 'contest keen' was for them the thing that mattered. Nowhere does this philosophy come out more strongly than in Digby's account of a very strange match in which he once participated, when on holiday at Mersea. This match typified his notion that the game was more important than its location, that 'white' game of Fenner's, which represented the supreme challenge, whether it was played beneath the gasometers of The Oval or by the oyster beds of an Essex seaside town: 'It is a strange thing to be alive; it is a far stranger thing not to be dead – at least this is what I thought as I emerged, bent and broken, from the first and last cricket match of my holidays.

'I was standing in a field in an Essex village; the game was about to start. "You play cricket, don't you?" I modestly admitted the fact. "Well, we're one short – make up the side?" I did. I asked which was the wicket. "Right in the centre." I walked in that direction; I looked at the pitch; it was plantain, oyster shells, bits of anchors, tar, concrete and more plantain! I looked for a roller; there was none; but suddenly six men with six spades arrived on the scene and hammered our wicket flat. Then the play began.

'There were no pads, no gloves, and each side had only one bat! This necessitated the non-striker carrying a stump, and as the batsmen crossed they changed weapons, which did not lessen the chance of being run out. I went in first. I thought Richardson, Lockwood and Kortright were fast, but their pace was as nothing compared with the speed of those six-feet sons of the sea. I had five balls. The first landed on an oyster shell – it just missed point; the second struck an anchor and hit square leg; the third smote me on the chest; the fourth nearly throttled me; and the fifth, having found a plantain, sent the middle peg 16 yards. We made 18.

'Then six of our opponents went out with six new spades, and again rolled the wicket. During the interval the plantains seemed to have grown; they are indeed excellent herbs to have on one's side. They made 14.

'But still, as at Lord's, The Oval or Fenner's, so on this village field with its wicket of oyster shells, anchors, tar and concrete, with its tall longshoremen, the spirit of fairness, of the grand old game is just the same. At any time it is a strange thing to be alive, but it is a far stranger things not to be dead after a cricket match at Oysterville!'

The Essex County Ground Leyton

5
Lobs and bouncers

It was in 1892, just months after he had come down from Cambridge, that Digby first began to bowl lobs. A Wanderers' tour had taken him to a match against Reigate Priory. 'I said to myself, "If you can't bowl round, you must try underhand."' The experiment was very successful. Digby took 5 wickets for 27, thrice tempting batsmen down the wicket to be stumped by the Wanderers' wicket-keeper, Arthur Behrend. The Lobster's career had begun.

His decision to bowl lobs was unlikely to have been one lightly and suddenly taken. As a 13-year-old schoolboy, watching an Oval Test Match of 1884, his interest in lobs would have been aroused by the action of the England wicket-keeper, the Hon. R. H. Lyttelton, who, at a critical moment, removed his pads and bowled lobs. He took 4 wickets and so defeated the Australians! Later, at Cambridge, Digby would have often heard the story of A. W. Ridley. In the Varsity match of 1875, Cambridge, with 2 wickets standing and 4 runs to win, were suddenly confronted by lobs from Ridley, the Oxford captain. He won the match for his side and was ever after known as 'Jammy' Ridley. Digby himself, in his final Varsity match, had experience of an Oxford lob bowler. John Barry Wood, later a famous KC, lodged many successful appeals as he lobbed his way to victory over Stanley Jackson's Cambridge XI. But the man most likely to have influenced Digby was the Surrey and England player, Walter Read.

Reigate was Read's home club and, ever since Digby had first arrived at The Oval as an undergraduate to play a game for the 2nd XI, Read had taken a tremendous interest in him, acting as his guide and mentor. Walter Read was only an occasional lob bowler, the extra turn pushed on to the stage when the regular acts had fallen flat. But he was good enough to have taken a first-class hat-trick and he was especially tantalizing to sloggers. When Charles was one day having a moment of glory with the bat, celebrating an invitation to open the Essex innings by thrashing Richardson, Lockwood and others all round The Oval, Read's 'innocent-looking but insidious' lobs troubled him greatly and he ultimately succumbed to one, when caught at square leg off a skier, mistiming a big hit. It is likely therefore that it was a quiet word of encouragement from Read that afternoon at Reigate which finally prompted Digby to become a lobster.

In bowling lobs Digby was associating himself with a very small group of players who had continued to ply the art long after it had ceased to be popular. Round-arm bowling had been legalized as long ago as 1835, but underarm bowling did not go out of existence at once. Like the horse-drawn vehicles at the advent of the motor car, old ways combined with new for a time. Indeed, in the person of William Clarke, lob bowling reached its highest form of expression around the middle of the nineteenth century. Clarke, a Notts professional and the creator of the All-England XI, took an enormous number of wickets in spite of having only one eye. He was particularly successful in middle age. In his seven best seasons he claimed over 2000 wickets.

Twenty years later, however, around the time that the Demon and Lobster were born, great changes were afoot. Most important of all was the legalization of overarm bowling. Within a generation, lob bowling and round-arm had gone right out of fashion. At the same time top hats and braces disappeared from the cricket field. Pitches improved. A sport, previously enjoyed by only a few, became a sport enjoyed by many. Cricket turned into an English institution. Schools had previously merely tolerated the game. Now the public schools led the way in championing its cause, seeing it, in fact, as a necessary part of the education of an Englishman. 'Mark me,' said the Revd Edward Thring, Headmaster of Uppingham, 'cricket is the greatest bond of

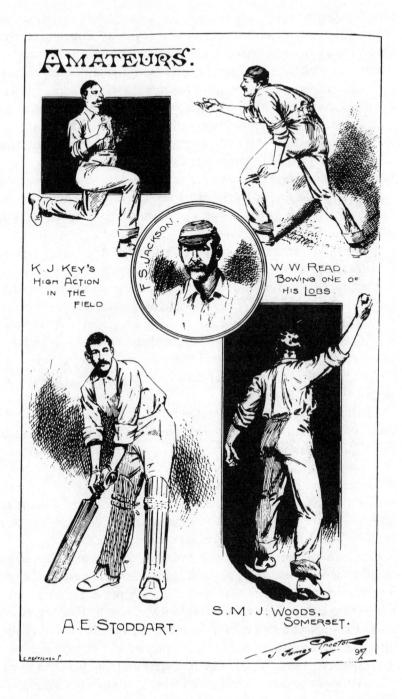

Amateurs.

K.J Key's High Action in the Field

F.S.Jackson

W.W.Read. Bowing one of his Lobs.

A.E.Stoddart.

S.M.J.Woods, Somerset.

the English-speaking race, and is no mere game.' Andrew Lang, famous as a man of letters but also as a devoted admirer of cricket in general and Charles Kortright in particular, went further in his claims: 'Cricket is a liberal education in itself, and demands temper, justice and perseverence. There is more teaching in the playground than in the schoolroom and a lesson better worth learning.'

It was in such an atmosphere of enthusiastic support for the game that county cricket began to emerge as the most important area of activity for amateur and professional players, with W.G.'s Gloucestershire to the fore. Grace was 16 years old at the time when overarm bowling was legalized in 1864, and the young, slim-line medic was in the 1870s proving a powerful exponent of the new bowling technique.

In the 1890s, at the beginning of the Golden Age, as the careers of Charles and Digby began, further changes were occurring. It was as if the Industrial Revolution, which had speeded up the pace of life in general, was now finding its expression on the cricket field. 'We travel faster, make love faster, gain and lose money faster, and exhaust our vitality faster than did our forefathers,' bemoaned one newspaper of the period. The speed of the changes in cricket came faster in the Golden Age than at any other time (except, perhaps, in the last 20 years).

Charles' tearaway bowling was symbolic of the new age. There had been fast underarm jerkers and there had been fast round-arm slingers, but Charles was in the vanguard of an entirely new concept, fast bowling as one knows it today. He used the short-pitched ball deliberately (although he would always gruffly deny this). He cared little about the physical well-being of the batsman. He was the most ungentlemanly gentleman the cricket field had yet seen. He was as modern as the Dreadnought and about as thick-skinned.

One must turn to the printed word to obtain a clear picture of what Charles' action was like as he heralded in the brave new world of fast bowling, for his career was just over when George Beldam was pioneering close-up action photography. Prior to Beldam, bowlers tended to pose by the wicket, one arm in the air. There is such a photograph of Charles, taken in his prime; it is depressingly static. The only action shots of Charles' day were long-shots, taken from the ring without the aid of a telephoto lens. One such photograph now hangs in the pavilion at Edgbaston. It was taken to celebrate

Warwickshire's first Championship match in 1895. It purports to show Charles bowling to the Warwickshire captain, Herbert Bainbridge. A stocky man of medium height is delivering the ball to the obvious unconcern of most of the fielders. His arm is 40 degrees from the vertical. Tom Russell, behind the stumps, has not even bothered to bend down. The field placing is that of a conventional medium-pacer. Although it is likely that the photograph was taken on the third day's play, when the match was a certain draw, it is difficult to believe that this really is the 24-year-old Demon. It is more likely to be Harry Pickett, bowling one of his many fast-medium overs that match. There are only two other known photographs of the Demon in action, both taken at Leyton. In the first he has just released a quick ball towards a Yorkshireman in 1897. The field is surprisingly defensive. Wicket-keeper and third man have clearly eaten too good a lunch. The batsman is stepping out to drive with a back-lift of extreme audacity. Either he is about to lose his middle stump or Charles is indulging in a warm-up ball. The second is from a match in 1900. Charles had just beaten Gloucester's Edgar Thomas outside the off stump. There is a greater tenseness about the fielding. Tom Russell is actually bending down this time to take the ball. But neither photograph tells us much about the bowler.

From the written word one learns much more, even though Charles' chief panegyrist, E. H. D. Sewell, must be treated with great caution. Sewell never saw the Demon at his best. His highly coloured prose owes much to the imagination. Fortunately there are enough small insights from contemporary sources for one to build up a picture, synthetically, of the Demon bowler:

As he passes the umpire on the way back to his mark, he stoops to rub the ball in his own foot-marks. Satisfied that the ball is sufficiently roughened for him to get a good grip, he walks back to the beginning of his run-up, 20 paces from the stumps. As he waits impatiently for the batsman to ready himself, he is a formidable sight. Loosely built, strong-backed and long-armed, he stands just six feet tall. For a big man he moves lithely. There is something of the panther about him. By modern standards it is a short run; to his contemporaries it is fearsomely long, nearly 15 yards. He begins to run. There is no gradual acceleration. He is flat out all the way. He runs dead straight, as if he cannot wait to get at the batsman. As he runs, his long arms pump to and fro. The left arm is thrusting forward. The hand which grasps the ball makes a curious rotary movement. He does not decelerate as he reaches the wicket. There is a sudden, sweeping, hurling action – arm very high – and down the wicket he rushes, carried by his own impetus.

Charles never varied from this flat-out style. He had tried bowling a slower ball, but it proved rarely successful. He was happy to leave swing to George Hirst and movement off the seam to Lockwood and Richardson. Occasionally he only bowled from two or three paces, but this was to conserve his breath rather than to introduce variety. His contemporaries were convinced that he was the fastest bowler of the period. Many believed him to be deliberately dangerous. There were stories of direct hits, of batsmen who had cocked their toe at him and had it broken. He let fly viciously at anyone to whom he took a sudden, personal dislike. An apt summary of Charles, the most modern of bowlers, came from Lancashire's Johnny Tyldesley. When asked about Charles' repertoire of tricks, he shook his head. There was none to report. 'He bowled fast,' said Tyldesley simply. 'There was no time for anything else.'

In strong contrast to Charles, Digby turned his back on modernity. The bowling styles of Demon and Lobster were an expression of their differing personalities. Charles was an uncomplicated man, aggressive, proud. So too was his bowling. He liked applause and hated criticism. He took his sport and himself very seriously. Digby, on the other hand, was many-sided, gentle, humble. Aware of the serio-comic nature of life, he perceived acutely the amusing incongruity of an underarm bowler in an overarm world. He wrote little of his triumphs, but frequently of his disasters, and, when he did, it was always with humour and without a trace of self-pity. A typical anecdote involved a 2nd XI match against Lancashire at The Oval: 'A tall, stalwart yokel arrived at the scene, and I tossed up the usual slow half-volley; a swoosh, a swirl, and the ball cleared the old pavilion. Again the same half-volley, again a six. Five of them – 30 runs in the over! It was a long over, quite a long one. As we crossed, I said to the aggressor: "Have you ever played lobs before?" "Noa," he replied, "but I should like to play 'em again." "Not today, baker," I said, as I went to ruminate at mid-on . . .' Digby relished championing the art of William Clarke and the more remote underarm bowlers of Hambledon. It was an act of homage to the deep traditions of the game and it minimized any ridicule involved. He seemed unbothered by the

54

inevitable charge of eccentricity. Indeed, as he grew older, he may even, like Hamlet, have assumed an antic disposition. Certainly there was a bland acceptance, with no sense of outrage, in his summary of the lobster's difficult lot: 'We, the solitary few who still strive to uphold the tottering pillars in the ruined temple of lob bowling, unto whose shrine the bowlers of olden times ever flocked, today we are of but small account; but there is scarcely a ground in England where derision is not our lot, or where laughter and taunting jeers are not hurled at us.'

Most of the 'solitary few', the latter-day lob bowlers, were characters if not eccentrics. In the 1880s Kent's irascible Lord Harris turned to lobs and so too did E. M. Grace, W.G.'s brother. The latter could never be persuaded to take himself off. His idea of a bowling change was to have a go at the other end, even though, according to Lord Hawke, his lobs were 'merely an invitation to hit the cover off the ball'. The most successful professional lob bowler of the Golden Age was Walter Humphreys of Sussex, 20 years Digby's senior, a shoe-maker by trade. Nicknamed 'Cobbler', Humphreys was a very difficult individual, whose arguments with fellow professionals were legendary. Once, when one of them called him as cross-grained as the cobbler in *The Arabian Nights*, he replied: 'I don't know nuffin o' that, but I'd as soon 'ammer your ugly 'ead as shy a good ball at it!' But, for all his cantankerous manner, Humphreys was a splendid bowler. His accuracy enabled him to take over 700 wickets for Sussex. In his best season, 1893, he took 150 and he lasted long enough to be able to tour, at 45, with Stoddart's team to Australia. A distinguishing feature of his bowling was his flapping sleeve, to which batsmen sometimes took exception. It seemed to have the same subtle psychological value in that relentless battle between bat and ball as, in more modern times, the coloured headbands of Dennis Lillee or the cap always worn by Sonny Ramadhin. It was something which Digby was to copy.

One very eccentric lob bowler of Digby's day was Captain Teddy Wynyard. Ten years older than the Lobster, Wynyard was an army officer, who did much for Hampshire cricket. Lob bowling was but one unconventional facet of his very unusual character, for Teddy Wynyard was as colourful a personality as the I Zingari 'pill box' cap which he used to wear as a young man. The laughter of spectators would not have troubled him, a decorated war hero, a European toboggan champion, a member of an F.A. Cup winning side, a man outspoken enough to indulge in public acrimony with the idol of the nation, Ranjitsinhji, foolhardy enough to upset the Commandant at Sandhurst by dressing up as W. G. Grace during an important army fixture. He was very self-opinionated. Such an extrovert would have revelled in the fun of bowling lobs, and bowling them well enough to have got Bobby Abel stranded down the wicket on at least one occasion.

A more successful amateur, George Simpson-Hayward, enjoyed some good seasons with Worcestershire and even played in five Test matches in South Africa in 1909–10, where he found the matting wickets most helpful to his spin. But Simpson-Hayward was not an orthodox lob bowler. He flicked the ball away with his fingers in an inimitable fashion, causing a very sharp off-break. He bowled with an audible noise, and when, for variety, he bowled a perfectly straight ball, he flicked the fingers of his non-bowling hand, so it was alleged, thereby leading the batsman into erroneous expectation of a sharp break.

Digby, then, was more in a direct line to William Clarke than Simpson-Hayward, as he employed all the traditional craft of the old lob bowlers. There are no known photographs of him in action, but through drawings and descriptions one can build up a clear picture of his style. His action was described thus: 'Stooping very low, he made two or three shuffling paces to the wicket and delivered the ball in the exact attitude of a man putting down a bowl, except that the bowl would be tossed up in the air at the last moment almost from the ground.' Another eye-witness account emphasized his flapping sleeve and the nonchalance of his approach to the wicket. The Spy cartoon, published in *Vanity Fair* in 1902, gives a lively record of Digby on his approach to the wicket. He is bent double, left leg forward and bent, right leg well back and bent, back nearly parallel to the ground. The ball is held comfortably in the right hand, enclosed by thumb and fingers, first and second finger protruding beyond the ball. He is about to bowl a leg-break. But the most vivid thing about the cartoon is the facial expression. Digby glances appraisingly down the wicket, determined to deceive. Robert Tinley, the underarm successor to William Clarke at Trent Bridge, was once described as being like Odysseus, 'full of wiles'; the epithet would have suited Digby even better. He loved the craft. He himself said as much: 'Captain Wynyard and I both bowl in the old, old way, and we bowl of a persistence born of tentative success – occasionally we hook a fish and great is our rejoicing. We are both fond of this bowling, I particularly so, and when on many a ground there has arisen on every side the gentle sound of "Take him 'orf! Take him 'orf!", were it not that the side comes ever before oneself, I would bowl, and bowl, and bowl, until at eventide the cows come home.'

The lobster had a big repertoire of tricks. First, there was the leg-break, the natural break, bowled with a gentle turn of the wrist. This break had sufficed for William Clarke, who was so concerned not to impart too much turn that he used to bowl at the pavilion end at Lord's, so that the slope would limit the amount of spin. Digby, however, like most other lob bowlers, spun off-breaks as well. Of these two deliveries it was the off-break which, according to C. B. Fry, gained Digby the more wickets. Another useful delivery was the surprise straight ball, delivered with a top spin which made it hurry off the pitch. 'Often enough', noted Fry, 'Mr Jephson clean bowls a man with a straight, low ball.' Then there was Digby's 'guileful full-pitch', also known as a 'toss', which he usually aimed on the leg-side. One pundit who favoured this ball, reckoned that 'a full pitch, delivered at the batsman's body about the height of his ribs, should often provide one of the three fieldsmen stationed near the square-leg umpire with a catch' – an early form of bodyline! But, with catches and stumpings being the main aim of the lob bowler, and the flight being all-important, 'tices' were useful deliveries too. 'Learn to bowl tosses and tices', wrote James Pycroft in 1851. 'With a stiff player, before his eye is in, a toss often succeeds. But especially practise high lobs – a most useful variety of ball.' Tices were steepling, high deliveries, which enticed, and Fry commended Digby for just such a species, 'the high ball which drops short'. P. F. Warner likewise commended Digby's change of pace, particularly his use of quite a fast, good-length ball.

There were, finally, two somewhat mean deliveries, which Digby seems to have been too good a sportsman to employ. One was the Donkey Drop, falling on top of the bails, a difficult delivery to achieve with precision and one fraught with danger for the wicket-keeper. Hot-blooded amateurs like Sir Timothy O'Brien of Middlesex were not averse to smashing a full-toss straight at the unfortunate wicket-keeper (which might be why insurance firms were beginning to show an interest in the game). The other ball which Digby rejected was the Daisy Cutter or Shooter. Daisy Cutters were considered bad form in Digby's day, which is probably why they were also known as 'sneaks'.

Good field placing was crucial to the lob bowler's strategy. Humphreys employed a 5-4 offside-onside distribution, copying an overarm slow bowler's field (except for the dispensing of short slip). Simpson-Hayward favoured a 4-5 distribution, with an inner ring on the leg-side and two outfielders. By way of contrast, Digby pioneered a radical leg-side approach, with a 2-7 distribution, a system demanding a high degree of accuracy from him. Fry described a typical Jephson field as 'two short legs, two mid-ons, a long leg, a long-on, a man in the country behind the bowler, and a mid-off, rather wide'. This leaves one other fielder, presumably a point or cover. The philosophy behind these odd placings was explained thus: 'The "pokey" batsman gets caught by the near fields on the on-side, the hitters risk their wicket to long leg or long-on.' The Jephson leg theory seems to have been sufficiently accepted by the time Ranjit-sinhji wrote his *Jubilee Book of Cricket* for the Indian Prince to offer a 3-6 distribution as an ideal field for a lob bowler. As part of his leg theory Digby took to bowling round the wicket (a practice which the overarm leg-break bowlers of the 1900s came to copy).

Lob bowling was still enough in evidence in the 1890s for cricket manuals to offer batsmen advice on how to deal with it. The favoured method was to try to run out and hit the ball on the full toss. This done, some caution was advised: 'Reaching the ball full pitch, it is not necessary to hit it out of sight. It will usually pay better to hit it along the ground for a single.' Ranji agreed with this: 'I am convinced that most batsmen fall victims to lobs not so much by reason of intrinsic difficulty, but on account of their own nervousness or anxiety to score. A firm-footed batsman, who does not leave the crease, is most vulnerable to lobs.' At this stage it is probable that his co-author, C. B. Fry, was leaning over his shoulder, for Ranji added as an afterthought: 'Still, Mr Charles Fry has, in this way, taken innumerable runs off Humphreys.'

At the appearance of a lob bowler the most somnolent of crowds would waken to life. Digby's spells were usually accompanied by good-natured banter from the ring. 'One ball, one nut!' yelled a wag at Tonbridge, imitating the cry of an attendant at a coconut shy. 'Take off them . . .ing lobs!', yelled a chorus of Derby miners less imaginatively. One gentleman took Digby sternly to task. It was not fair, he said, to bowl lobs at all, for cricket was a progressive game and to go back 40 years was absurd!

The gentleman was of course right, in that cricket *is* a progressive game. Batting progress, with improved technique and wider acceptance of defensive methods, would have made lob bowling a profitless occupation in the days which followed the Golden Age. Digby's bowling of lobs, moreover, was a backward step in the march of cricket progress. There were too many new bowling ideas afoot in the Golden Age for there to be a serious reassertion of the old ways. It is not altogether surprising that, after Digby and George Simpson-Hayward, there was little more lob bowling in the first-class game.

Over the years there have been vain calls for its return. As early as 1907 it was being championed, Philip Trevor devoting a whole chapter of *The Problems of Cricket* to its plight. Trevor saw the decline of lob bowling as a temporary change of fashion and believed its time would come again. Forty years later E. H. D. Sewell saw the dearth of lob bowlers as an affront to the game: 'The answer to why there is no lob bowling is simple. It is because Games Masters are, in many cases, *funks* . . . A Humphreys, a Jephson or a Simpson-Hayward would have been worth his weight in platinum in England during 1919–39. Will nobody at our public schools start in, here and now, and help remove this reproach from our cricket?' Alas for his hopes, nobody did. Since the last War underarm bowling in first-class cricket has been limited to a few very special circumstances, most notably when Wilf Wooller made his protest against some intolerably slow batting and Trevor Chappell bowled his infamous underarm delivery, all along the ground, to eliminate the possibility of six runs. The last serious lob bowling occurred as far back as 1921, when Trevor Molony won a small place in cricket history by taking 4 wickets for Surrey.

The spectator of the Golden Age was very lucky in the variety of bowling on view. There was much on offer in addition to the Lobster in the rearguard of underarm bowling and the Demon in the vanguard of a new style. There were the new-fangled leg-break bowlers, like Vine and Braund, and the pioneering of the googly by Bernard Bosanquet. There were off-spinners in plenty and their left-handed counterparts, both highly encouraged by the uncovered wickets. Medium-paced bowling had many talented adherents, men like William Attewell, Jack Hearne and George Lohmann, none of whom ever considered themselves as mere run-savers, stock-bowlers. The

Golden Age was indeed golden in the variety of its bowling and the high value which it attached to the art of spin. Frequently a slow bowler would be given the new ball with a fast bowler. Playing for the Gentlemen in 1900, Charles and Digby opened the bowling against the Players. It may not have ultimately proved a match-winning combination, but it typified the Golden Age's imaginative blend of the old and new.

6
The Demon
at Lord's

KORTRIGHT BOWLS.

In 1893 the Demon ceased being merely a local phenomenon. His furious bowling had attracted the attention of the MCC and he was selected for two very important matches at Lord's. He had not played first-class cricket before, but his fine performances for the MCC v. the Australians and the Gentlemen v. the Players turned him into a nationally known figure. It was then only a matter of time before a 'Korty' became schoolboy slang for a really fast ball and the phrase 'as fast as Kortright' became a common-place comparison.

Australian tourists have always been a huge attraction. Those of 1893 drew vast crowds not merely in their three Test matches but all over the country in their exhausting itinerary of nearly 40 games. Each match played was, in its own way, a Test. The public interest in the tourists was, by modern standards, extraordinary. Thirty-five thousand people had been known to watch a single day's play at Sheffield and 44,000 had attended the very first Test match in England, at The Oval in 1880.

The popularity of the Australians could be partly attributed to their comparative novelty value – it was only 15 years since the very first Australian tour of England – and partly to their great charisma, which was as strong as that of the Varsity Blues, but of a very different kind. It depended on an unusual fusion of the gentlemanly and the ungentlemanly, of the amateur and the professional. First of all, in the amateur spirit, the Australians were *real* tourists. Their tours could be of as much as nine months' duration. On their travels they would stare at the scenery of Honolulu, take donkey rides at Port Said, walk down the ancient streets of Pompeii and take snap-shots with their ever ready cameras of Samoan girls at Fiji. They were tourist-adventurers. Frank Laver, player-manager of the twelfth tour, re-met his ship at Naples, having driven through Europe in a recently purchased Rover, a vehicle which, today, would impress if it were to chug successfully down from London to Brighton. They were an independent, though representative, group of the best cricketers of their land. An Australian board of control might be in the offing, but as yet there was more board than control, so the tourists were privateers, unencumbered by the sanctions of officialdom. They were organized, but not too organized. What could be more in keeping with the amateur spirit than a team meeting up at Liverpool, many thousands of miles from home, and deciding there, by a democratic vote, who was to be their captain? In the amateur spirit they sometimes brought their wives and their young families, and for five months they made their headquarters at the Inns of Court Hotel, London. In the amateur spirit, they would travel down to Mitcham Green for their first practices, where the pitches might be lively, but the beer was very reliable.

Yet they were not really amateurs at all, but the hardest-headed of professionals. Their image might be that of rough, tough buccaneers, but they were in fact on-the-make businessmen. They played the game hard, really hard, because that way their financial reward would be all the greater. The Australians' share of match receipts was the envy of the English professionals (and it led, indeed, to the latter striking for better pay before one Test match). The Australians might have paid for their own passage as amateurs, but it was on the clear understanding that they would make a sizable profit from the whole undertaking. And they would return home, like some ancient army, laden with spoils. Frank Laver's men had trunks bursting with gifts: books, bats, other cricketing goods, knives, razors, gold keepsakes, whisky, champagne, tobacco, cigars, medicine chests and underwear . . .

Throughout their time in England the Australians were entertained on a grand scale. The Midland Railway put at their disposal a specially equipped carriage plus luggage van, and undertook to attach them to any train on any network in the country. At every venue the tourists were inundated with invitations to attend luncheons and banquets. Also, because they played as amateurs, they had access to the patronage of the upper classes. Typical of the latter was the opening match of the tour which often took place against an XI of the cricket-loving Lord Sheffield at one of the grandest of country-house settings. In 1896, 25,000 spectators were at Sheffield Park for the first day's play, among them the Prince of Wales, who was met at the railway station by Lord Sheffield and Lord Harris, and then driven in a procession of carriages to the stately home. Ranji travelled in the sixth coach and Fry and Jackson in the seventh (but W. G. Grace, although captain of Sheffield's XI, was not thus honoured, his lack of public school and university background seemingly making him less socially acceptable than the three young Varsity Blues). The Australians were duly introduced to the future king and had luncheon with him. They did not make any money out of this fixture, for entrance to the game was free, but as publicity for the rest of the tour it was unrivalled.

The Australians, therefore, were a glamorous attraction and well promoted. The result was near hysteria. Men fought with each other to obtain their autographs or for a chance of slapping them heartily on the back as they came off the field. The opposite sex was even more susceptible to their Antipodean virility. Frank Laver reported strange goings-on at the sylvan Canterbury ground, that idyllic setting for carriages and picnics, where many a pretty girl lost her head watching cricket in the shade of an expensive marquee: 'Ladies of title and their daughters and friends spoke to one of our side whenever he went near enough to them in the outfield. Some made eyes; others smiled. Two beautiful daughters of one of the peers of England waited, after the game was over, to have a few words with two of the eleven. Introductions were at a discount . . .' Perhaps the problem may have lain in the Australians' easy accessibility, for, in some instances, the dressing rooms were not secluded from the public gaze: 'Ladies seated in the Reserves were now and then able to see us putting on our flannels. This was, however, quite interesting to a number of them, if we may judge by the close attention with which they watched us.'

The Australians of 1893 were captained by John McCarthy Blackham, who had participated in all seven previous tours. Blackham had done more than anyone to further the art of wicket-keeping. He was the first to demonstrate the possibilities of standing up to the wicket and the speed of his stumpings became proverbial. The Australian stars were the big-hitting J. J. Lyons, the stone-walling Alec Bannerman and the off-spinners, George Giffen and Hugh Trumble. If there was a weakness in the party it was in their lack of a really fast bowler. This probably prompted the MCC to take a chance and select the unknown Charles Kortright.

It was a proud moment for the 22-year-old Charles as he followed the other three amateurs down the stairs of the Lord's pavilion, through the Long Room thronged with frock coats and top hats, and down on to the pitch. Leading the way was the large figure of W.G., followed by two Middlesex favourites, Andrew Stoddart and Tim O'Brien. Stoddart was the best batsman in England that year, O'Brien a larger-than-life Irishman. A little later, from the professionals' side gate, came the seven other members of the MCC, the tall figure of Billy Gunn leading the way. Two other Notts professionals were in his wake, all-rounder Wilf Flowers and fast bowler Francis Shacklock, whose problems off-field were to bring a premature end to his first-class career a few weeks hence. The wicket-keeper was Bill Storer of Derbyshire, like Charles a player from a second-class county. There were 12,000 spectators watching as the two parts of the MCC side joined together and took their positions for Kortright's first over. It was a bright June day, freshened by recent rain. In the stands there was already a large proportion of animated ladies. Lyons and Bannerman were very enthusiastically received as they came out to start the Australian innings.

Charles opened the bowling from the nursery end (partnering J. T. Hearne with his slow-medium off-spinners). His first over was auspicious, a maiden to J. J. Lyons. After that, however, things became less easy. At 22 for 1 he was involved in a blundering piece of cricket. Lyons cut a ball from him down to third man, where Gunn came running in. Giffen called Lyons for a single, but for some reason the latter stood his ground and both Australian batsmen ended up at the Pavilion end, to which Gunn had erroneously thrown the ball. Storer threw it, less than accurately, down the wicket to Charles who, perhaps through big-match nerves, completely missed it. The crowd hooted with merriment. Charles scowled blackly and O'Brien, who was backing Charles up, walked up to the wicket and removed the bails, for Giffen had given up and made no attempt to return. Charles, cross and over-enthusiastic, now totally lost his length and was later accused of bowling dangerously short! After lunch Grace gave him the Pavilion end, but several long hops were punished fiercely by Lyons, and the afternoon was well advanced when, in his third spell, Charles took his first first-class wicket, having Gregory caught behind by Storer. This was his turning point. He began to relax. There were two tail-enders left. He hurtled in at them, grimacing horribly, and bowled them out.

Despite the counter-attraction of Ascot, there was an even bigger crowd on the second day's play and every stand was full to overflowing. The pavilion itself was bursting at the seams and this forced the MCC Committee to insist that, in future, members should be required to show their passes on entry at big matches. The crowd was particularly excited because W.G. was 71 not out at the close of the first day and yet another century from the Champion was anticipated. In this there was to be disappointment for, although W.G. had earlier survived a loud, general appeal for lbw and a confident one for caught behind, he was now, indisputably, caught at point. Wickets fell steadily and, when Charles took stock at the crease, the score was 215 for 9 in reply to the Australians' 231. The tourists seemed likely to gain the honour of first innings lead. Charles had other ideas. He smote Macleod to the off for 4 and to the on for an all-run 5. Next over he hit Trumble 'straight to the canvas' for 4 and, next ball, off-drove him for 4. Loud and prolonged cheers greeted the last hit. The MCC had first innings lead and it mattered little to Charles that Trumble knocked back his middle stump next over.

It was in the Australians' second innings that Charles produced a true Demon's performance. Put on for his second spell of the afternoon by Grace – 'none too soon' according to the critics – he dismissed the last five batsmen with the same rapidity as had been customary at Wallingford and Hythe. He may have been goaded into this furious action by an incident a little earlier. Fielding at mid-off he got his hands to a ball driven tremendously hard by Lyons, just failing to bring off a remarkable catch. The pain in his hands was very soon avenged! His yorkers wrought havoc. Shots were played far too late. Tail-enders failed to stand their ground. And, in due course, the MCC reached a 7-wicket victory. Charles' match analysis of 8 for 129 made him the talk of the Long Room.

The other talking point was the wicket-keeping of Bill Storer. Tradition relates that Storer stood up at the wicket to Charles for part of the match, a piece of bravado inspired by the presence of the great Blackham in the pavilion. Conclusive proof is given by the report of Trumble's dismissal, bowled by Charles. *Sporting Life* relates: 'The ball, after just touching the wicket, rebounded onto it, causing many people to think that the man was not out.' The ball can only have rebounded off the pads of Bill Storer, bravely standing up to the wicket.

The second match at Lord's, in which Charles played in 1893, was an equally impressive occasion. Since their inception in 1806 contests between the best eleven amateurs and the best eleven professionals had been the feature of the season. Even the development of Test matches in the latter part of the century had not yet taken away the popularity of these meetings at Lord's. The reason for this was largely the emergence of W.G. For many years the professionals had been hard to beat. Then came Grace. With his massive presence on the scales, the balance shifted. And so, in the public imagination, the fixture became identified with the classic struggles of the Champion, fighting like Leonidas against the odds, and, unlike Leonidas, often winning.

There was also, just under the surface, the excitement engendered by the clash of classes. The social struggle shortly to be fought out in Britain was already being enacted on the turf at Lord's. The working man, freed by the Factory Act from labour on Saturday afternoons, could come to Lord's to indulge his most lurid phantasies, as Bobby Abel, cricket's version of Charlie Chaplin (both men were born close to The Oval), defied and punished the bowling of his social superiors. It was more easy to overturn the social order at Lord's than at Westminster.

There was, of course, strong support from all classes for the Gentlemen. In an age when the lower orders gathered at Hyde Park on Sundays to admire the upper classes out riding, there was bound to be much awe for the gaily bedecked amateurs, each brightly striped blazer a symbol of the wearer's superior status, each beribboned boater exaggerating the essential dullness of the professional's monochrome cap. Varsity Blues now formed the nucleus of Gentlemen's XIs. In 1893, four of Digby's fellow Blues were taking the field with Charles: MacGregor, Ford, Wells and Jackson. The Gentlemen proudly thought that they played the game in a much more sporting way, sentiments with which Digby concurred. Lilley, the Warwickshire and England professional, might be a good wicket-keeper, but, to Digby, MacGregor possessed an extra, vital dimension: 'He never asked "How's that?" unless the man was out. And he never asked in vain. He was a grand, clean stumper, clean in every sense of the word.' The myth of a differing philosophy between the teams persisted, even though there was another side to the Gentlemen which fitted ill with the philosophy of Fenner's. There were some amateurs who happened to make money out of the game. In 1893 this category was well represented by Grace, Walter Read and Andrew Stoddart. Likewise John Ferris, who had twice toured England with the Australian mercenaries, had now settled in Gloucestershire to earn his living as an amateur. Charles lacked such financial acumen, just as he lacked a Varsity Blue, yet he fully subscribed to his team-mates' philosophy. 'To play cricket', he said in his old age, 'was to play a clean game and that was always the understanding in my day that you played clean, and, if anyone didn't play clean, well, he heard about it . . . If a man played cricket, he was understood to be a good sportsman.' This was largely self-delusion. But the Gentlemen of 1893 – even W.G. – undoubtedly believed in their own essential 'cleanness'. So this fixture, with its strong social undercurrents, was just the game to bring out the worst of the Demon's prejudices.

An event nearby, in a terraced lodging house in St John's Wood, had added a terrible poignancy to this particular match. William Scotton, a famous Notts professional and an England player in the 1880s, had put a razor to his throat only hours before it was due to start. During the game an inquest was held, which aroused national curiosity. Since being dropped by Notts three years before at the age of 34, Scotton had tried to make ends meet by doing some umpiring and continuing as a bowler on the Lord's ground staff. This brought him a subsistence wage during the summer but nothing during the winter. He had no savings. He had taken to drink and a letter had just been sent to him from Lord's telling him to mend his ways. He was also worried by a wrong decision which he had given in a recent county match. Scotton's untimely death, which highlighted the unhappy lot of many retired professionals, must have heightened the tensions inherent in the match.

A contemporary of Scotton's at Nottingham, the wicket-keeper Mordecai Sherwin, was captain of the Players. Too many lunch intervals spent in the beer tent had helped fill out his ample frame, making for a solid, if immobile, barrier behind the stumps. But at least he was a physical match for Grace as the two captains tossed, and, with this threatening adversary, Grace might not have dared try out his rumoured dodge of calling 'Woman' and claiming both Britannia and Victoria as his own. Still, Grace *did* win the toss and soon, in bright, warm weather, he and Stoddart were opening the Gentlemen's innings. The ground, brimming with a colourful humanity, over-flowed with applause for the two heroes.

There had been a considerable amount of rain before the start and the uncovered pitch was therefore helpful to the bowlers as it dried out in the July sun. The ball bumped about disconcertingly. With not a run on the board Mordecai Sherwin appealed for a catch at the wicket. It was turned down, in Grace's favour, and the crowd sighed with relief. Grace himself then enjoyed a scintillating hour, delighting the crowd with one delicate late cut off Briggs for 4 and several good blows, before falling lbw, not his usual method of dismissal. At lunch, the amateurs were 103 for 3, with W.G. gone.

After lunch Walter Read, Digby's patron, took control of the innings. Some spectators no doubt recalled how, nine years before, it was Read's stand with the late-lamented Scotton which had saved England against Australia at The Oval. Now the Lord's crowd was treated to a typical innings, full of orthodox defence and unorthodox aggression. He was particularly severe on the spinners, Briggs, Hearne and Flowers, employing time and time again the stroke which he is said to have originated, the pull. 'In my youthful day', wrote Digby, 'we used to call it "the donkey's cross" and we regarded it as a symptom of poor batsmanship. Walter Read changed all that.' Later, both Trumper and Ranji employed the shot and gave it a greater respectability. Walter Read also favoured a shot now seen regularly in one-day cricket. 'The hardest hit which Mr Read makes', wrote Ranji, 'is off a short ball outside the off-stump. He moves his right leg slightly back from the wicket – that is, he moves slightly backwards himself, and, as the ball passes him, hits it somewhere in the direction of cover point with extraordinary force.' Finally, Walter Read took one liberty too many, at 77, and was bowled. The Gentlemen were eventually 258 all out, leaving the Players about 40 minutes' batting before close of play.

It was a situation which all fast bowlers relish. Stanley Jackson opened from the nursery end, medium-fast, and Charles from the pavilion, very fast. Some say that these Kortright overs were the fastest yet seen at Lord's. The recipients were poor Arthur Shrewsbury, just recovered from a blow on the head, and Frank Sugg, Lancashire's tall, burly, front-footed hitter. The evening light was very fitful. The sun kept peeping out coquettishly from behind dark banks of clouds. The Demon always drew inspiration from uncertain light and by close of play the Players were 35 for 3. Jackson removed the uneasy Shrewsbury and Charles claimed Billy Gunn and Sugg. Gunn lost his off stump to a ball which he never saw and which he claimed was a yard faster than anything he had previously experienced. Frank Sugg was quite clearly only too pleased to return to the pavilion. The manner of his dismissal, however, was remarkable. MacGregor had initially stood back several yards to Charles, with the slips very deep indeed and Archie MacLaren 'sharp leg, to save the boundary'. But after a couple of overs, MacGregor moved up to the stumps, apparently influenced by Sugg, who was taking his guard outside the crease. One or two balls, which beat Sugg for pace, MacGregor took neatly, 'as easily as if Kortright were a lob bowler', according to one enthusiastic witness. Then Sugg got a thick edge and MacGregor caught him, low down, in his right hand. It was, in Plum Warner's opinion, probably the best catch ever made by a wicketkeeper. MacGregor was later very modest about it. It was, he said, a great fluke and he had afterwards moved back, having learnt sense. But perhaps he was too modest, for on the second day's play he again stood up to Charles for limited periods.

The next morning, Charles, urged on by another large and very demonstrative crowd, again bowled at a tremendous pace and finished off the Players' innings, forcing them to follow on. He had taken 7 wickets for 73. He could have taken even more. Walter Read dropped Wilf Flowers at cover, the ball spinning high up but straight to him. And MacGregor, even Digby's MacGregor, dropped a catch too. The Players put up spirited resistance. Maurice Read, the Surrey professional, batted long and pluckily. Charles got more and more irritated with him and eventually struck him a powerful blow on the hand with a ball which reared sharply. The same over, Read, fighting back, drove him hard and straight, only to see Charles, galloping down the wicket on his follow-through, hanging on to a very difficult catch. Surrey's Bill Lockwood, who was a fine batsman as well as an

England opening bowler, applied himself well, off-driving Charles for a magnificent 4. Charles responded, in the same over, with a ball which knocked the bat out of Lockwood's hands! Nothing daunted, Lockwood put Charles away for 4 on the leg and for another to square leg. The latter boundary infuriated Charles, because a small boy, running out from the crowd, fielded the ball well before the ropes. With eyes glinting like an angry Jove, Charles ran in again, sending down a thunderbolt, which had Lockwood caught in the slips. The crowd tittered as the ungainly Sherwin faced the Demon. Sherwin himself smiled, but not for long. He was bowled second ball by a delivery which 'carried away his bails like a whirlwind'. Johnny Briggs' dismissal was even more spectacular. His leg stump was knocked out of the ground some 17 yards. In its progress the stump made three complete revolutions. The leg bail was sent 60 yards. Briggs, a small man with a large sense of humour, turned to MacGregor. 'I s'pose I'm out, sir?' he asked.

When the Players followed on, the tiring Charles was less effective. His temper flared as Stanley Jackson dropped a very easy catch in the covers and he began to spray the ball about very wildly. Grace, however, seemed not to notice his fatigue and kept him going, as Arthur Shrewsbury cut him with precision every time he pitched short, or hooked him round to leg. W.G.'s captaincy rarely showed much subtlety. 'He worked me off my legs,' was Charles' terse comment. But, with 70 to win with 6 wickets left, the Gentlemen were still well placed, when heavy rain, sweeping across Lord's, put an end to the Players' discomfort.

In those two first-class matches of 1893, therefore, Charles made his reputation as a demon bowler. He would also have gained many insights from his experiences at Lord's. He would have discovered to his surprise the sharpness of the needle atmosphere between Gentlemen and Players. He would have perceived something of the very deep resentment in the professional ranks towards money-making amateurs like Grace and Walter Read. At Lord's he tasted firsthand the bitterness of this conflict.

It was also Charles' first opportunity to gain some insight into the character of his famous captain. In 1893 Grace was having a comparatively lean year. He was rising 45, suffering from a recurring knee injury and having problems with a dissatisfied Gloucestershire Committee. Retirement would be in prospect for most men in such circumstances. Not so for W.G.! He was far from finished and was yet to enjoy his magnificent Indian Summer and to score another 31 first-class centuries. Charles, in these two matches, would have seen something of Grace's strengths and weaknesses. He would have approved of his hard, opportunistic approach to the game, his ability to overcome opponents by superior mental strength and his resilience in adversity. He would not have been shocked by Grace's philistinism, his scorn of literature and cultural pursuits. He would have sympathized with Grace's total devotion to all things sporting, although he would not have understood how Grace could spend his winters in medical practice, for Charles found the compulsion to work difficult to comprehend. He would have been shocked by the considerable sum of money which Grace received, as expenses, for these two matches.

We cannot be sure of the nature of Charles' insight into the touring Australians of 1893. Possibly he found their volatile and abrasive approach to life not to his own conservative taste. Unlike many other amateurs of his day, Charles had both the leisure and the means to tour overseas in the winter, but he never availed himself of the opportunity. At this period, tours were still organized by enterprising individuals rather than the MCC. Other countries besides Australia and New Zealand were visited: South Africa, North America, India, the West Indies, Egypt . . . Charles' friend, Freddie Fane, by contrast, spent five winters playing cricket abroad in the space of eight years. Similar opportunities were undoubtedly there for Charles to play abroad. The fact that he never took them suggests that he disliked foreign travel and displayed a chauvinistic lack of interest in cricket on other shores. Whether or not he found the Australian tourists of 1893 unsympathetic, at all events he was not inspired by them to undertake similar ventures.

Both the Demon's games at Lord's in 1893 show the Golden Age to advantage. There was more than just good, three-day cricket, played out before large, enthusiastic crowds in these big matches. There was a real sense of occasion, a real excitement in the air. Today, it is the one-day, rather than the three-day, fixture which attracts a similar big-match atmosphere. The sustained excitement of the three-day game has almost disappeared. Docile wickets, defensive bowling tactics, the demise of the leg-break, cautious professionalism – even the advent of television – have contributed to a lack of public interest. The shape of the game has changed to correspond with the demand for quick results and the faster tempo of modern life. One Golden Age player anticipated such a change, for in 1905 the Australian Frank Laver forecast an even more drastic situation than that existing today. 'I shall not be surprised,' he wrote, 'if one day a rule is brought into force abolishing the second innings altogether . . . Life is too short for long contests.'

7
*Demon
versus
Lobster*

A *Stampede
for Shelter*
SURREY v. ESSEX.

The 1890s were boom years for county cricket, the 'Grace Boom', as it was sometimes called, years in which the County Championship took the shape which it knows today. Not long before the birth of Demon and Lobster, Surrey had won the very first County Championship in 1864. They beat only six other competitors to this honour: Kent, Middlesex, Nottinghamshire, Sussex, Yorkshire and Cambridgeshire. This small group was soon augmented by Lancashire and Gloucestershire and diminished by the loss of Cambridgeshire. The Championship then stayed fairly static until the 1890s, when no less than seven counties (Derbyshire, Essex, Hampshire, Leicestershire, Somerset, Warwickshire and Worcestershire) were admitted (or readmitted) to the Championship. Surrey was by far the most successful of the counties in the 1890s, winning the Championship six times. Yorkshire and Lancashire were the other winners, while Notts and Gloucester had already established a tradition of success.

The huge general public interest in cricket in the 1890s and the soaring attendances at county matches derived particularly from the developing cult of personality. This cult came about with the spread of newspapers and popular journalism. Of all cricket's personalities in

73

the 1890s, of course, the figure of Grace dominated. Quite unexpectedly, in the middle of the decade, W.G. re-found all his old skills with the bat. No public relations consortium could have fabricated a better scenario. In 1895 W.G. scored his hundredth hundred and achieved the extraordinary feat of making 1000 runs in the month of May. Amidst much national celebration of these achievements there were loud and insistent calls that he should be knighted. In the end he had to be content with a congratulatory letter from the Prince of Wales: 'His Royal Highness cannot allow an event of such interest to all lovers of the national game to pass unmarked by him.' Indeed, he could not, for it had been noted at Osborne that the marked revival of affection for the monarchy was only surpassed by the phenomenal rise in the popularity of the national game. Cricket and royalty were the two things closest to the heart of most Englishmen. When Victoria had celebrated the sixtieth year of her reign in 1897 with a Jubilee, the nation's thoughts automatically turned to that other monarch, the Champion, who, happening to reach 50 in 1898, was accorded his own form of Jubilee.

The Demon and the Lobster were fortunate that their first-class careers should begin in such a euphoric atmosphere. The Demon had already experienced, in 1893, the excitement of playing in a big match with Grace and, a year later, Digby played under W.G. for the Gentlemen too. For both Digby and Charles 1894 was a very special year. It was in 1894 that Charles Green's ambition that Essex should become a first-class county was realized, and, accordingly, Charles was able to test himself against the best batsmen in the country. Later the same season Surrey, the county champions, decided to include the Lobster in their 1st XI. The result was that the Demon and Lobster met each other in a county match for the first time in 1894. Of the two men it was Charles who made the quicker impression in the first-class game. Indeed, the meteoric rise of Essex to prominence in the 1890s was inextricably linked with his own personal successes.

For the first five of Essex's first-class seasons Charles was the spearhead of their attack and he waged a campaign of terror around the counties of England. 'What a prodigious run Korty takes!' wrote one onlooker. 'No wonder the batsmen are frightened of him! It is no joke to see a man come running at you at full speed and sending a ball down straight at you at 90 mph.' All batsmen were susceptible to his great pace. Surrey's famous team 'shivered before Kortright's expresses', their Test players still making their shots when the ball was safely in Russell's gloves. When Yorkshire crashed to 26 for 5 at Leyton, 'there was only one reason for the failure of the batsmen, sheer funk'. As he took 6 Hampshire wickets for 8 runs, there was 'the ludicrous spectacle of batsmen beginning to play the ball at the time their bails were flying behind the wicket'. On a lively wicket, the Demon was especially lethal. At Huddersfield, even Stanley Jackson, who was certainly no coward, was seen drawing away on certain occasions, while Charles pitched ball after ball halfway down the wicket. Eventually, when he did pitch it up, he landed it on Jackson's toe, Jackson's pain increasing as the ball ricocheted onto his stumps. The Yorkshire crowd was convinced the Demon was bowling at the batsmen and not the wicket, and told him so. Later, the young professional Bob Moorhouse was hit, first on the elbow, then on the arm. He was forced to retire to the pavilion while a lump, the size of an egg, was treated with cold water. During the ten-minute delay the crowd hurled abuse at the Demon. He, characteristically, felt outraged that his honour should be so rudely impugned. When Moorhouse eventually returned, he sent him back with the most vicious ball of the day.

Such bowling was very helpful to the man at the other end. Charles often bowled for Essex in tandem with F. G. Bull or Walter Mead, both slow bowlers. They formed a deadly triumvirate. Bull was a small, dapper man. He peers out of team photographs with a twisted, sphinx-like smile, sensing perhaps that the Fates were spinning his thread particularly thin. For a limited time he enjoyed spectacular success. He turned the ball both ways, more violently than Mead, but with equal guile. Mead, two years older than Charles, proved the professional backbone of the Essex XI for 20 years. A quiet, philosophical personality, strictly teetotal, he belonged to the new generation of professionals who looked after themselves and were cautious for the morrow. He was an inventive bowler, of great perseverance, spinning a big off-break and a gentle leg-break off a hunched, 'wobbling' eight-yard run.

Apart from Walter Mead Essex had only three other professionals of significance in 1894, Harry Pickett, 'Bob' Carpenter and Tom Russell. Pickett, who came from the docklands near Barking, had bowled fast-medium for many years. The arrival of the youthful and athletic Demon only served to emphasize Pickett's steady loss of pace and figure and probably hastened his abrupt departure. H. A. Carpenter was the youngest son of one of the outstanding professional batsmen of mid-Victorian times, R. P. Carpenter of Cambridgeshire and All-England. As a man, Carpenter was taciturn. As an opening batsman, he was a quiet craftsman, who played for preference off the back foot in the manner of Shrewsbury. Tom Russell was a typical professional of the time. He came from a poor background and saw cricket as the most likely way of improving his position in life. He had never played as a wicket-keeper before joining the Essex ground staff, but spotted the need and adjusted to the position. He acquitted himself honourably in keeping to the Demon. There are many stories of metal-shod stumps whirling over his head or nearly transfixing him, so there was need of courage. Gloves of the period lacked good protection. The sticky substance sometimes put on the palm, to aid adhesion, was no substitute for proper padding. Russell's greatest problem, however, was his own weight. Photographs show him ageing from youth to middle age with alarming rapidity. Like Pickett, he enjoyed the years of the Grace Boom too carelessly.

Essex relied very heavily on amateur batsmen. Bunny Lucas still played whenever pressure of business allowed – he was for 30 years a member of the Stock Exchange – and maintained his reputation as one of England's most stylish bats. Digby considered that, for pure style, a schoolboy could do no better than copy Lucas. Short and stocky, he possessed every stroke, including a much-admired 'chop cut'. He was a most lovable and modest man, a devout Christian. When cheering crowds would flock to the Leyton pavilion, he would quietly slip away by the back door. He hated any fuss.

The captain, Hugh Glendwr Owen, had never been an adventurous batsman, but a nudger of twos and threes. He was a gentle giant, a man who asked nothing more from life than a quiet smoke of his pipe on the pavilion balcony. His unruffled calm was a soothing influence on all around, but it did not make for dynamic captaincy. He was timid towards the Demon, disliking the arguments which would ensue if he tried to take him off, and therefore he quite frequently over-bowled him. He was not quick to adjust his field placings and, again, Charles suffered. At The Oval, for example, it was once noted: 'Kortright had not got his men in the slips suitably placed, there being too wide a gap between the three slips and third man, but eventually Fane was placed on the spot where three balls had dropped.' Owen was also too amiable in the face of his team's poor fielding. 'If he has a fault', said Harry Pickett carefully, 'it's that he's a little too considerate with our feelings when we have made a mistake in the field.' There were other signs of weakness. Sudden changes of batting order were sometimes left to the club secretary, Oswell Borradaile. When Essex were in the happy position of considering a declaration, it was often Charles Green and Borradaile who led the discussion.

Perrin and McGahey, two young amateurs whose Essex careers began in the Grace Boom, enjoyed many high-scoring partnerships, but they were very different personalities. Percy 'Peter' Perrin played straighter than McGahey and successfully modelled himself on Lucas. Perrin was a tall, gaunt man; many thought him gruff and morose. But those who came close to him discovered enormous charm. His pleasures were all of the outdoors. Even as a young man he preferred a day's fishing to a day's county cricket. Bird-watching was a passion, which he could indulge easily from his home in Norfolk, where he kept a big ornithological museum. He would go out duck-shooting at dawn and shared a shoot which attracted visitors like George V.

Charles McGahey was an inelegant batsman, an effective, natural player. He developed into a useful bowler of non-breaking leg-breaks, following Digby's lead in leg theory, sometimes employing all nine fielders on that side. He played football in the winter, on occasions for Tottenham Hotspur, for he lived nearby. Whereas Perrin was a slow, serious thinker, McGahey was light-headed and light-hearted. As a young man he was frequently in various troubles. Life later took its revenge for the liberties he took with it, but he never lost his sense of fun. '*I* drink the drinks which *he* refuses', he once said of Perrin. It was a typical contrast.

From public schools came two other amateurs, A. J. Turner and F. L. Fane. 'Johnny' Turner first played for Essex as a 19-year-old Woolwich cadet and was an immediate success. Photographs show him jumping out to drive with the same authority as Victor Trumper, while his cutting was magnificently executed. Freddie Fane, an Oxford Blue, was a front-foot player, especially good on the off-side and nimble in using his feet to get down the wicket. He lived not far from Fryerning, so he and the Demon became good friends, sharing a common passion for cricket and shooting. The friendship endured for 60 years, Fane's imperturbability coping with the other's gruffness. As the son of an army officer and a relative of the Earl of

Westmorland, Freddie Fane was especially welcomed by Charles Green into the amateurs' dressing room. He even came complete with a Latin family motto: *Ne Vili Fano*, 'No Fane will ever give his wicket away'.

In contrast to Essex, searching hard for success, Surrey had already found it. Under the captaincy of John Shuter they had won the Championship in six consecutive years from 1887 to 1892. They were champions again in 1894, the year that they invited Digby to play for them. His many successes in club cricket and his useful Surrey connections had won him his place. He received, however, a most hostile reception from both Ovalties and Press. 'In these modern days', wrote one of the few sympathetic observers. 'when every first-class cricketer has to live in a glass-house at which all and sundry may throw stones, Mr Jephson has attracted more than a fair share of the attention of the throwers.' He was considered a second-class cricketer, unworthy of a first-team place. Dozens of other players, said the Press, were more deserving of selection. People scoffed at him because he chose to take lob bowling seriously and, with his limp, he hardly looked a cricketer. Nevertheless, Digby played 15 matches for Surrey in 1894 and, although given very little bowling, he performed usefully with the bat and brilliantly in the field, justifying his selection.

Surrey's new captain in 1894 was Sir Kingsmill Key. In photographs he does not look much of a player, with his ungainly stance, his corpulence and his generous walrus moustache which made him the delight of cartoonists. Yet he was good enough to score a century in a Varsity match and intelligent enough to gain a first-class degree. Digby had great respect for his batting: 'Should runs be wanted, the massive figure would be seen to move, slightly, one step, and the pitched-up ball is gone – probably into the pavilion. Should it be necessary to play out time, we find in him a wonderful exponent of the "goose game"; he is back on his wicket; the bowler searches in vain for his stumps: they are hidden by the ponderous pads . . .' Temperamentally, Key was far removed from Digby: 'He was a taciturn man . . . one of the few cricketers who preferred the gold of silence to the silver of speech, and yet he was of a jovial heart, and in his eye there was always a merry smile for those who cared to seek it. He was of a dry rather than caustic wit, that by some men was never understood.' Key, who, according to Digby 'purchased at the commencement of his career a 99-years' lease of mid-on', had one habit which must have caused great irritation. He invariably threw the ball back to the wicket-keeper, even when the bowler was only a yard away from him, 'no doubt to gain time for deep meditation of his policy of attack', as Digby commented loyally.

Certainly Key had a fine cricketing brain and brought the best out of his talented team. There were seven England players in his XI of 1894, including Tom Richardson and Bill Lockwood, a formidable pair with the new ball. Although they couldn't match Kortright for speed, they both bowled very fast and had the advantage over him in the variety of their bowling; they both moved the ball off the seam and had well-disguised variations of pace.

Surrey's opening batsmen were both England players too. Bobby Abel, small and wiry, who regularly accumulated large scores and topped 2000 runs season after season, and Billy Brockwell, a stylish stroke player and hard hitter. Among the many all-rounders was the brilliant Tom Hayward, whom Digby had met in the nets at Cambridge, a strong off-side player of the cut and drive, as well as a useful medium-pace bowler. Behind the stumps was Harry Wood, who made no pretence to be anything but a good professional wicket-keeper, sacrificing style for dependability. He was a good enough batsman to have made a century for England against South Africa.

Surrey, then, was a team at the very peak of success. Essex, on the other hand, had an inexperienced side which lacked Surrey's depth of bowling and batting. The Essex XI approached the fixture at The Oval with considerable relish – it was an opportunity of showing the cricket world that they had merited their promotion – though Surrey approached it with the greater confidence. But the biggest difference between the two teams lay in the manner of their composition. Surrey's success was based entirely on professional expertise. Other successful counties, like Yorkshire, Lancashire and Notts, had likewise shown the wisdom of developing a large professional nucleus. Essex, however, partly on the whim of Charles Green and partly through economic necessity, fielded a largely amateur side. It was a policy which Gloucester and Middlesex had shown could work and one which several other less affluent counties were pursuing.

Most matches at The Oval in the 1890s attracted huge crowds.

Delivery boys outside the ground would stop their carts and jump on the back of them to peer over the walls for a glimpse of the play. Horse-drawn trams would slow to a halt, so that those on the top deck could read the scoreboard. And when Abel and Brockwell were batting, traffic outside would grind to a halt in the most modern of manners. On Essex's visit in 1894, however, the prospect of bad weather had limited the attendance. Only the hardy regulars waited under lowering skies for the twelve o'clock start. They were cheerful and expectant. They had heard much of the young Essex demon bowler, but were otherwise scornful of the opposition. Was old 'Bunny' Lucas really still playing? Why, it must be 50 years since he failed to save that Test match here! And H. G. Owen? The old beggar must be all of 60! They were sad at the absence of their own captain, unable to play in this match, but by way of compensation they had their own idol, Bobby Abel, captaining the side, for the first (and, as it proved, the only) time. Quite right too, thought the Ovalites, casting a glance at the scorecard. Mr D. L. A. Jephson was the only amateur in the Surrey XI and the captaincy could hardly have been entrusted to him. Why, as everyone knew, he wasn't even worth his place in the side . . .

Charles looked out at the famous pitch and scowled his familiar scowl. The weather was dull and threatening, but, worse, it had rained overnight, so the run-up to the wicket was soggy and he would not be able to keep his footing. Tom Richardson, however, was looking more cheerful. The soft turf would give him movement off the seam. The wet conditions might mean a more cautious approach and loss of pace, but the extra movement could be crucial . . . and so it proved. Essex had the misfortune to bat first. In the very first over Richardson produced an off-cutter which went right through Carpenter and bowled him. Thereafter, the Essex batsmen hurried to and fro at Richardson's behest. When rain interrupted play after an hour, Essex were 55 for 8, the Demon still not out, and his face was as thunderous as the sky above. All eight wickets had fallen to Tom Richardson. While the faithful Ovalites waited in the rain for the resumption, they debated earnestly the chances of 'Long Tom' claiming all ten. Fifteen minutes' play mid-afternoon settled the issue. Walter Mead came and went. Just one wicket to go! But Charles was certainly not going to surrender without a struggle. When Essex wickets tumbled, his resolve always strengthened. As Richardson ran

Demon versus Lobster, Leyton, 1898

Essex: Back (L-R): Mr F. Street, Mr A.J. Turner, Russell, Mead
Seated: Mr C. McGahey, Mr C.J. Kortright, Mr H.G. Owen, Mr A.P. Lucas,
          Mr P. Perrin, Front: Carpenter, Mr F.G. Bull.

Surrey: Back (L-R): Lockwood, Lees, Brockwell, Mr V.F.S. Crawford, Wood.
Seated: Holland, Mr D.L.A. Jephson, Mr K.J. Key, Richardson, Hayward,
          Front: Baldwin, Abel.   *(British Library)*

Charles Kortright, c. 1896
(MCC)

Kortright, flanked by Fane and Perrin, returning to the Leyton
pavilion during his come-back match v Gloucs., 1900.

Digby Jephson batting at The Oval against Yorkshire, 1900. The non-striker is Bill Lockwood. *(British Library)*

Digby Jephson in his early twenties. *(British Library)*

Charles Kortright in his late twenties.

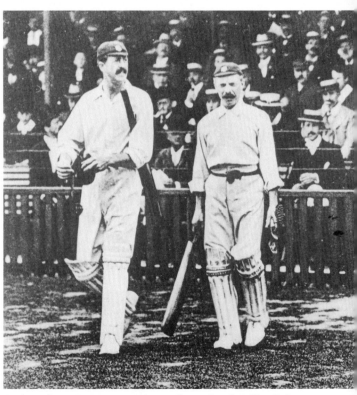

Digby Jephson (L) going out to bat at The Oval with Bobby Abel, c. 1902. *(MCC)*

Yours truly
D. L. A. Jephson

Yours faithfully,
C. J. Kortright.

Lobster and Demon, as featured in Alcock's *Famous Cricketers & Cricket Grounds* (1895).

up to him, the Demon meditated as to which part of South London he might direct the ball. Alas, instead of a fine drive, he achieved only a thick slice. The ball ballooned up over the slips and the youthful Tom Hayward came racing in from third man to hold a remarkable catch and give Tom Richardson his tenth wicket. Thereupon, with Essex all out for 72, the heavens opened.

Tuesday was as fair as Monday foul. Surrey's two senior professionals, Bobby Abel and Maurice Read, began the Surrey reply with the sun shining and only an occasional cloud scudding above the gasometers. The ground was still very damp, however, and Abel thrived as Charles bowled much below his usual pace. Soon the Essex total had been passed and with no Surrey wickets fallen! Runs piled up, and though Abel went for 65, Billy Brockwell excelled with his crisp driving, and, when the third wicket fell, the 200 had just been reached. A gasp of surprise and irritation greeted the new arrival. Scorecards were scanned despairingly! Yes, it really was Mr D. L. A. Jephson! Wasn't it bad enough to pick the fellow let alone to bat him at no. 5! 'Go back to Clapham Common,' shouted a wag. Charles watched the arrival of the newcomer with interest. There was a look of diffidence on Digby's face which spelt encouragement to Charles. He demanded the ball. The ground had been drying fast. With his feet no longer slipping, the Demon proceeded to give Digby that special test which he reserved for tyros. For the first time that day, he stretched out his strides and gathered true momentum. Soon Digby was ducking and weaving. The Demon, warming to the job, dug the ball in shorter and shorter. Digby stopped one ball with his neck, another with his head. The crowd could see that these were painful blows but Digby shrugged them aside; the crowd watched approvingly. More short deliveries followed and the Ovalites shouted abuse at the bowler, but it soon subsided, for Digby was now weathering the dying storm more confidently and Brockwell was driving his way to an aggressive century. When Brockwell went, Digby took control. Basking in the sun, the Ovalites started to realize that the young man from Clapham was a much better batsman than they had given him credit for. He was now driving powerfully, in the style of Brockwell, and his back-foot defence looked most secure. Walter Mead trundled away, Harry Burns toiled with his left-arm slows, Harry Pickett carried on gamely, off an economical eight-yard run. Even H. G. Owen bowled a few overs. The total had passed 400 and now the

81

Ovalites were anxiously looking at the scoreboard. Could Mr Jephson score a century before he ran out of partners? For a time, the slow bowler Frank Smith stayed with him, but then the Demon came back for a final burst. Tail-enders were always his by right. Frank Smith stood his ground well, until at last he gave a sharp chance to A. P. Lucas at cover slip. Lucas dived and made the catch, but Smith stayed, certain that it was not a fair one. Umpire Lillywhite humbly apologized. Mr Kortright, running down the wicket, had obstructed his view. The Essex amateurs turned, as one, towards Umpire Thoms at square leg. Out, he said decisively. That left only Tom Richardson. He would dearly have loved to have stayed long enough to give Digby his century, but, as so often with him, the spirit was more willing than the flesh; Digby was left without partners, 94 not out. Sensing his disappointment, the Ovalites gave him a rousing reception. He was on his way to acceptance.

By the time the match had reached its concluding stages on the morning of the third day, Charles was in a thoroughly bad humour. Losing he disliked; losing ignominiously he loathed. The scoreboard showed 53 for 7 when he arrived at the crease. He and McGahey stayed for a while and then, with an innings and 300 runs in hand, Bobby Abel gave Digby a bowl. The Demon's record against lobs was not too good, but he always fancied himself against them. Visions of 30 runs an over arose in his mind. He sensed the Lobster's nervousness and knew his own strength. As Digby made his low approach, Charles came charging down the wicket, taking the most mighty of swings. He completely missed the ball – but so too did Marshall, the reserve Surrey wicket-keeper. After a terrible fumble, he collected it up, but Charles by this time had been able to make his ground, moving only as fast as his wounded dignity allowed. He flailed more successfully at some subsequent lobs, raising the hundred in the process. Then McGahey, attempting to emulate the Demon, swung right across the line and was bowled by Digby. Soon after that, the Demon, slogging at Tom Richardson, was caught in the long field and Surrey had won by a crushing margin. The result was as the Ovalites had expected. It is not every day that David conquers Goliath.

Much of the entertainment of the visiting amateurs would have devolved on Digby, the only Surrey amateur playing. So it is possible that during the course of this match he and Charles were able to discuss their common family background. But it is doubtful that Digby would have found Charles congenial company. He himself was an inveterate pavilion gossip, enjoying nothing better at the end of a day's play than to mull things over, 'to chew the rag' late into the evening with a glass or two. He would have found Charles distressingly uncommunicative, for the Demon tended not to unwind in the company of fellow cricketers. Charles McGahey had a telling story. On one occasion at Old Trafford, when rain had meant a lengthy postponement, he and the Demon had gone for a long constitutional round the streets of Manchester. They had walked for miles. All the time Charles stayed in grim silence, as if concentrating on the battles ahead, resistant to all of McGahey's conversational gambits. Back in the pavilion, they had silently parted. 'Thanks for the chat,' muttered McGahey.

Later that summer of 1894, Digby made the decision to go on a three-week tour with Crystal Palace rather than play for Surrey. The consequence of this was that he was not picked again by the aggrieved County for three years! Understandably, the Surrey Committee felt let down. Only the month before they had given Digby a game for the Gentlemen v. Players at The Oval, always a less representative match than that at Lord's, but an honour nonetheless for a young, unproven player to play for the Gentlemen.

By the time of his return to first-class cricket in July 1897, Surrey had won yet another Championship and were still a very powerful side. While Digby was absent from first-class cricket, Charles had enjoyed three years of unbroken success. He was on the verge of selection for England, as one of the most feared bowlers in the country. Inspired by Charles in 1897, Essex were now challenging Surrey and Lancashire for the Championship. Record crowds of 15,000 a day had watched the defeats of Yorkshire and Lancashire at Leyton. When, in mid-August, Surrey visited Leyton, Essex needed only to win and the Championship would be theirs. Another record crowd was confidently expected. New stands had been erected. Extra trains were organized by the Great Eastern Railway. The national newspapers added to the pre-match frenzy with massive coverage of both teams' prospects. The match was hailed as 'The Last Big Task for the Eastern County'. Locally, from Walthamstow to Stratford, there was the keenest of anticipation. The weather too was obliging. The long-awaited Thursday was a dog-star day, oppressively hot.

Ominously for Essex, it was a day more suited to a lobster than a demon, and, as luck would have it, Digby had been recently reinstated by Surrey after his three-year exile, as part of a deliberate Committee policy to play more amateurs.

Essex won the toss and chose to bat. The first ball proved sensational. Tom Richardson bowled Carpenter, by way of Carpenter's arm. Some steady batting by Perrin, Turner and Fane, however, took the score along with misleading ease. The turning point of the Essex innings came when Kingsmill Key decided to give Digby a bowl, with the score at 92 for 3. Digby now was a much more mature cricketer than the last time he had played for Surrey. Success in club cricket had filled him with self-belief. Turner had been playing majestic shots off the overarm bowlers. Against Digby's underarm lobs, he became strangely apprehensive, his only tactic being to scamper up the wicket to kill the spin with a defensive prod. Freddie Fane was similarly ill at ease. Eventually, Fane went dancing down the wicket, failed to make contact and was comprehensively stumped. This marked the beginning of the Essex débâcle. Richardson accounted for Turner. Now much depended on Hugh Owen. Digby tossed up a straightforward leg-break, pitching just outside the stumps. Owen watched it suspiciously, trying at the last minute to nudge it to leg, but missing. It hit his pads. Not out! A titter went round the ground, releasing the tension. Nothing looked sillier than a big man being perplexed by a lob bowler. The next ball was again well flighted, pitching this time around middle stump. Owen essayed, a little clumsily, to lift it over Digby's head, but instead of breaking from leg, it ducked into him, beat the bat and again struck the pad. Surrey appealed as one, and the umpire, with some sorrow, signalled the retreat of the Essex captain. Out strode the Demon to replace him and Essex hearts were cheered. So often in the past Korty had hit them out of trouble. They cheered their hero all the way to the wicket, until, bare-headed, he glanced imperiously around the field. He noted the seven leg-side fielders with grim disdain. So much, he thought to himself, for good sportsmanship! So much for the good, clean off-side game! He determined to settle Digby's hash, to belt him all over the field. Digby came crabbing in; from low, ground level, up he tossed a delicate tice. The Demon waited for it to fall, bat at the ready. Porters must have heard the impact, willow on leather, far away at Leyton Station. Momentarily the crowd applauded. High the ball flew skywards; but it then began its long descent, coming to land with an awful inevitability in the strong hands of Billy Brockwell at square leg. The Demon stared in disbelief and then began the silent journey back. When Tom Richardson, bowling in tandem with Digby, finished off the tail, Essex, who had been 92 for 3, were 143 all out. For the home supporters it was a terrible disappointment. Loud was their outcry against the Essex batsmen. They should have practised in the nets against some lobs. They should have played with greater circum-spection. 'As for Jephson's "underhands",' said the *Essex County Chronicle* sadly, 'a little care and patience would soon have enabled the batsmen to deal with them, but they rose to the bait – and were "hooked"!'

Only a great effort now from the Essex bowlers could save the match and the Championship. Charles bowled magnificently from the pavilion end. Abel and Brockwell looked anything but secure. Abel had a lucky 4 through the slips. Brockwell was all but bowled. Abel played uppishly, just wide of a fielder on the leg-side. But a wicket did not fall and, gradually, the Surrey openers found the middle of the bat and the initiative shifted. As the afternoon sun beat down and the fielders began to wilt under it, Abel and Brockwell started to play more freely. The crowd became strangely subdued, and, when Charles induced Brockwell to give a catch and F. G. Bull had Hayward caught in the long field, there was a restraint in the crowd's celebration, for they eyed the board and saw that, with only two wickets down, Surrey were already past the Essex total. But, when Charles came on for his third spell, he brought his county fresh inspiration by his renewed hostility. Abel may have roused his ire by driving him for 2 boundaries. Charles increased his pace and the Guv'nor, in attempting a third drive, lofted the ball and Charles, following hard down the wicket, caught it. As the little man retired, with 82 to his credit, he was given a very generous reception. The Leyton crowd readily identified with his 'cockney sparrow' image. They were still standing and cheering Bobby Abel as Digby emerged from the pavilion. All the humiliation of his dismissal by the Lobster welled up in the Demon's heart. And all his hatred of Digby's foul leg theory went into his next delivery. Digby had never experienced a ball of such pace. He attempted to get his bat on it, but the bat was still coming down, ever so heavy and slow, as the ball whistled through.

He had been bowled by the Demon, all ends up, first ball, and the crowd exulted in his discomforture. When 'Shrimp' Leveson Gower managed to save the hat-trick, a great sigh rose up all around the ground. But the Cambridge captain, Norman Druce, soon lost his off stump to Charles and then the rotund Charlie Baldwin fell to him too. By the time Kingsmill Key reached the wicket, just before the close of play, Charles had bowled Essex back into the match. Many people, not least the bowler, believed that Key was lbw to the first ball the Demon sent him. But the umpire found an element of doubt from somewhere and at close of play Surrey were 205 for 8, with Key still there.

The early play on the Friday morning swung the match conclusively Surrey's way. Key smote the Essex attack and, in half an hour, the last 2 wickets put on 59 invaluable runs. Surrey were now 121 ahead on the first innings. It was a bleak situation for Essex, but by lunch it was bleaker. Tom Hayward's medium pace was their undoing and, at 76 for 6, Essex had as good as lost the match. Inevitably it was left to the Demon to give the crowd something to cheer. He struck Tom Richardson first ball for an all-run six (the portly Surrey captain giving chase). Again and again he attacked Richardson. One ball bounced off the seats of the pavilion. Another ended up in the ladies' enclosure. At last he perished, when Leveson Gower caught a towering catch in front of the pavilion rails. It was a catch which the fielder treasured 60 years on!

The 10-wicket defeat cost Essex the Championship and great was the mourning in East London. There would have been even more sorrow, had it been known that Essex would not win their first Championship until 1979.

A few months later, at the start of the new season of 1898, Surrey again came to East London. Leyton had now become a rival to The Oval in terms of the partisan support around the ring. Yet there remained a subtle difference in the atmosphere of the two grounds. 'Though the Leyton ground has acquired importance attaching to fame and ability, there is still something rustic in the environment,' commented one writer. 'The dramatic keenness of The Oval is toned down here, and the cricket is not desperately serious.' This just misses the mark, for the cricket *was* certainly serious. But it was conducted at Leyton in a cavalier spirit, a spirit not unconnected with Charles Green's lost ideal of an exclusive club.

It was something the Surrey Committee would soon covet, at considerable cost.

Much had happened to Digby since the last encounter. His return to the Surrey side had been extremely successful, and he was now welcomed not only as a batsman but as a serious bowler of lobs. Suddenly his star was in the ascendant. He was beginning a period of five consecutive seasons with Surrey. His place was assured and he wore his brown cap with pride. As the county's most successful young amateur, he found himself hurriedly promoted to act as vice-captain. The critics vied with each other in his praise: 'Mr Jephson is a cricketer from the crown of his head to the soles of his feet,' said one. 'Mr Jephson has not many superiors among the amateurs at the present time,' said another.

Memories of the previous exciting encounter drew massive crowds. Surrey chose to bat, Brockwell and Abel opened, and Charles started the match off from the pavilion end. The Demon was at the height of his powers in 1898, faster than ever, faster than anyone. He had many spectacular successes through the season, helping Essex win a record 11 matches. His first two balls to the Guv'nor flew past the little man, who did not seem to have got sight of them at all. The third ball, outside the off stump, Abel felt for and got a thin edge. McGahey held on to the catch: 0 for 1! Brockwell was clearly unnerved by the Demon's pace and soon both he and Baldwin had gone. It was left to Digby and Tom Hayward to withstand the blistering attack and they did so bravely. Right up to lunch they battled, when Hugh Owen tried one of his more enterprising pieces of captaincy. To the merriment of the rest of the XI, he put on Johnny Turner, who bowled very bad lobs. The last time he had bowled, some of his balls had hardly reached the other end. Tom Hayward hated lobs. In the last over before lunch he got into all kinds of difficulties with a very high flighted one and ended up by snicking a catch to the wicket-keeper. Surrey were left 118 for 4, with Digby not out.

The resumption was delayed until after three o'clock, so that photographs of both teams could be taken. These contain some interesting expressions. Abel and Brockwell look shell-shocked. Hayward's ludicrous dismissal is still on his mind. The 19-year-old Frank Crawford, about to go out to bat, is looking pensive. Digby himself looks like a fugitive from a chain gang. The heat of the present battle is there on his brow. But he also looks, and was, unwell. In the Essex group, the Demon seems preoccupied, brooding perhaps about further Surrey wickets.

In the afternoon there was some fascinating cricket. 'Everyone was anxious to see how young Crawford would shape', wrote *The Morning Leader*. 'He had to face Kortright and I do not think that any young cricketer could pass through a severer ordeal in his first county match. Kortright was early at him with yorkers. Crawford stopped two of them right enough, and the next he cut beautifully for 2 and made us think he was in for a score. He was in too much of a hurry, however, and in lashing out at the next, he was bowled.' Thoroughly intimidated by Charles, Surrey were bowled out by Mead and Bull, Digby being last out for a very defiant fifty. Thanks to a century from Turner, Essex enjoyed a big first innings lead.

Surrey's second innings began in dreadful light. Charles pitched deliberately short and the ball flew around dangerously. The Surrey professionals were in great discomfort. Brockwell was soon bowled. 'I fancy that Brockwell does not like fast bowling,' observed *The Morning Leader*, 'and in the bad light of yesterday I don't wonder at it!' He was bowled by a beautiful ball, which cut in off the pitch and hit the top of the off stump. Twice in one over Tom Hayward had to duck to avoid being hit. It was impossible to see the ball clearly. Frank Crawford stood up bravely to Charles but could not lay bat on ball. Digby and Hayward made another brave stand, Digby taking 50 minutes over 11 bitterly contested runs, before succumbing to the Demon, with a snick to Russell. So it was now simply Tom Hayward v. Essex, a frustrating contest for the home side. Hayward much preferred fast bowling to slow and he took as much of the Demon as he could. He was, said Digby, the best professional batsman against pace, 'a fine player off his chest or throat'. Eventually Hayward, last man out, succumbed to the Demon. There was a gale blowing, and, to take advantage of this, Charles had switched to the Walthamstow end. The extra speed was too much for Hayward, who sliced a ball over the slips, and Carpenter, dashing in from third man, took a wonderful low-down catch. Essex had won by an innings and avenged their last defeat! The crowd surged onto the field. Charles evaded their attention, but the professionals, Carpenter and Mead, were carried shoulder-high back to their enclosure.

Such enthusiastic demonstrations were common during these years at Leyton. Hardly a match there ended without a jubilant rush of spectators towards the pavilion, When Essex had beaten Yorkshire in 1897 'the crowd roared with delight, hats were thrown into the air, and a vast crowd surged in front of the pavilion. There were repeated calls for Mr Kortright and, after a time, the hero of the match presented himself for a moment or two in front of the pavilion and acknowledged the enthusiastic cheers by raising his cap.' A big match at Leyton affected the whole neighbourhood. As Essex neared a famous victory over the Australians in 1899, 'it was marvellous to see all the thoroughfares round about, how housewives stopped their Saturday afternoon cleaning, how butcher boys pulled up their fast trotting ponies, and middle-aged gentlemen, enjoying a quiet smoke at the garden gates, let their pipes go out, in order to learn the result of the match and to listen to the details.' Inside the ground there was pandemonium: 'The shouting in front of the pavilion, the speeches, the condolences, the explanations, the wild wonder of the natives, and then their hysterical delight – who will paint the scene in appropriate colours? The rejoicings over the battle of Waterloo were nothing to it. Trafalgar was a mere whisper. Omdurman sank in the shade before the hysterical heroics of the Essex camp followers.' Post-match speeches needed no microphones. The crowd hushed for its heroes. Joe Darling, the Australian captain, spoke a few words from the balcony and was cheered rapturously. Charles Green delivered a speech of passion. He then caught hold of Hugh Owen and dragged him to the front: 'Mr Owen blushed, bowed and then, breaking away, dived through a doorway behind him like a rabbit into a hole. Mr Green then declared that he would bring out Mr Kortright . . .'

Of course a county's victory over the Australians was a particularly special event, but ordinary county matches could produce just such extraordinary scenes. Never before or since has the three-day county match attracted such devoted interest as it did in the Grace Boom years of the late 1890s. It is difficult for us today to believe that county matches, such as those played between Essex and Surrey, could cause a spectator's pulse to race so fast. This intensity of interest in county cricket, however, was comparatively short-lived. It was not long before football, with its emphasis on towns rather than counties, began to exert a greater mass appeal. But county cricket, for the moment, while Grace remained as its champion, could fairly call itself the national game. As each new season dawned and cricket awoke from slumber, there was a stirring of the national consciousness. Digby expressed it thus:

> And so, my hibernating friend, you wake,
>   Full fresh from out your winter hours of rest!
> And they that wept to lose one single day
>   Of your brave company, – now laugh, – now jest;
> As you return. Your call is heard throughout
>   The land, and English hearts and English eyes
> Go out to you, and English hands stretch forth
>   To show their love for you, that never dies.

8
Demon
and
Doctor

In 1898, the year of Grace's fiftieth birthday, the Demon played in two famous matches with the Champion. In the first, at Leyton, where Essex entertained Gloucester for the first time, a tremendous feud arose between the two men, each accusing the other of unfair play. In the second, at Lord's in W.G.'s Jubilee match, came a reconciliation.

Grace, of course, was known and praised for his wiliness. 'No subtlety by which a batsman might be legitimately dispossessed of his wicket was unknown to the doctor,' wrote Dick Lilley, with a reverence typical of the times. The legitimacy of some of W.G.'s manoeuvres, however, is very questionable. Stories abound about his loud, off-putting comments in the field, his cries of 'Miss it!' when he had put up a catch, his ruining of the wicket with his spikes, his unjustified appealing and his manipulation of the umpires. He would seem to have resorted to fair means or foul in his desire for success and to have been a most inventive and forceful exponent of the art of gamesmanship. He could catch out even the wary. Once, for example, he had thrown his arm round Bobby Abel, 96 not out at lunchtime and very nervous, and had promised a ripe full-toss on the leg-side immediately after the resumption. Abel was duly grateful for this promise and ate the more heartily. However, while Abel practised his cow shots after the interval, the Doctor quietly put an extra man on the boundary rope. He then produced the promised full-toss and Abel fell into the carefully prepared trap. 'An artful toad' was Sammy Woods' appropriate description of him.

Demon and Lobster reacted differently to W.G.'s massive personality. Digby never once criticized. Strangely, he, the champion of the 'whiteness' of the game, was always full of unqualified praise for Grace. Lord Harris, a stickler for etiquette, who knew all about Grace's gamesmanship having played with him for England, did not blush to write that W.G. was 'the most prominent exponent that there has ever been of the finest and PUREST game there has ever been'. This apparent willingness to condone W.G.'s sharp practices may seem like mere Victorian hypocrisy. But that is to ignore the extraordinary way in which cricket viewed its Champion. For years he had been the nonpareil. Now too he was the Grand Old Man. His achievements had placed him above petty considerations of abuse of amateur status and an over-zealous aim to win. W.G. was untouchable, and knew it.

Charles' clash with Grace, therefore, in 1898 of all years, tells us much about his own character. Like W.G., he was a gentleman cricketer with ungentlemanly habits on the field. Of course, both men believed that they played fairly and would have been shocked to have been told otherwise. Like Grace, Charles was sparing of words and those he used were generally blunt and unvarnished by finer feelings. The Demon was too similar in temperament to the Doctor ever to have an easy relationship with him. He cared nothing for reputations. He cared nothing for the Doctor's awesome seniority. It meant nothing to him that, in the year of his own birth, the Doctor had scored ten centuries and topped the national averages for the third consecutive time. He was perfectly prepared to speak his mind about the Doctor, even if he was a national hero.

Gloucester's visit to Leyton, then, in 1898, tells much about both men. There had been feelings of animosity before the game ever began. Charles had long been critical of the refusal of E. M. Grace, Gloucester's long-standing secretary, to grant Essex a fixture. Only now, in Essex's fifth first-class season had one been arranged. There were rumours that W.G. had not fancied facing the Demon on the sporting Leyton turf. These rumours were surely ill-founded. Wickets had been much the poorer in the 1870s and yet had not upset W.G. then. Besides, Leyton was the one county ground where he had never scored a hundred. But the rumours persisted and helped crystalize the personal conflict between batsman and bowler.

Leyton gave Grace a rapturous reception. Charles watched dourly from the Essex balcony, as W.G. was fêted in the members' enclosure. It was the same everywhere he went, for Grace was one of the few instantly recognizable Victorian celebrities, the constant object of spontaneous demonstrations of affection. Gilbert Jessop, who often travelled with him, remembered extraordinary scenes at railway stations: 'Luggage was left to take care of itself until the wielder of the barrow had taken his fill of the colossal bearded figure, or even perchance pressed the Old Man's hand with his grimy fingers. I never remember W.G. refusing to shake hands with anyone who possessed sufficient self-assurance to ask it of him.'

Gloucestershire fielded first and the spectators marvelled at the Doctor's bulk, as he led his fellow amateurs out of the pavilion. 'It seemed to me impossible', wrote Jessop, 'that a man of his years, carrying so heavy a burden of flesh, could persist at the game.' He had always been big-framed, with size 14 boots, and, even in his prime, had weighed as much as 15 stone. Now, in his fiftieth year, he was two stone heavier and would shortly reach 20 stone. Most appropriately, he was known simply to his fellow cricketers as 'The Big 'Un'.

Essex made a disastrous start to the match. By lunch they had been bowled out for 128. W.G. was the cause of their downfall. Bowling his curly slows from the Walthamstow end he had taken 7 wickets for 44, his best performance for a very long time. His very first over heralded things to come. He completely beat Hugh Owen with his first two balls and bowled him with the third. Then McGahey, playing tentatively forward, across the line, was bowled round his legs first ball. It was not long before Perrin, Turner, Mead and Bull followed. Charles came out to bat, exuding aggression and defiance, but he was hit on the pads by what the Doctor and umpire considered a straight one. Only Bunny Lucas played Grace with confidence; he knew Grace of old. W.G. bowled with an old-fashioned, round-arm action. Digby recalled 'a few short shuffling strides, the arm a little above the shoulder, the right hand a shade in front of him, the curious rotary action before delivery, and the wonderful length. The hand is large and the ball is well concealed, and, as you face him, for he stands full-fronted to you, it seems to leave by the back door, as it were, that is, over the knuckle of the little finger.' In another appreciation of Grace's bowling, Digby wrote: 'I have played with him many times, but he does not seem to me to do very much, but some come a little higher, others a little lower, some a little faster, some slower; on the middle-leg is his favourite spot – two or three off the leg stick with a square deep who is not asleep, then a straighter one with "a bit of top on it" – the batsman tries to push to leg – there is a somewhat excited "'s that?" and the would-be run-getter is sauntering pavilionwards.'

Some of the Essex batsmen, dismissed by Grace, had sauntered very angrily pavilionwards. Perrin returned in a fury. He had spooned up an easy chance, but Grace was slow to move to it and caught the ball very low down. To many it seemed that Grace had caught the ball on the half volley. He, however, clinched Perrin's departure with the triumphant cry, 'Not bad for an old 'un!' Perrin appealed to the umpire, whose view had been obscured by Grace, as usual. He appealed in vain. Gilbert Jessop, in a good position at cover point to see what had happened, was adamant that Grace had caught the ball on the first bounce. Most newspapermen, loyal to the Champion, remained reticent, apart from the correspondent of *The Walthamstow Guardian* who was more forthright than most: 'The general opinion was that the ball touched the ground before it reached Grace's hands, and the action of the Champion in tossing the ball up before the umpire could have given his decision was a subject of general comment.'

Worse things followed. That lunchtime Grace had telegraphed news of his success back to Bristol. From there came a congratulatory wire: 'How cruel of you to bowl the rabbits out!' Grace could not resist pinning this message up in the pavilion where the Essex amateurs would see it. Charles, for one, was outraged at this act of hubris.

It is possible that Grace deliberately enraged the Demon in this way, hoping that, in his fury, he might lose control and be easier to play. *The Morning Leader* set the scene well as their duel began: 'The Old Man went in first and I understand he was somewhat doubtful about facing Kortright, while the fast bowler for his part was anxious to do his best against the Old Man, whom he had never bowled to before. It was bad light too when Grace went in and I for one did not think he would be equal to stopping Kortright, who bowled from the pavilion end with a mass of spectators for a background.' The crowd hushed, watching the familiar figure walking to the wicket with Harry Wrathall, and gaped in awe at the famous beard, now flecked with grey, contrasting strangely with the vivid MCC cap of red and yellow hoops. He removed a bail, as was his custom, and marked his guard in the popping crease, and the battle commenced. Gloucester lost 3 quick wickets, but W.G., playing himself in with a great deal of care, mastered the situation and with the help of his godson, Charles Townsend, a stylish left-hander, he guided Gloucestershire to a total of 230 for 8 at the close. He himself, in just over three hours, had made a heroic 126. 'On his retirement Grace was accorded a magnificent reception,' noted the *Daily News*, 'the occupants of the pavilion seats rising and cheering heartily as he passed the steps.' Charles had bowled superbly, with great fire and accuracy, taking 5 for 41 in 24 overs. But he had not managed to dislodge the Champion.

Fifty years later, Charles talked to John Arlott about Grace's remarkable innings. W.G., he said, kept fisting the ball down to third man: 'He wasn't attempting to hit the ball with his bat outside the off stump, but was punching it – punching it – with his thick felt gloves through the slips, and I was bowling fairly fast then . . .' It is a marvellous story, but difficult to believe. Contemporary reports make no mention of such a drastic manoeuvre. But in Grace's *Memorial Biography* one reads: 'Kortright was banging ball after ball down with almost reckless virulence, but Grace never seemed perturbed, even though severely knocked on the hand several times.' The action would seem to have been involuntary rather than deliberate. *Sporting Life* also challenges Charles' story: 'Some of Grace's strokes past third man were excellent to watch.'

During his century Grace also played particularly well on the leg-side, scoring freely between mid-on and short leg. His strength in this area is borne out by the evidence of precious film, made in 1899, of W.G. batting in the nets. This demonstrates how, in his fiftieth year, Grace was still able to master top-class bowling. First, the film reveals evidence of a copybook style. There is a high back lift. When Grace is playing on the front foot, there is a strong top hand, his left elbow very prominent, bent at 90 degrees. But he modifies the copybook style, to counter his physical limitations. Eschewing the full-face drive, he turns the wrists on impact, and, with much sweetness of timing, flicks the ball away in the direction of mid-wicket. On the back foot too, there is the same flick of the wrists, sending the ball scudding away to leg. They are shots which only a few modern batsmen, such as Vivian Richards, can play successfully, because they require a magnificent eye. W.G. could still see the ball like a young man.

Seldom can any 49-year-old have had such a wonderful day's cricket: 7 wickets and 126 runs! 'THE GREAT WG COMES TO LEYTON AND WORKS WONDERS', cried one paper. 'UNDER MEDICAL ORDERS THE HOME TEAM SUFFERED A RELAPSE', wrote another.

The next morning Grace arrived a little late at the ground. In such circumstances it would have been usual to have delayed, but Essex were in no mood for making friendly gestures to Grace and insisted on a prompt start. Gloucester, with their last 2 wickets falling quickly, had to take the field without him. However, they had the better of the incident, for by the time Grace arrived to take charge of proceedings, Townsend had already bowled out Hugh Owen.

Essex fared a little better in their second innings, playing W.G.

cautiously and, this time, losing no wickets to him. There were further incidents, as Essex suffered some poor umpiring. Johnny Turner was surprised and dissatisfied at being given out lbw to a ball which turned in from outside the leg stump. Tom Russell was very doubtfully stumped. Worst of all, Bunny Lucas was wrongly given out caught at the wicket. Perhaps the ball brushed his shirt, perhaps it hit his thigh. It certainly got nowhere near his bat. Lucas, normally so mild a man, was outraged. He retired crossly to the pavilion. 'Cheats never prosper!' he cried loudly as he approached it. Charles nodded grimly on the balcony.

With Perrin scoring a slow 81 and Carpenter cutting and off-driving his way to a fifty (before being caught off one of Harry Wrathall's lobs), Essex were able to give their bowlers a small chance, setting Gloucester 148 to win. 'It might seem a rather insignificant total', wrote Jessop, 'on a plumb wicket, which this one at Leyton certainly was, but this was no ordinary occasion. For here we had the fastest bowler in the world bowling with a determination which I never saw exceeded . . .' Jessop, who had already lost his middle stump to Charles in the first innings, was writing from experience.

As Grace and Jack Board opened for Gloucester, the crowd sensed the importance of the moment. 'Kortright opened the bowling amid a dead silence, as if on the wearing pitch the crowd were expecting him to do something out of the common.' They were not disappointed. Grace managed a single and then Charles sent Jack Board's stumps flying. Two balls later, Walter Troup's middle stump sailed back some six or seven yards and the cheering, loud at the first wicket, was deafening at the second. Gloucester were 1 for 2!

Slowly Grace and Cyril Sewell began to weather Charles' furious onslaught. But not without cost. At one stage the game was halted, when W.G. was struck in the left side by a ball from Charles, the thud being clearly audible all round the ground. Batsman and bowler glared at each other. The ball left a lurid bruise, the seam visible the next day and, some said, the maker's name too! As the shadows lengthened in the cool of the evening, there were two final troubled overs.

Walter Mead was bowling to Grace. 'Grace hit a ball hard to the ground', wrote *The Sporting Life*, 'and Mead, rushing in, secured it from the bounce. Under the impression that he had caught Grace, he threw it up and was considerably disappointed when, on appealing to the umpire, he was met with a negative answer.' The crowd, however, seemed astonished at the decision and so too were many of the players in the middle who had witnessed a somewhat different sequence of events. To them the catch had been perfectly genuine, but W.G. ignored it and took up position for the next ball. Thereupon Mead, with the strongest of support from Charles and other distressed Essex players, appealed to the umpire, George Burton, an old Middlesex professional. 'Out,' said Burton decisively. 'What, George?' thundered Grace down the wicket, a picture of menace. 'Er, not out,' muttered Burton, capitulating. Charles never forgot that decision. Fifty years later he still remembered it and it still rankled.

Beside himself with anger, Charles now bowled the final over of the day. He subjected Grace to a deplorable barrage of intimidating bouncers. Off one of these Charlie McGahey missed the hardest of slip catches and the ball rushed past him to the boundary. As the players came off the field shortly afterwards, Charles suggested to McGahey that he might have done better with the chance. The bruised and battered Grace, overhearing this, quickly seized his opportunity. 'Cheats never prosper,' he said.

On the final morning Gloucester were faced with the task of scoring 67 more runs to win with 7 wickets left. *The Morning Leader* commented: 'The Champion is still in possession with 36 to his name and the man who gets him out today can join a mutual admiration society with Bull, who took his wicket on Thursday. I believe Kortright is a very eager candidate.' He was. Fresh from a night's rest, he was swooping in like a Fury. Sewell was caught off a skier. Townsend's off stump was sent spinning. And Grace himself, who had reached 49, was bowled. This dismissal has taken its place in cricket legend. Two balls earlier the Demon had beaten Grace for pace and caught him well and truly leg before wicket. But the umpire disagreed. One ball earlier the Demon had beaten him outside the off stump, the Doctor had snicked, Tom Russell had clung on and the fielders jumped in triumph. But the umpire stayed unmoved. This time, however, there could be no doubt. The leg stump was uprooted, rearing high in the air, as if in celebration, before coming to rest seven yards back. The middle stump was uprooted too. The Doctor made his usual dumbshow of astonishment and then began to walk away. 'Surely you're not going, Doctor,' said Charles, half smiling, half snarling. 'There's one stump still standing.'

The runs nevertheless continued to come. Gloucester, at 132 for 6, with only 16 more runs needed, looked well placed, particularly as Jessop was still in at one end. Wrathall had a lucky snick for 4 and survived an lbw appeal. Jessop meanwhile had the temerity to rush down the pitch at one ball from the Demon, mis-hitting it for a single. Then Mead had Wrathall caught in the slips: 3 to win with 3 wickets left! There was another single and then Charles bowled out Jessop's new partner: 2 to win with 2 wickets left! The incoming batsman, Edward Wright, was a young Oxford Blue. Charles landed one on his toe and broke it. Lbw! Still 2 to win, but now only one wicket left!

That wicket belonged to Fred Roberts, a good professional quick bowler, but no batsman. In the pavilion he received some last-minute instructions from W.G. He was not to draw away from the stumps, but must stay there with his bat. 'But what about my wife and family, Doctor?' Roberts is said to have muttered. 'Kortright may hit you, but he can't kill you,' replied the Doctor. Roberts, still looking uncertain, was then given further food for thought. There would be an extra £1 for him if Gloucester won, but he would have played his last game for the county if they lost. Quaking in his boots, Roberts left the pavilion. 'A great silence came over the spectators,' wrote *The Morning Leader*, 'as the batsman made his way to the wickets and they were evidently preparing to send up a huge shout, being nearly certain that he would not be able to resist Kortright.' Charles had three balls left. Off the very first Roberts snicked a single and a huge sigh of anxiety and disappointment came from the Leyton ring. The match was now tied. According to Jessop's later account, that was the end of the over. Match reports suggest, however, that Jessop then received two balls from Charles, without scoring. At all events, Roberts was left as the recipient of the next over. Jessop watched nervously and helplessly. It was a match which he very much wanted to win: 'The sense of ill-feeling brooding over the game made the idea of losing the match, after all that had gone before, extremely distasteful.' Mead bowled to Roberts. There were appeals for a catch at the wicket and for lbw, both turned down. One ball was said to have brushed the wicket without dislodging a bail. Somehow, Roberts survived and salvaged his county career. Charles now bowled to the crouching Jessop, the fastest-scoring batsman of the whole Golden Age, who only had one style of play. Jumping two or three yards down the wicket, bravely and against all the laws of probability he drove the first ball to the long-off boundary, to win the match.

There was left a residue of bitterness between the two counties. Charles Green's friendship with W.G. suffered another setback, and he was loud in his condemnation of Grace's 'sharp practices'. The feud between Demon and Doctor endured. Grace's *Memorial Biography* stated erroneously; 'A good deal of feeling ran high between the great batsman and the fast bowler, but thanks to the friendly offices of C. E. Green all ended happily.' As Green was not on speaking terms with Grace, he was hardly a useful intermediator. Hugh Owen, not a man easy to rouse, commented publicly after the match: 'We can take a beating in good spirit, when we are fairly beaten, but we have not been fairly beaten in this match.'

Only nine days later, Demon and Doctor were playing on the same side at Lord's, for the Gentlemen v. the Players. It was W.G.'s Jubilee match, the most important match of the season. The MCC had arranged for the fixture to start on 18 July, W.G.'s fiftieth birthday, and had kept the date clear of county matches, so that the strongest available sides should make it a memorable occasion. Charles very nearly turned down the invitation to play, so strongly did he resent the Doctor's gamesmanship at Leyton. Although Bunny Lucas ensured that wiser counsels prevailed, neither Demon nor Doctor were on speaking terms at the start of the match. Other quarrels were sooner mended, for, among Grace's birthday telegrams, was one from Hugh Owen: 'Heartiest congratulations to the greatest cricketer of the age.' This remarkable volte-face typifies the Age's ambivalent attitude to its Champion.

W.G.'s fiftieth birthday party was a happy confection of cricket, sunshine and goodwill. It was the talking point of the nation. Everywhere the names of Grace and Gladstone were being bandied around as the two greatest Englishmen of Victoria's time. The familiar bearded figure smiled seraphically from every newspaper. His every cricketing statistic was scrupulously detailed and avidly read.

Lord's was en fête on 18 July 1898. Long before the start, spectators formed a long queue outside the gates. Cabs were arriving by the dozen. The mid-summer heat was already so intense that several roads were blocked by hansoms, their horses collapsed with fatigue within the shafts. The ground was full by 11.30 a.m. but a few thousand more were allowed in, to squat on the ground in front. Straw-hatted men formed the majority, but lady enthusiasts thronged the covered stand south of the pavilion. There were over 20,000 people in the ground, but it was an orderly crowd. The only time the police were called into action was when a gentleman in the grandstand disregarded the sign 'No smoking allowed' and was forcibly ejected.

Before the game even started there was much to cheer. Those who would get a poor view of the match ensured that they had a good view of the net practice. When W.G. took a stroll on the north side of the ground to visit the telegraph office, he was accompanied by tremendous bursts of applause. Everywhere he was confronted by a sea of smiling faces, a channel of outstretched hands. W.G. himself is said to have smiled non-stop for three whole days.

The Players won the toss and elected to bat on the hard, true wicket. So, shortly after noon, W.G. led his team onto the field. All round the ground he was given a standing ovation, the men cheering again and again until they were hoarse, the ladies fluttering their handkerchiefs. Only a few of them had been present 33 years before, when W.G. had first represented the Gentlemen. Of those who now followed him onto the pitch, Dixon, Wynyard and Stoddart had been infants at the time and the others not yet born. The hysteria was understandable. W.G. was so much more than the Champion of cricket. He represented continuity, resistance to the ravages of time and change. To the spectators he seemed as indestructible as their own values, society and Empire. He was certainly worth cheering.

Only one man out of many thousands remained unmoved. Charles looked haughtily around him. He knew more intimately than these cheering thousands the real nature of cricket's Champion. He knew him as a cheat and braggart and would not readily forgive. W.G. threw the ball to him. Charles caught it. Neither man spoke or caught the other's eye. Charles was to start the match off at the pavilion end. Silently he measured out his run. Bobby Abel and his captain, Arthur Shrewsbury, had come out, almost unnoticed, to open the Players' innings. An aggressive field greeted them. There were three slips, Teddy Wynyard, Jack Mason, Kent's young captain, and Andrew Stoddart. Archie MacLaren was at short third man, almost a fourth slip. W.G. was in his usual position of point. John Dixon, the Notts' captain, was at very deep third man. Stanley Jackson was at cover point and Charles Townsend at mid-off. This only left one fielder on the leg-side, Sammy Woods at mid-on. Gregor MacGregor was standing a good dozen paces back, behind the wicket. He did not intend to move closer. He had observed the Demon's thunderous looks.

Shrewsbury and Abel looked anxious. The Demon was known to be at his worst when fresh in the morning. This he now proved, giving vent to all his pent-up feelings. 'He simply let himself go', commented one writer, 'like a steam engine.' Time and again he hurled the ball half-way down the wicket: 'The batsmen frequently had to play him off their eyebrows.' Neither batsman could score off Charles or Jackson. The crowd went very silent. When, eventually, Shrewsbury pushed a single, Abel's turn came to face the Demon. He was very scared and it showed. Several times he drew away, allowing a big gap between bat and body. Nonetheless, when Charles overpitched, he managed an off-drive for 4, to much applause. Charles responded, as Abel knew he would, with something extra fast and extra short. 'I doubt whether I ever saw anyone bowl so fast', wrote R. L. Hodgson 30 years later, 'as C. J. Kortright on that Monday morning. He always took a tremendous run; if I remember right, when walking back towards the pavilion each ball, his strides numbered 30 . . .' Eventually, the inevitable happened. Charles bowled Abel, removing his leg stump as he played tentatively forward, groping for a ball which he could not see. Soon afterwards, Shrewsbury followed Abel, caught brilliantly at slip by Charles. 'Shrewsbury never looked like making many runs,' noted the *Morning Leader*, 'yet he was a trifle unlucky in getting out to a quite remarkable catch by Kortright, who took the ball well behind his body.' Billy Gunn came in. While playing his first over from Charles he looked the picture of misery. Three balls flew past him, one perilously close to the off stump. The Notts professional, now aged 40 and weighing 14 stone, still possessed a delicate touch and a good eye. Despite a most uncomfortable stance (feet splayed out, heels together), he was a graceful stroke player and now the wristwork of his cuts and the forearm power of his drives began to be seen. But he was hit several times by the Demon and was so badly bruised by the end of his innings that he was unable to field the next day.

W.G., impressed by Charles' magnificent efforts, now decided to break their mutual silence. He slowly sauntered across to Charles, a twinkle in his eye. Neither man was accustomed to using many words. 'Well, Korty, want to come off?' The Demon regarded the Doctor suspiciously for a moment. 'Well, I can keep on,' he said, mopping his brow. The Doctor smiled and this time the smile was reciprocated. For the first occasion that morning Charles' frown disappeared, and for the rest of the morning session he pounded away at the pavilion end, from twelve till two, allowing the Players no respite.

One of the excitements of the Jubilee match was the first appearance at Lord's of a cinematograph man. Sadly there is no extant film of the actual cricket, but there do exist moving pictures of the two teams, walking together two by two, a Gentleman with a Player. It was possibly taken on the occasion of the presentation of specially struck commemorative medals. Alternatively, it may be an artificial procession, arranged for the cinematographer. Most of the cricketers walk past the new-fangled device with a self-conscious disdain, as if having been told to act 'naturally' and managing to achieve the exact reverse.

Little conversation is taking place between the two sides. The captains, Grace and Shrewsbury, leading the parade, are within shot for the longest and neither exchanges a word with the other. Grace himself looks cheerful and moves comparatively easily. He is the only cricketer to play up to the camera. As he approaches, the schoolboy within him rises to the surface and he doffs his cap at the bioscope, grinning conspiratorially. Stoddart and Gunn, who follow, look serious. Gunn, with a modern white sun-hat and wearing no blazer, is a towering figure. Stoddart, with the sleeves of his blazer rolled up at the wrists in the fashion of the day, seems quite small beside him. Dick Lilley, the England wicket-keeper, and Sammy Woods come next. Woods, puffing clouds of smoke from a cigarette which does not leave his lips, whispers a quip to Lilley. It is the only point of contact between the two sides. Bobby Abel and Captain Teddy Wynyard follow, both looking very solemn, each with one hand grasping the lapel of his blazer. Two Yorkshire players, Tunnicliffe and Jackson, are the next pairing. Tunnicliffe is tall, almost gypsy-like with his curling moustache and sideboards. Jackson's thoughts are elsewhere. He cuts the cameraman stone dead and his county colleague too. A brief glimpse of the taciturn Middlesex players, Jack Hearne and Gregor MacGregor, leads to the stony-faced Storer and Dixon, the former as brightly blazered as his amateur counterpart. Bill Lockwood and Archie MacLaren look an irritable pair. Lockwood's expression is sour, MacLaren's aggressively haughty. One is left in no doubt that these two certainly have exchanged no word in the past and have no intention of doing so in the future. Billy Brockwell grins, his pipe adding a homely touch; his partner, the gangling Townsend, towers above him.

Charles brings up the rear, a cigarette dangling from his lips and the broadest of grins on his face. He has ignored instructions and forsaken his professional partner, preferring the company of Wykehamist Jack Mason, leaving three professionals moving uncertainly in his wake, Schofield Haigh, Alec Hearne and the twelfth man, Wilfred Rhodes. One can hazard the guess that the film was shot at lunchtime on the day of W.G.'s fiftieth birthday. Certainly the Demon looks like a man who has been enjoying himself enormously and the special solemnity on the faces of Abel, Shrewsbury and Gunn would have a rational explanation.

After lunch Billy Gunn took command, delighting the crowd with a succession of drives between mid-off and cover point and reaching a fine century. The Players passed 300 before the close of play. The Doctor had clumsily overbowled the Demon and, in the end, Charles had little to show for all his hostility and effort: 1 for 90 off 37 overs! As usual, he had fielded magnificently. One left-handed stop from a full-blooded drive by Brockwell provoked much praise: 'The ball came wide to him and he not only stopped it and picked it up in the same action, but standing deep mid-off 80 yards from the batsman, he returned the ball so smartly that not a single run was got from the hit. Never was there a drive more deserving of 4 runs and never was there a finer piece of fielding seen on any ground. Kortright is a masterpiece in the field.'

It rained early on the Tuesday. With the turf soft on the top and hard underneath, the wicket gave bowlers like Lockwood tremendous help. The ball cut back off the seam all day and often reared unpleasantly. This was bad luck for the Gentlemen, the Players having enjoyed such a perfect wicket. It was a dull day, with rain threatening often.

Grace opened for the Gentlemen with Andrew Stoddart. W.G. was suffering from an injured heel, which rendered him quite lame, and a bruised hand, legacies from Leyton. It was painful to watch him limp along the pitch. When he had only scored a single, he snicked a ball from Lockwood, and Dick Lilley, fumbling with the ball, finally dropped it at the third attempt. There was an enormous crowd again present, 18,000 people, who had come to pay an emotional salute to just one man. Grace had strong views that those who had paid to see him should always be allowed to see him! So it is probable that the fielders were under instructions to avoid the Champion's early dismissal. Alternatively, Lilley took the decision himself. The Warwickshire professional, who rose from obscurity as a Bournville chocolate factory worker to middle-class respectability, was a devoted admirer of W.G. At all events, the Doctor was 'fortunate to be missed' but then played well, though the ball was not easy to time. 'Although often in difficulties, he was soon making many fine hits, mostly in front of the wicket.' He also enjoyed a couple of lucky fours through the slips. Finally, Lilley made sure of a second chance – he had his England place to think of – and W.G. was out for an honourable 43. The Gentlemen, with Jackson and MacLaren to the fore, did remarkably well to top 300 on such a difficult wicket.

There were 45 minutes left for play. Charles was delighted at the prospect. It was a quarter to six and it was getting very dark. Abel and Shrewsbury looked pale in the evening light. There was great excitement in the pavilion. 'Someone asked whether Kortright would be accused of murder or manslaughter, presuming he killed one of the professionals.' Fortunately he did not succeed in killing anyone, but, after Abel had boldly hit him for a single and cut him for 4, he knocked out his off stump. This was no surprise. Abel, with his eye problems, was understandably ill at ease. 'With the shadow of the pavilion behind him,' noted a reporter, 'Kortright bowled so fast in the waning light that it was impossible in the Press box to follow the ball.' Indeed, the brightest item at Lord's was the glint in Charles' eye as he ran in at Shrewsbury. In the end, it was Woods who bowled Shrewsbury out, but the wicket largely belonged to Charles. Storer, playing for his batting and not his wicket-keeping, had his bat knocked out of his grasp three times by Charles, but he bravely withstood the bouncers and was there at the close, with the Players on 42 for 2.

That evening W.G. was entertained to dinner at the Sports Club. Among the guests was his complete team. Sir Richard Webster, Surrey's president, presided, with W.G. in the place of honour on his right. Webster gave a witty speech, even if some of his jokes were predictable: 'I remember a Gloucester schoolboy who, on being asked, "What are the Christian graces?", said, "E.M., W.G. and G.F.," and a young Etonian who described them as "Grace before Dinner, Grace after Dinner and W.G. . . .".' After a toast to him had been liberally drunk, Grace rose to propose the toast of 'The Game'. He quickly admitted his inadequacies as a public speaker. 'Gentlemen. You know that I am a man of few words. When I am pleased, the words might be all right. When I am not, they may be all wrong!' That night the words were all right, and he ended a vigorous speech by picking up a reference made by Webster: 'Sir Richard has referred to my kindness to young players. Well, I remember one colt I was kind to. When we brought him up to Lord's, my first two balls went into the garden by the old armoury and my second two went into the pavilion. We never played that colt again!' It was a good story with which to raise a laugh, but it was hardly in accord with the code of good sportsmanship to which all amateurs were said to adhere.

The next day, unsurprisingly, the Gentlemen were not very effective in the field. Charles was again overbowled. In bowling his 74 overs in the match off his 20-yard run, he covered some eight miles! In perfect weather Gunn and Storer again batted well and, when the Players' innings ended at twenty to four, a tame draw was in prospect as the Gentlemen needed 296 in just three hours. However, the enormous crowd enjoyed one of the most exciting of conclusions. 'If a stage manager, with all the limelight accessories of modern times, had been conducting this game,' wrote one witness, 'he could not have wished for a more dramatic finale.'

Jack Hearne of Middlesex had found a couple of bad patches on the wicket, off which he was spinning the ball viciously, sometimes as much as a foot. The hard-driving amateurs were quite unable to cope with this and, at 77 for 7, W.G. came in. He had held himself back because of his lameness. He was still at the wicket when the ninth wicket fell. The ensuing final 70 minutes have been delightfully recorded by R. L. Hodgson:

'There was still over an hour to play, and but 80 on the board, when C. J. Kortright – loose-limbed, bareheaded – joined the Champion. Any hope left? Of course not! How could there be? No one regarded the fast bowler in the light of an accomplished batsman. He had made 17 not out in the first innings, but it was unthinkable that he would succeed when so many of the great ones had failed!

'We had made such remarks to one another as Kortright walked to the wicket. We continued to make them for some minutes after he had

106

reached the crease. Then we ceased to talk and merely shouted. Clapped and cheered! For the hands of the clock moved forward and the Essex man did not get out. He played well, and he scored freely. W.G. stood like a rock. He might be disabled and lame, but his bat was as broad as ever. Seven bowlers beat and battered against it in vain. He was still – at 50 years of age – the greatest batsman in the world!

'Six-thirty arrived and the last pair remained together. Six-forty-five and the great stand went on. Each moment the excitement grew. Would they hold out? We longed for them to do so. A drawn match has always been part of cricket, and if ever two men deserved to succeed in an effort to save a lost game it was then!

'Almost on the stroke of seven o'clock Kortright made his first mistake. He had batted with admirable judgment for nearly 70 minutes and his score stood at 46. Was it the glamour of the coveted fifty which warped his judgment? Was it some mischievous sprite, whispering the promise of a certain four, that lured him to destruction? I cannot tell: I only know he lashed out recklessly at Lockwood, and the ball – hit in the air – instead of travelling to the boundary, found a haven in the safe hands of Haigh at cover point. The last wicket had put on 78.'

There was triumph in defeat. The crowd, with one accord, rushed onto the pitch, surging around their smiling, limping hero. And W.G., for his part, slipped his arm into Charles' as they returned to the pavilion. The reconciliation was complete. The cheering crowd gathered by the pavilion rails. They were not satisfied until Doctor and Demon appeared together on the balcony, to bow their acknowledgements.

The harmonious end of W.G.'s Jubilee match is justly famous and seems a perfect expression of what was best in the Golden Age. But it cannot obscure all the acrimony and bad sportsmanship which went on at Leyton only days before. These two matches serve to emphasize the many contradictions of the Golden Age and, in particular, the enigmatic nature of its Champion.

It is difficult to categorize W. G. Grace. He was the country's leading amateur, yet he made more money from the game than anyone else in the Golden Age. Cricket was a game to which the Victorians attached great moral value, and nobody laughed when Lord Harris likened the cricket field to God's classroom. Yet in that classroom W.G. often acted like a naughty boy, playing all manner of dirty tricks. He had no public school or Varsity background himself, yet for years he packed the Gloucestershire team with those who boasted one.

In his medical career the contradictions are equally strong. He qualified late, at 31, and retired early, at 50; as such, he was probably the least motivated of all famous doctors. As a perfectionist, used to winning, he possibly became frustrated by his inability to master other people's physical ailments as well as other people's bowling. Then too, as a doctor, he would have witnessed the terrible conditions under which the less affluent lived, conditions which led to illness and early death. As a much-loved public figure, he could have done much to help turn public opinion towards the urgent needs of the poor. Instead he seems to have accepted the situation for what it was.

His popularity, itself a thing of contradictions defying simple explanation, transcended all class barriers. Although he eschewed the opportunity of championing the cause of the poor, he himself was championed by them. Through him they enjoyed, vicariously, triumph, and they readily identified with the essential roughness of his nature. For all his middle-class origin, he was a man of the people, who enjoyed dirtying his hands. Indeed he was said to have had a life-long aversion to soap and water. His sense of humour too was of the earthy variety. As a practical joke, he sometimes put a dead rabbit in a vanquished opponent's cricket bag. To the middle classes he was the ideal expression of their own potential for prosperity, while the upper classes welcomed him for his great achievements.

It is not surprising then that he has remained a 'great Victorian', competing with writers, musicians, politicians and empire-builders to be chronicled in series of 'Great Lives', for he was truly very special in his own time, worshipped as no other cricketer has been, before or since. E. H. D. Sewell, the contemporary and friend of both Demon and Lobster, provides one small example of the special veneration paid to him. It was Sewell's boast, for 40 years, that he had unbuckled the great man's pads after his last appearance for the Gentlemen! That act of homage done, he had performed another, taking a photograph of the bat which had just scored 74 runs – 74 first-class runs at the age of 58! Therein is clearly some measure of his greatness. And therein lies a major reason for his popularity. For it is possible that W.G. was most of all admired because he so successfully challenged life beyond the boundaries of probability.

9
Reflections at Hastings

The Hastings Festival, providing the final first-class matches of the season, typified the glamorous festivity of cricket weeks in the Golden Age. There were older weeks, like Canterbury, and rival weeks, like Scarborough, but Hastings was something very special in the late Victorian cricket world. When, in 1898, Charles and Digby both received – for the first time – invitations to Hastings, they accepted with alacrity, delighted to be spending the first days of September by the sea. They found the town crammed with visitors, with few lodging houses or hotels offering vacancies. Hastings was one of the most popular south-coast resorts, with its three-mile esplanade, its pleasant beaches and gaudy bathing machines, its pier, its hydropathic spa, its royal concert hall and its theatre, the Gaiety, with lilting musical comedies. Most of all, it boasted a week of marvellous cricket, when the very best competitors of the day, invigorated by the ozone, played in an appropriately extravagant holiday spirit.

Record crowds queued up to pay their shilling entrance money, twice the usual county charge, inspired by the final opportunity of watching W.G. in his Jubilee year. In the first match, W.G. was captaining the Rest of England, for whom Charles was playing, against the team which Stoddart had led to Australia the previous winter. This was a needle match. There had been much criticism of the composition of Stoddart's team and, before he sailed, he had promised to prove his team's strength by this fixture. In the second match, Digby was playing for Surrey and Sussex against another Rest of England XI, again captained by W.G.

There was glorious weather all week. It was so hot on the Monday morning that Charles was pleased to learn that W.G. had won the toss and chosen to bat. The Demon could enjoy at his leisure the sea air and the Hastings atmosphere. The little Central Ground was festooned with bunting, its ring surrounded by a medley of brightly covered stands, makeshift pavilions and elegant marquees. The unusually high percentage of ladies present added to the colour of the occasion. In the clear light, the cliff, topped by the ruins of Hastings Castle, dominated the ground more forcefully than usual. The sandy hill was a marvellous vantage place for hundreds of people who stood in bold relief on the skyline. The match, once started, justified the predicted needle atmosphere. With W.G. scoring a careful fifty, others adopted a cautious approach and it was left to the Demon to bring the first touch of festival spirit to the game with a vigorous partnership with 'Stork' Ford. After a lucky start, with a snick for four off Hirst and another snick off Richardson, he delighted everyone with some powerful blows: four to long leg off Hirst; four with the sweetest of off-drives off Richardson; four for the most delicate of late cuts off Hirst; another four off Hirst, this time through the covers, four for a slashing cut off Jack Hearne. It couldn't last, and it didn't. Charles perished, as he played, festively, with a lofty straight drive off Jack Hearne, which allowed Archie MacLaren to make a showy catch in the long field.

As the game proceeded, Charles enjoyed it enormously. W.G. gave him some very long bowls, nearly 60 overs in all, and he banged the ball down on the bone-hard ground with considerable pleasure, taking a number of expensive wickets. As in country house cricket, so too in festivals, Charles could never be relied upon to adhere to the rules of the occasion. As soon as the ball was in his hand, the holiday spirit left him: 'In Mr Kortright's third over Hayward was very badly hurt and, shortly afterwards, clean bowled by the same trundler.' Even in the face of intimidating bowling by Charles and a truly festive century by Gilbert Jessop (in 60 minutes), Andrew Stoddart was finally able to prove his point and the side which he had taken abroad beat the Rest of England.

Charles was immediately at ease in Hastings. He enjoyed the formality of the social occasions in the evenings and he found the friendly fraternity of amateurs, with its strong bachelor element, congenial. He even forgave their ostentation, the exaggerated care which they took in their appearance. Charles had little time for colourful cravats or negligent neckties. When the Gentlemen had posed resplendently for a Jubilee match photograph, he managed to appear without his blazer!

At 27, Charles was very set in his ways. He was now living with his mother and two unmarried sisters at a large house in Fryerning, known as The Tiles. A year before, on the death of his father, he had been bequeathed Furze Hall, but had opted for the comfort and modernity of The Tiles (bequeathed to his sister, Caroline) because, with three devoted ladies to make all the necessary domestic decisions for him, he was left to pursue his cricket, golf and shooting. Fryerning was the centre of his life. His married brothers lived close by, William at St Leonards and Mounteney, when home on army leave, at Furze Hall. Bunny Lucas and his family were at the nearby Rectory. Freddie Fane was two miles away across the fields and often invited Charles and William to shoot on his land, while annual shooting trips to Scotland were a sacrosanct part of the Kortright existence. William and Charles played some cricket and much golf together locally.

For Charles it was a very contented existence and he himself never expressed regrets that his life lacked much purpose beyond that of his sporting pleasures. When asked, years later, why he had devoted himself so assiduously to cricket, at his own expense and for no profit, he frowned in some perplexity before replying brusquely, 'There was mightly little else to do in the summertime.' He never acknowledged any emptiness in his life, but there was little obvious love or affection in it, even in his attitude to his closest relatives. One of his nieces could remember him only for his caustic tongue and frightening appearance. On that occasion he was clearly irritated that his sister's visit should have disturbed his own routine. Worse still, he was unable to be demonstrably appreciative of the devotion of his mother and sisters towards him at The Tiles. Rather, he accepted it as his due, like the new ball at Leyton. Women found him attractive, but he kept his distance. He did not mix easily with men from other walks of life. In this apparent reluctance to involve himself in human relationships, there is a reflection of the way he played his cricket. There was an emptiness about the whirlwind batting, the clouting of a few quick fours before the inevitability of dismissal. It contrasted with the more responsible approach of others, who recognized the need to build an innings. Charles seems not to have been prepared to put the needed time into relationships. His bowling, too, reflected only too well his aggressive response to those around him. To intimidate and hurt could only alienate, yet he persisted. Charles, then, was a proud and somewhat lonely man, but his cricket and life were one. For all his temperamental failings, he was still a genuine amateur gentleman, on the field and off it, and, as such, there was a place for him at Hastings.

There would always be a regular place at Hastings for Digby too, for, in the second match, he played the innings of the 1898 Festival. As Surrey and Sussex were struggling at 24 for 4 against the Rest of England, Digby singlehandedly transformed things with some ferocious hitting, to score 143 out of his side's total of 254. 'He ran tremendous risks,' said *Wisden*. 'Some of his pulls approached the miraculous!' By what he himself described, modestly and inaccurately, as 'blind slogging', Digby attacked some of the very best bowlers of the day. One straight drive off Wilfred Rhodes landed in a hedge. Twice in one over he lifted balls from Charles Townsend over the ropes, near the sightscreen. Cutting fiercely, he upset the impeccable length of Jack Hearne. George Hirst was hit all over the Central Ground, twice by brilliant 'forward cuts'. After Digby had reached a quick fifty, the hard-pressed W.G. suggested to the England spinner, Johnny Briggs, that he might try the chapel end. Digby took 28 off his first three overs, including six fours, mostly taken from the off stump, bouncing up against the canvas at square leg. Briggs turned to Grace, looking very aggrieved. 'That's not much of a stroke, Doctor,' he complained. 'It's all right if you can do it, Johnny,' said the Doctor, and took him off.

Lobs were a delight at festivals and Digby found himself opening the bowling with Tom Richardson. But the partnership of MacLaren and Grace was a difficult one to break. While MacLaren indulged in imperious drives, W.G. played pragmatically: 'Dr Grace played the lobs cautiously, but, an opportunity occurring, he sent one round the long leg for four.' Like the Demon before him, the Lobster bowled long spells at Hastings, with limited, expensive success. With Abel spilling a vital catch in the deep, when George Hirst mistimed a lob, the Rest of England eventually defeated Surrey and Sussex by 4 wickets. It had been a close, exciting game.

To the casual observer at Hastings, Digby, with his flamboyant batting and eccentric bowling, must have seemed a very typical cavalier amateur, every bit as genuine a gentleman cricketer as Charles Kortright. But this was far from being so. Digby seems to have been playing the part expected of him, but it was a role very different from his real character and situation. The more closely one looks, the less true Digby appears.

In the first place, his amateur status was bogus. During his years out of Surrey's favour he had endeavoured to earn money by journalism but with only spasmodic success. His private means by this time were distinctly limited. Digby's good performances in 1897 had made him eligible for the County Committee's patronage. Through the good offices of C. A. Stein, a powerful figure in the City and on the Surrey Committee, Digby was bought an introduction into stockbroking. Surrey's generous, but illegal, sponsorship of amateur talent was well known. Only the previous year the headmaster of Whitgift School had written to The Oval about Frank Crawford, then a schoolboy cricketing prodigy. Crawford's father was unable to pay for an Oxford education. Would Surrey, asked the headmaster, be interested in sponsoring the boy? The Match Committee, impressed by Crawford's batting average, believed that he 'deserved encouragement', but the full Committee jibbed at the idea. Instead, Crawford was diverted from Oxford to London, where he joined Digby as a stock-jobber.

Despite his Cambridge Blue, Digby continued to feel socially insecure years after he had left the university. He was only too aware of his modest background, his parochial schooling and his parents' split marriage. So, the older he became, the stronger he championed the philosophy of the Varsity Blue, as some kind of compensation.

Then there was the question of his marriage, which occurred only one week after the end of the Hastings Festival. It is tempting to believe that it was the presence of his fiancée at the Central Ground which inspired Digby, but there are a number of points about the marriage which remove it from the annals of high romance. There was, for example, a very big age discrepancy. Digby was 27 and his bride, Lina Behrend, 39. In this there is a remarkable similarity with the marriage of C. B. Fry, which took place earlier this year. Fry had married a lady eight years older than himself. Not only was she wealthy, she possessed a wealthy patron. Fry accordingly was able to give up teaching at Charterhouse and to concentrate on his cricket. It is tempting to view Digby's marriage as a similarly shrewd move towards financial security. Lina Behrend's father had come from Danzig as a young man and prospered as a merchant. He became very wealthy and lived for many years in an imposing house overlooking Clapham Common. The marriage was no sudden romance. Lina was the sister of the Wanderers' wicket-keeper, Arthur Behrend. Bride and groom would have known each other for many years. Above all, it was a suspiciously timely union, coming, as it did, just after Digby had established himself in the Surrey side. There is one further unusual aspect to the marriage. Digby not only gained a bride but also a father figure, in the shape of Arthur Behrend, Lina's elder brother.

J. Arthur H. J. T. Behrend was much more than just a keen club cricketer. In the late 1880s and early 1890s he had become nationally known as a composer of light music. He had discovered in the setting of ballads a very profitable occupation. His music was technically beyond reproach, within the limited confines of Victorian harmony. It hints of Sullivan and Mendelssohn, but modern ears would find it sentimental and insipid! Behrend made his name with a setting of Hood's 'The Song of the Shirt' and a very maudlin piece called 'Auntie', which was taken up by Madame Patey and sung with tremendous success at the popular London Ballad Concerts. Encouraged by this, Behrend put to music Mary Mark Lemon's tear-jerker, 'Daddy', in which a little girl talks about her dead mother to her much-harrassed, working-class father. Hundreds of thousands of copies of 'Daddy' were published. It was one of the biggest ballad successes of the 1890s. From this song alone Behrend made the large sum of £4000.

A. H. Behrend was a devoted cricketer. He had been in the Haileybury XI as a boy and he was a keen member of the Wanderers as a man. No Wanderers' gathering was ever complete without his own rendition of 'Daddy', for he had been trained as a singer and possessed a high, strong tenor voice. He continued to play for the Wanderers in the 1900s when in his fifties. Behrend and Digby were the firmest of friends before and after the marriage. In the absence of his father, it was to Arthur Behrend, 18 years his senior, that Digby often turned. It was he who encouraged him in his literary aspirations and who put him up for membership of the Savage Club.

Of Lina herself one knows tantalizingly little. Lina Rosa Eleonora Jephson has left few traces behind her. One can be sure, however, that the marriage was, at the very least, one of true minds rather than mere convenience. Digby and Lina were united by their deep love of music and poetry. Music was in Lina's blood. Her mother was the daughter of the composer Balfe, today remembered chiefly as the creator of *The Bohemian Girl* and of the archetypal ballad, 'Come Into The Garden, Maud'. The Behrend children used to stay with their famous grandfather at his home, Rowney Abbey, Hertfordshire, Arthur precociously playing violin duets with him. Lina and Arthur were allowed to turn over the music while their mother and grandfather played violin sonatas.

Lina was a very competent lyricist as well as amateur musician. She worked within the conventions of the day, a strong metre prevailing and a love of dialect. Her heroes are often working class, with hearts of gold. Sometimes, indeed, they exhibit the 'clean' philosophy of the Varsity Blue. 'Submarine Jack', for example, would have felt quite at home at Fenner's:

> Oh! Jack, he's a middling decent chap,
> He's a wholesome brew from the good old tap.
> Ye may sample him morning or noon or night,
> If you're ripped and down, he will set you right:
> For Jack, he's learned it's a useful thing
> To take's life rough as you takes your fling,
> With a smiling face and it pans out best
> Just to do your level and to chance the rest.

Digby and Lina were married in St Paul's Church, Cambridge, very close to Union Road, where his mother lived and even closer to Fenner's. It is odd that they were married in Cambridge, for Lina's home was with her brothers in Clapham. Surrey were quick, however, to mark the marriage of their new vice-captain and a grant of £50 (half a working man's annual wage) was made for a wedding present.

After the wedding Digby and Lina set up home with Arthur Behrend in north Clapham. Number 41 Larkhall Rise was conveniently only a mile from The Oval. It was a tall, four-storeyed house, standing in a road of similar, newly built houses, big-roomed, capable of accommodating a useful number of servants. Today many of the houses are split into flats, but the Jephson residence still stands and the road retains something of its original character. This was to be the most affluent period of Digby's life. Surrounded by friends, admired as a sporting celebrity, courted by Surrey and loved by his wife, Digby had money to spend and spent it with a *fin de siècle* flourish. For Digby and Lina these were days of laughter, music and good living. Like Submarine Jack, they did their level, and chanced the rest.

Yet, for all the apparent happiness of the marriage Digby seems to have been obsessed by the fact that they could have no children. Time and again he invented imaginary children of his own in his writings. In 'The Way To Watch Cricket' (penned for *The Cricketer*) he began with an apparently real situation: ' "Hurry up, daddy – we're late", and I felt the small hand take a firmer grip, as that wee, bright atom of humanity that I call my son dragged me down the road. "All right, sonnie, we're in time," as the pressure on my arm grows stronger; I look into the little face, and I see there that golden eagerness of youth – that world's wealth of anticipation that has no resting place on this earth but in the eyes of a child . . .' The theme of his children is one on which Digby plays innumerable variations. In 'Beach Cricket', written for the *Daily Mail*, he is as misleading as ever: 'I am, like a good many people, a parent. So as it is my duty at this season to provide a holiday for my little bunch of humanity, I invariably suggest the seaside . . .'

It is no surprise for the reader, so grossly misled about Digby's 'sons', to come across a poem which erroneously suggests that he played for England. Although this can be put down to poetic licence, Digby's determination to mislead, at least on the subject of his marriage, his social position and his financial status, may well have become such a motivating factor in his life that he eventually was able to imagine himself in *any* role. He had played the part of the slightly eccentric gentleman cricketer so long that a few embellishments could be easily acquired.

All this, however, lay ahead. As Digby travelled in a first-class carriage on the train bearing him away from Hastings in September 1898 towards Cambridge, marriage and a new phase in his life, his thoughts were different from those of Charles three days earlier. Charles, too, had travelled first-class, the amateur's privilege. For him it was his right and he had been content as he looked forward to a weekend's good pheasant-shooting and looked back on a first-rate game, played hard in the right festive spirit, at the end of which winner and loser had enjoyed generous hospitality. Digby, too, had enjoyed himself and he joined in the high-spirited banter of the Varsity Blues on the train, the schoolboy humour of Grace and Murdoch, the verbal fencing of Archie MacLaren. But part of him would have been more at home in the down-to-earth company of the third-class compartment, where Tom Richardson and Bill Lockwood, 'two big powerful men with big powerful pipes, smoked powerful tobacco'. For him the future seemed less certain, less stable, than it did for Charles Kortright.

Meanwhile, at Hastings, as the crowds drifted away from the resort, it was agreed that it had been the best Festival ever, a tremendous financial and social success. As the bathing machines were dragged up the beaches for the long winter, everyone was of one mind that W.G.'s Jubilee year could not have ended better, with the Doctor's side winning the very last match.

Friday afternoon at the Oval.

10
Strains and stresses

In 1899, the very next year, the Demon played no cricket at all. His absence from the Essex XI was closely connected with the atmosphere of discontent within the game, for, ironically, at the very peak of the Golden Age, problems were rampant and the health of first-class cricket was a topic of constant debate.

Officially, however, Charles missed the whole year through injury and no other cause. He had attended the usual pre-season nets at Leyton and had been picked for the country's opening match against the Australians. Then the injury happened. One rumour suggested that he had a back strain, and it was easy to imagine the Demon straining his back at the nets as he strove for the extra length necessary for his speciality, the yorker. On an earlier occasion Tom Richardson, when asked by Ranji why he did not bowl more yorkers, had replied: 'An extra yard is too much effort. I want to last the season out, sir.' A second story, however, was also circulating, suggesting that Charles was nursing a strained side. Neither rumour was correct. In reality, Charles had strained a tendon to his leg at home at Fryerning. It is difficult to assess the extent of the injury. The national Press was evasive about it all year and the local Press was little more forthcoming,

118

although one report in May suggested that Charles was under the care of a Mr Allison. As there were no doctors or surgeons of that name practising in London or Essex in 1899, Charles would seem to have been merely in the hands of a local masseur. In strong contrast, Surrey's Bill Lockwood, when suffering from a leg injury, was given regular treatment by a Harley Street specialist. It is very strange, therefore, that Essex did not take similar steps, if Charles' injury was at all serious, to safeguard the fitness of their most vital bowler.

As the season progressed, hopes were sometimes expressed for his swift return: 'Mr Kortright is sorely needed. When he makes his reappearance on the field, he will receive such a royal greeting that it will do sore eyes good to see it.' But sore eyes remained sore, for Charles did not reappear. Then, in August, the county club published a statement. Mr Kortright, it said, had *not* had a row with the Committee and there was no truth in the rumour that he was qualifying for Kent! Such, however, was the lack of information forthcoming about his injury, its nature and treatment, that it seems very likely that Charles had indeed had a disagreement with the Essex Committee. Over what, one wonders, might this have been about? There are two possibilities.

A disagreement about the captaincy is probable. There had been rumours that the 40-year-old Owen was retiring, which, at the annual general meeting of 1899, Charles Green was at elaborate pains to suppress: 'I tremble to think what will happen to our county when Mr Owen drops out of it! But he has assured me that he will continue in it until it becomes necessary to wheel him to the wicket! If you had seen Mr Owen at practice recently, you would be of the opinion that he would be good for another 20 years!' Owen replied: 'I am afraid that I shall not have many more opportunities of addressing you in this capacity! Already there are silver threads among the gold! But, as long as my services are of use to the club, I will be glad to serve you!' It is possible that Green, in loyalty to Owen, was suppressing a growing desire in some Essex circles for a change of leadership. On considerations of both prowess and seniority, Charles had the greatest claim to assume the captaincy. Clearly change *was* under discussion, for later that year it was mooted that Freddie Fane might be taking over from Owen, though nothing came of this and Owen was to continue for another three years. It may be, therefore, that Charles, irritated beyond endurance by Owen's passive handling of the team and seeing it as an impediment to Championship honours, had made an unsuccessful bid for the captaincy.

An even likelier possibility is that he and Green had a disagreement over the legality of his bowling action. The unfair bowling issue was the bane of the Golden Age. For the past 30 years, ever since the legalization of overarm, the problem had periodically surfaced. There had been some obvious throwers in the 1880s. The stumbling block to their suppression had been the passivity of the umpires. As ex-professionals themselves, the umpires feared to no-ball the amateurs and were unwilling to jeopardize the careers of fellow professionals. But in the 1890s an Australian umpire, Jim Phillips, who had played for Middlesex, took decisive action, championed with fervour by Sydney Pardon, the editor of *Wisden*, who waged a long, zealous campaign against the evils of throwing. In 1897 and 1898 Jim Phillips no-balled Ernest Jones, the fastest Australian bowler, and Charles Fry, whose medium-fast deliveries had long been in hot dispute. Some other umpires began to consider following Phillips' lead. In 1898 a young Warwickshire bowler was also called for throwing. The problem was still far from resolved – 'Fry could fairly urge', wrote Pardon, 'that bowlers far more formidable than he had been permitted to bowl without protest' – but at least the campaign was now well under way. At the beginning of 1899, the time of Charles' mystery injury, there was much speculation as to which bowlers would next incur the umpires' displeasure. Among names freely bandied around were the four most formidable bowlers in England, Arthur Mold of Lancashire, Bill Lockwood, Tom Richardson and Charles Kortright.

It is ironic that Mold and Charles should have been bracketed together, for Charles considered that Mold's action was as illegal as his own was impeccable. A little earlier, at Old Trafford, he had made his own protest. Enraged, it is said, by some flagrant throwing by the Lancastrian, he made no effort to bowl one ball fairly, but threw it, with all his might, at the unsuspecting batsman. The umpire, concentrating on his foot, failed to notice, and wondered why the crowd suddenly erupted in fury. E. H. D. Sewell told the story later in somewhat more general terms. During snooker the previous evening, a discussion had been raging as to whether the umpire at the bowler's end could spot a throw. There were mixed views among the Essex players. 'Bet you five bob I fling one tomorrow and am not called,' said Charles. The bet was taken up and, with the second ball of his

second over, Charles proved his point. The law was shortly afterwards altered, to allow the square leg umpire to call! Arthur Mold was
a quite notorious thrower and had been so for ten years. Off the
shortest of runs he was one of the fastest of bowlers. Digby's
description of his bowling, while making no accusations, gives a
strong hint of illegality: 'No other bowler ever attained a similar pace
with such a minimum of exertion – two or three long, loose strides,
two at a trot, and an arm swinging like a flail, a good length, great
pace, and on any wicket a considerable flick back from the off . . .'

While people talked openly about Mold, they muttered quietly
about Charles and had done so for a long time. As soon as he had
appeared on the county scene complaints had been made about his
action. Its description, as 'full-chested', sows seeds of doubt, for the
early turning of the trunk is the mark of the thrower. Charles himself
described his action as 'deceptive' and said: 'Players attribute my
success to the delivery, which they describe as "baulking".' Baulking
could suggest that Charles' delivery arm paused for a moment in its
circular motion, in which case the elbow might not have kept
perfectly straight. For the next three years, as the debate raged,
Charles' name featured regularly. Norman Gale, the writer of popular
cricket verses, thought the theme of Charles' doubtful action a fair
topic for satire. 'Fast he is, but is he fair?' he queried, in a parody of
'Who is Sylvia?'

While Charles absented himself from first-class cricket, the controversy grew and grew. It culminated a year later in a meeting of
county captains, who compiled a list of the worst offenders whom
they agreed not to bowl, and a second list of those who were to be
warned. Although the MCC eventually revoked this unilateral action
and substituted a milder plan, urging moral pressure to be brought to
bear by the counties, the battle against throwing had been won. The
throwers were steadily eliminated.

Charles, somewhat luckily, was not on either list. Only the most
blatant amateurs were. One of these was his Essex partner, F. G. Bull.
Bull's fate was a terrible example of what could happen to the victims
of the controversy. After the storm broke, his employment as
assistant secretary of Essex was abruptly terminated. He attempted to
alter his bowling style, but in 1900 he took only 5 wickets at 50 runs
each. He was finished. For four years he had enjoyed great success,
often bowling in deadly partnership with the Demon. He had been

one of *Wisden*'s Five Cricketers of the Year. He had toured America with P. F. Warner. He had played with distinction for the Gentlemen v. Players. But now, at the age of only 24, he quietly slipped away from the first-class game. The rest of his life ran to a tragic conclusion.

At first a mysterious Surrey patron seems to have offered him a lifeline. There was talk of him joining the London Stock Exchange. Surrey were in need of a top-class spinner, but it was only the briefest of flirtations. The clamour against illegal bowling may have frightened Surrey off, for, with McGahey and Sewell performing his duties as assistant secretary in the Leyton pavilion, Bull packed his bags and moved north, to sell insurance in Blackburn.

Later, Bull became a professional, both in Scotland and the Lancashire league. At the end of a successful season with Rishton, in 1910, Bull went to Blackpool, out of work and in need of winter wages. After a few days, failing to find the answer to his problems, he waded into the sea not far from St Anne's pier. Twenty-four hours later he was found dead, face down in a pool. He had filled the pockets of his trousers and his Norfolk jacket with stones. He had tied a handkerchief around his neck, attached to another, in which was wrapped a seven-pound stone. On the body were found only a pen-knife, a latch key and an empty leather purse. He was 34.

There can be little doubt that Bull *did* throw. His action was very odd. It reminded one spectator of 'a picture in which a gallant soldier has just received a bullet in the breast and is staggering backwards with upthrown arms'. An action photograph endorses this description. It is taken seconds before delivery. Bull is leaning right back in the posture of a javelin thrower. The right arm has nearly reached horizontal and there is a discernible bend in the elbow. His chest has already opened up, a little early, towards the batsman.

The throwing controversy ended the careers of several established professionals, most notably Arthur Mold and Edwin Tyler. Mold had attempted to carry on, for a while being shielded by Lancashire from umpire Phillips. Finally the two met. Phillips no-balled Mold 16 times and finished his career there and then. Digby was playing for Surrey at Taunton on the day that Tyler was no-balled. Tyler had played a leading part in Somerset's rise to prominence over the last ten years. Like Mold, he had played for England. He bowled left-arm, extremely slowly, and that was why he had been allowed to bowl unchallenged for so long. He was unlikely to hurt anyone. There was much indignation when Jim Phillips called him. His fellow umpire, Walter Wright (who had coached Charles at Tonbridge) refused to add extra balls to the over, as a protest. Sam Woods, the Somerset captain, was outraged, and Digby wrote soon afterwards in most sympathetic terms: 'I was sorry that Tyler should have been no-balled at the close of his career, for the day on which he was penalized there seemed to be no difference whatever from the action he always had, and which was universally passed for years.' Digby's position as a pacifist in the throwing controversy fits oddly with his philosophy of 'clean' cricket. His views were so mild that he seemed not to believe in the no-balling of throwers at all: 'No one could mistake the driving of C. B. Fry for the driving of F. S. Jackson, or the cutting of John Tyldesley for that of A. O. Jones. It is hard to explain where the difference lies as it is to define a throw; in other words, it is almost impossible.'

With mild views or strong, there was no escaping the controversy. Both Demon and Lobster were embroiled in it. Digby found himself uncomfortably in the centre of the debate on the captains' unilateral action in 1900, when he took over the captaincy of Surrey. Charles, as one of the biggest suspects, was the object of much unpleasant gossip and he reacted with predictable vigour. That he was genuinely injured at the beginning of 1899 is unquestionable. He was not a man to be dishonest. But, with the throwing controversy becoming more and more unpleasant, he may temporarily have lost his appetite for the game. He played for pleasure. He was an amateur in the purest sense. He saw himself as the fairest of bowlers, as a gentleman of honour. If his simple pleasure was going to be spoilt by accusations of unfair play, if his honour was to be impugned, why then should he continue to turn out? The strained leg, whether a light or serious injury, may have been the deciding factor in what had been a growing disenchant-ment with the Essex hierarchy and with the atmosphere within the game.

The atmosphere of the Golden Age certainly left something to be desired. Opinions clashed, not just about the illegal bowling question, but about many other aspects of the game. Also, underneath there was a deep malaise, as the conflicting relationship between amateur and professional remained largely unresolved. Double standards flour-ished. There were faults on both sides. Deceit was met with mistrust; blithe unconcern with a deep-rooted sense of injustice.

The tone was set by the County Committees, which tended to be unyieldingly autocratic. The Surrey Committee was ruled by Sir Richard Webster, for many years Attorney General in the Salisbury government and later, as Lord Alverstone, Lord Chief Justice. He was a boisterous man, very genial when playing snooker or singing lusty ballads, and very opinionated on the subject of cricket. Although he himself was very keen on the game and possessed a cricket ground of his own at his home at Cranleigh, he himself had never progressed beyond being a good long field for Charterhouse. However, he saw his appointment as president of Surrey in 1895 with missionary zeal as the opportunity to lead a campaign for the purity of Surrey cricket. This meant, to his mind, playing as many amateurs as possible. 'Too many professionals are played continuously by our leading counties,' he stated contentiously. Over the next few years of his presidency he pursued his ideal, 'the spirit of unselfishness' in cricket. There happened to be not enough Surrey amateurs of independent means to help him in his mission. So he left the necessary, sordid financial arrangements to members of his Committee.

The reactionary nature of the Surrey Committee under Webster can be seen in its handling of a dispute with Middlesex over the conduct of Sir Timothy O'Brien. After batting for Middlesex at The Oval one year, Sir Timothy had lost his temper – he frequently did – and had sworn at an Oval clerk. The clerk complained about this to the Surrey Committee, which debated O'Brien's fall from grace late and long. The result was a letter, sent to Lord's. Unless O'Brien was dropped from the Middlesex team, it said, Surrey would cancel the return match with Middlesex. The latter obligingly omitted O'Brien from this fixture, but the Surrey Committee was not yet satisfied. Middlesex were instructed to drop O'Brien in both the Surrey matches next season as well. Surprisingly, they did. Two years after the original incident, Gregor MacGregor, as captain of Middlesex, sent a precautionary cable to The Oval: 'Presume if we want O'Brien to play you have no objection.' Swiftly came the Surrey reply: 'Regret we have strong objections!' MacGregor responded very reasonably: 'Surely after this long time matter should be forgotten. Kindly wire if your Committee refuses to fulfil engagement if he plays or merely strongly prefers that he doesn't.' Webster remained unrepentant: 'Committee very much regret that they must adhere to their letter of 1 July 1897, stating that they would be compelled to decline to play if

Sir Timothy O'Brien plays.' The matter was only finally resolved when O'Brien retired from the game.

The uneasy relationship between amateur and professional is highlighted by a dispute between Ranjitsinhji and the old Lancashire and England professional, Dick Barlow, umpiring at The Oval. Ranji, as captain of Sussex, was getting very irritated as runs came fast from the bats of Abel, Crawford and Jephson. When Ranji thought a brilliant piece of fielding had saved a boundary, but Barlow signalled 4, he swore forcefully at the umpire, trying to get him to change his mind. But Barlow, a man of much character, refused to alter his decision. The matter did not rest there. Barlow complained to the MCC about Ranji's bad language. Ranji lodged a counter-complaint that Barlow had called him a liar. The MCC, supporting the amateur, sent a letter to Barlow telling him to apologize to the Prince. Barlow refused, declaring that it was Ranji who should apologize. The Press began to show interest. One interviewer asked the embarrassed Indian: 'Do you deny the allegation that you bully umpires?' 'Emphatically,' snapped Ranji. 'If the fieldsman saved a boundary magnificently, that is no reason why a 4 should be given to the opposite side, because the umpire presumed it could not be stopped.' Ranji found it hard to compose the quarrel: 'The persistence with which Barlow tries in the Press to prejudice the public against myself, and attributes to me, either mistakenly or wilfully, the use of violent language towards him, almost makes it impossible for me to adopt a generous attitude.' Barlow was a literate man and may well have derived grim amusement from noting what Ranji had advocated in his *Jubilee Book of Cricket*: 'Obey the decision of an umpire at all times, without any outward sign of what you feel and show a sportsmanlike spirit by putting up in the most cheerful manner with occasional blunders on the umpire's part . . . I'm afraid that umpires meet with unkind and even abusive language. Never abuse an umpire!'

One obvious source of irritation to the professional was that the amateur enjoyed a better-situated changing-room and the sole use of the central gate to the field of play. Some counties were aware of this. Yorkshire were, as so often, impressively iconoclastic. For some years Lord Hawke and Stanley Jackson had invited professionals to change with amateurs at Bramall Lane. Only when Gloucestershire (and the unbending W.G.) visited, did the old system obtain. There was no sign of change at The Oval and Leyton. Accommodation for the professionals at Leyton was in small, cramped huts to the side of the main pavilion. Members looked askance in 1899 when the Yorkshire amateurs invited their paid colleagues to share their room within the pavilion. They were even more outraged that year when the ten professionals in the Warwickshire side joined the single amateur, Tom Forrester. Much ill-feeling arose when C. E. Green insisted that they should not use the central gate onto the playing area but take the circuitous route through to the usual side gate for professionals.

There was also professional dissatisfaction at the way amateurs sometimes poached on what might seem professional preserves. The endorsement of cricket products was one example of this. Although some professionals did make money out of putting their names to cricketing goods (notably those, like Gunn and Abel, who ran their own sports businesses), many amateurs did so too and received reward. Stuart Surridge, for example, in advertising the Patent Rapid Driver bat in 1897, listed its successful users. Abel and Hayward were the only two professionals. Many amateurs, however, endorsed the Surridge product: Grace, MacLaren, Jessop, Ranjitsinhji, Owen, Lucas, Perrin and the Demon himself. By 1901, several other amateurs, including Digby, had become advocates of the PRD bat. The Quaife brothers (who operated a sports shop in Birmingham with wicket-keeper Dick Lilley) championed their own product, 'The Patent Xylonite Spring Handle Bat', but those who endorsed it were all amateurs. W.G. declared: 'The bat is just what I like, the patent handle fits me exactly, and 'Tip' Foster said he used it for his record Test score of 287. Inevitably it was W.G. who made most money out of endorsements. There was scarcely a bat which W.G. did not advocate. His fad of using a different bat for each new innings may have developed from his popularity with the advertising world. He even endorsed many non-cricketing articles. He was a lifelong non-smoker – 'You can get rid of drink, but not of smoke,' he once said – yet he happily advertised Players tobacco. There he stood, bat in one hand, pipe in the other, beside a gigantic packet of tobacco. The legend read: 'The two Champion Players'.

It was disagreeable enough for the professionals, when amateurs were rewarded for endorsements, but the direct and indirect payment of amateurs by their counties was far less agreeable. Patronage, such as that enjoyed by Digby and Frank Crawford, was widespread. Several apparently 'pure' amateurs were only on the county circuit thanks to liberal 'expenses'. Hugh Owen, for example, was not a rich man. When he died, at 53, he left his widow very little. He would have been one of the obvious beneficiaries from the suspiciously high expenses in the Essex accounts of 1891, which an over-zealous member queried. Were these expenses, he asked, a reflection of large sums paid to leading amateurs? Charles Green's reply was abrupt and in the negative. Such was his influence that there the matter rested. For the future, however, the subsidy to leading amateurs like Owen was probably paid in a more discreet way. Before 'shamateurism' became a big topic of debate at the turn of the century, Surrey had been quite candid about some of their illegal payments. John Shuter, for example, was awarded £100 (more than the average working man's annual wage) 'for good cricket during the season' and the Committee donated £200 to his testimonial (in itself a questionable thing), whereas £50 was their usual contribution to a professional's benefit. Walter Read's financial situation at The Oval infuriated professionals. For skeletal duties as Assistant Secretary, he was paid a handsome summer and winter wage. He was, according to wicket-keeper Harry Wood, the best-paid professional in his county. Read was able to live in suburban ease and develop a business career in the City. He was even given a season ticket for the railway! Grace, of course, did things on a far greater scale than anyone. He died a very rich man. His testimonials in 1895 alone raised over £9000. He expected to be paid handsomely, wherever he went. His final tour of Australia cost the organizers £3000 and, in addition, he received his expenses and the fee for his locum. The professionals looked on quietly at all this, noting that there *was* big money in the game, if the right way could be found to extract it.

So in the 1890s the professionals began to fight hard for their share of the increasing profits of the boom years. There was a growing awareness among them that pressure on, or confrontation with, County Committees could produce a higher standard of living. One source of great discontent had been the lack of winter wages, something which Committees had long resisted, despite the hardships which many incautious professionals suffered during the eight months when there was no cricket. In 1896 Lord Hawke persuaded his Committee to establish a regular system whereby the leading Yorkshire professionals received £2 a week during the winter. Many counties reacted bitterly to this, claiming that they could not afford to pay a winter wage. *Wisden* abjectly sided with the dissidents, condemning Yorkshire's 'liberality' as likely to breed dissatisfaction elsewhere.

Surrey, however, quickly followed the Yorkshire lead, if a little less generously. Some leading players negotiated for one big winter payment. Thus Tom Richardson received £50 for the winter of 1898/99. Usually, however, there was a weekly winter payment, calculated carefully according to the player's usefulness. By 1902 Bobby Abel and Bill Lockwood were Surrey's top winter wage earners, with 30 shillings a week; some, like Brockwell, Holland and Stedman, received 25 shillings, others, including the young Herbert Strudwick, just £1. Tom Richardson, still on the ground staff but in decline, now received nothing.

Linked with the problem of winter wages was that of talent money. Some counties rewarded their professionals with an end of season lump sum. Again the amount varied, according to the player's current rating. In 1888, for example, George Lohmann had been paid an honorarium of £50, while six other professionals shared the sum of £100. The next year, the Surrey Committee, anxious perhaps to cut costs, offered only a sum of £100 to be shared between nine players, including Lohmann. The latter was quick to respond. His letter to the Surrey Secretary, Charles Alcock, was plain and business-like: 'Your cheque to hand, for which I thank you. I fail to see why my services should be less worthy of recognition in 1889 than those rendered the previous years. Kindly place this before the Committee.' The latter duly backed down and England's leading all-rounder received his £50, as before! Such a bargaining system of talent money could only cause envy and dissatisfaction.

The Essex professionals were much less well off than those of Surrey. Although Charles Green paid them out of his own pocket a sovereign for every fifty and ten shillings for every 5 wickets, they had no winter wages and no end of season talent money. Under such a system many Essex professionals left the club with no money saved and with no training for another job. At 33, Harry Pickett might say cheerily: 'The county itself has never paid talent money, but for all that is the best little club in the world to play for. . . .' At 45, impecunious, he walked into the sea off the coast of Aberavon and drowned himself.

If the professionals of the Golden Age needed any encouragement to press their Committees for better terms of employment, they only had to look at what had happened to the generation before them.

Humphrey, Pooley, Caffyn and Jupp, all leading Surrey professionals, reached such a state of financial distress as to appeal to The Oval
for aid. Thus, in 1890, £5 was granted to Richard Humphrey, the
opening bat of the 1870s. He made frequent subsequent applications
for aid, most of which were quickly met. And in 1900 Surrey made
a small payment to his wife on hearing that 'her husband had left
her for some days and had not been heard of and consequently she
was in great distress'. He reappeared, to receive some more aid,
before his body was suddenly found floating in the Thames. Edward
Pooley, Surrey's wicket-keeper for 20 years, was less favoured.
At one time he was receiving a donation of ten shillings a week,
contingent on keeping sober. When he failed to meet this stipulation,
he lost his money. However, supported by the word of a clergyman
and doctor, Pooley again became the recipient of Surrey help. Then he
again turned to alcohol. Pooley, an outstanding player who had
toured Australia with Lillywhite, died in the Lambeth workhouse.
William Caffyn, *the* leading batsman of his day, received a sum of £36
when he fell on hard times, and when Harry Jupp, a renowned
opening bat, died in financial difficulties, the club not only paid his
funeral expenses but allocated £100 to his sisters and sons to start a
business. There was clearly a need for the professionals of the Golden
Age to heed the warnings of the past.

Some did. Men like Dick Lilley set new standards of common
sense, gaining a new respect from their amateur brethren, which
helped close the big divide. Lilley, always impeccably dressed on and
off the field, enjoyed shooting parties with W.G. and went fishing
with Ranji. A letter which Ranji wrote to Lilley, after a Gentlemen v.
Players match in 1904, shows the beginning of a new relationship
between the cricketing classes: 'My admiration for you as a man
increases as I see more and more of you every year. May you live long
to adorn the profession which men like yourself raise yearly in the
public estimation.' Ranji added: 'It would afford me great pleasure to
spend an evening in town with you, if you happen to be here. We can
dine in company with some mutual comrades like Mr MacLaren and
do a theatre . . .'

Other professionals followed the old traditions of their calling.
Drink was constantly a problem. Indeed it was a national one, for this
was the age of temperance societies and temperance legislation.
Surrey's two fast bowlers are typical. Tom Richardson, it was said,

would already be downing his second pint when the rest of the team were undoing their bootlaces. By touring in the winter, however, he kept tolerably fit. One winter of inactivity wrought a terrible physical change in him. There was consternation at The Oval when he first reported back in April 1899. He was two stone overweight, his great muscles turned to fat. Swiftly he was summoned before the Match Committee. There he stood, awesomely flabby, his genial face half sunk in an excess of flesh. 'Why, Tom, what on earth has happened to you?' asked the Committee in dismay. 'Well, gentlemen,' replied Richardson candidly, 'I suppose it's because I like my creature comforts.' Bill Lockwood's loss of form in 1897 was equally dramatic. Severe family problems had driven him to drink. He was quite unable to bowl. The Committee recommended that his contract be terminated. Lockwood, only 29, was suitably aghast. He signed the pledge: 'I, William Henry Lockwood, do hereby solemnly promise to abstain from all intoxicating drinks.' Surrey regarded his pledge with suspicion. Lockwood was sent in the spring to Wiltshire, ostensibly as coach to the Awdry family, Wykehamist friends of Shuter, but in reality to be watched for signs of drink. Charles Awdry wrote a full report for Surrey: 'The trial given to Lockwood was, I think, a complete success; as a crack he was excellent and he behaved himself very well. I neither saw (nor have had any hint of) the least tendency on his part to lapse. I think you will find he is to be trusted and restored to self-respect and first-class cricket.'

Digby, watching the Lockwood drama from close hand, was sympathetic. He acknowledged that drink was often a central feature of a professional's life and he did not condemn. It would have been hypocritical of him, if he had. 'I can see no reason why cricketers should either be supposed to journey through life without this certain form of viscus, or without its playing a great part in their failures or successes. Every man is surely entitled to possess himself of a "liver", if its acquisition give him any pleasure. Cricketers certainly do possess "livers", but, as a rule, being physically thoroughly fit, are not troubled to anything like the same extent as men who are content to jog along without any serious form of exercise.' Digby himself had never lost the taste for rich food and drink, acquired at Cambridge: 'How many of us are there, I wonder, who have never at any period of our lives pondered thoughtfully over those dancing black specks that assail our vision after a dose of over-ripe lobster or similar cause? Very few, indeed, and consequently many a batsman's shaky start, many a bowler's faulty length, and dozens of chances missed by reliable fields . . .'

Just as Dick Lilley was reaching out from one direction, so too Digby from the other. The amateur-professional malaise would find a cure, in time. Attitudes would slowly change. In the meantime, there were other immediate problems of a more tangible nature. There had been a growing concern that too many runs were being scored, too many matches drawn. 'What's wrong with cricket?' became the question of 1900.

Artificial wickets were blamed. The Oval was cited, by way of example. For 12 years Sam Apted had devoted himself there to improving the square. His unique mixture of marl and loam had worked wonders, but not everyone approved. 'The Oval isn't an ordinary wicket,' went the grumble; 'it's a shirt-fronted arrangement and Mr Samuel Apted is its laundress.' Eventually, in 1901, there was so much concern that Apted was summoned before the Committee. With some cunning he described his preparation as a mixture of yellow clay and cow manure. 'What, gentlemen, could be more natural than that?' It was a good enough explanation for the Surrey Committee.

During the Demon's absence in 1899, the desire for 'sporting' wickets at Leyton ceased and the groundsman, Ted Freeman, came under much pressure from the Essex batsmen to improve his square. He sought advice from Apted and was advised to apply a liquid mixture three days before the next match. Freeman duly prepared his wicket and proudly promised Essex a perfect pitch for their match with Surrey. But Brockwell and Lockwood bowled Essex out for 37. Freeman complained bitterly to Apted and then learnt his error. The mixture should have been applied only *once*, not regularly. It was not long, however, before Freeman had turned Leyton into another 'shirt-front'.

The debate about drawn matches went on. One extremist lobby favoured a ban on artificial pitches, even a return to the days of the scythe! Few took this seriously. 'What would be the feeling', wrote the Revd Edward Lyttelton in 1900, 'of a man with a wife and family having to face Mr Kortright on a scythe-mown pitch?' Other lobbies called for a narrower bat, or a wider wicket, or a higher wicket, or even a fourth stump. Alteration of the lbw rule was widely championed, to prevent batsmen padding away off-breaks and leg-breaks.

Both Demon and Lobster were opposed to any radical changes in the laws. Charles favoured more punctual starts, the playing of longer hours and the abolition of the tea interval. Digby did not agree. He believed there was little wrong that improved fielding wouldn't cure:

'It is a curious thing to note how one month of bad weather and difficult wickets deletes from the columns of all the papers that deal with cricket every suggestion of heightening or widening the stumps, narrowing the bat, or raking the wicket instead of rolling it, or of starting at ten in the morning and playing till eight at night, with half an hour's interval for lunch. These suggested improvements are for the moment dead, but a fortnight of hard wickets will certainly produce a larger and probably more unhealthy crop. The game as it stands today is probably the finest game in the world. Why must we tinker with it? There are very few matches drawn that are played on anything but perfect wickets, except, of course, where rain stops play. Surely we don't wish to see sides make less than 36, as the Australians did at Birmingham, or less than 13, as Notts made against Yorkshire last year at Trent Bridge? The only remedy necessary is *to improve our fielding*. Catches are bound to be dropped as the sparks fly upward, but if half were held that today we with consummate ease put to the floor, the drawn match would become as the dodo – a thing of the past, a rare inmate of a dust-covered case in some dime museum.' These were comments with which Charles could not but agree. Essex were just as culpable in the field as Surrey. In one vital match with Yorkshire catch after catch had gone down, until the long-suffering Walter Mead had made his famous pronouncement: 'There be a hepidemic in this team, but it aint catchin'.'

Round and round the arguments ran in circles. Everything seemed wrong with the game. Dead pitches, boring batting, unfair bowling, feeble fielding, high wage demands, shamateurism, poor sportsmanship, drunkenness. There were even worries about crowd behaviour and the importation of foreign players. Could this really be the Golden Age? It all sounds so modern. Even the smaller crises have a familiar sound. An MCC member of the Golden Age had this to say of the catering in the Lord's pavilion. 'It is disgraceful . . . No member can obtain a mutton chop or steak after half past one, although the

Committee promised every reform when they took over the refreshments two or three years ago . . .'

At this time of debate and uncertainty, in 1899, Demon and Lobster experienced very differing fortunes. The former, at 28 at the peak of his powers as a bowler, and a certainty or as near a certainty for selection for England that summer as ever has been likely, gave up the game for an entire season. It was a set-back from which his cricket never totally recovered. The latter, however, went from strength to strength during the season of 1899. Runs continued to flow from his bat. And his lobs got better and better. Moreover, in 1899, Digby performed outstandingly well for the Gentlemen at Lord's, a match which, coming as it did straight after Grace's Jubilee event of 1898, attracted as much excitement as any match that season. Quietly helped, financially, by the Surrey Committee, he continued to act as vice-captain to Key and by the end of the season had captained his county for the first time. The balance, therefore, in the careers of Demon and Lobster was now at the point of change.

THE DOCTOR
RUN OUT

11
*Bats, balls
and Boers*

Despite all the public heart-searching and the private recriminations, the cricketers of the period possessed a combined strength of personality which communicated itself so strongly to the British public that it transcended all other considerations. Even when, in 1899, Britain went to war with the Dutch settlers in South Africa, cricket remained a national preoccupation. Indeed, the cricket ethos was reflected in the British attitude to the war. Typically, Baden-Powell, when besieged by the Boers in Mafeking and in receipt of his opponents' suggestion that a cricket match between the two sides might relieve the boredom, replied: 'I should like nothing better, after the match in which we are at present engaged is over. But just now we are having our innings and have so far scored 200 days not out against the bowling of Cronje, Snyman, Botha and Eloff and we are having a very enjoyable game.'

It was a professional soldier's war. Charles' brother, Mounteney, who had been serving as a regular officer in India, was transferred to South Africa. Several counties lost serving soldiers, among them Johnny Turner, who left Essex to join Sir Redvers Buller. Likewise, Major Poore, the leading batsman of 1899 with an average of over 90, left Hampshire for the front. Several volunteers enlisted, leaving further gaps in the amateur ranks. Frank Milligan, Frank Mitchell and Stanley Jackson all forsook cricket with Yorkshire for the war. 'At the moment one hears nothing but War! War! War!' said the old England captain, A. G. Steel. 'What numbers of gallant young soldier cricketers have gone to the front, eager for the chance.' Jingoism was rife. 'The Soldiers of The Queen' was more popular than any Behrend ballad. England confidently anticipated an innings' victory.

Rumours of impending war did little to spoil the renewal of conflict at Lord's between Gentlemen and Players. Both teams were fully representative. For the amateurs, W. G. again had a strong nucleus of ex-Varsity players, Ranjitsinhji, Stanley Jackson, Charles Fry and Gregor MacGregor, while there were England players in MacLaren, Mason, Bradley, Townsend and Poore. The Players, captained by Abel, largely depended on Surrey and Yorkshire, the leading counties. Rhodes, Jack Brown, Hirst, Hayward, Brockwell and Lockwood gave them a formidable look. Essex were to be represented by Walter Mead and Johnny Turner, but the latter had to return to his regiment. At the last minute, therefore, the MCC called up Digby, whose all-round performances during 1899 certainly merited his inclusion in such exalted company. Thus by the merest of chances, by the sudden decision of the War Office to make a further mobilization, the Lobster was given the opportunity to prove himself at the highest level of the game! And he took it.

A very good crowd of 12,000 came to the first day's play. Lord's looked fresh and green. A pleasant breeze blew across, tempering the rays of a powerful sun. W.G. pleased the crowd by winning the toss and MacLaren and Fry opened the innings. By the close of play the Gentlemen were 373 for 6, with Digby still to go in. Fry was top scorer with 104, made in three and a half hours, not slow scoring by modern standards, but it did not meet with total approval. There were periods, said the critics, when he was quite slow, and half a dozen times when he was beaten or missed. In contrast there were two short innings from MacLaren and Ranjitsinhji of a very different nature. MacLaren drove the opening bowlers, Lockwood and Hirst, with magnificent disdain and was followed by an even more inventive Ranji, whose nimble-footed forays against Rhodes, Mead and Trott made his partner Fry look very pedestrian. It was a great sadness to everyone but the eleven Players, when he slashed too wildly at Wilfred

Rhodes and was caught at third man. W.G. himself, who had been out of practice, batted at no. 7. Very opportunely, he was not out at the close, which ensured another big crowd for the second day. They were not disappointed, for he and Jack Mason made a big stand, the 51-year-old Doctor showing as good timing as ever. One of his most productive shots was the lofted pull to the on-side boundary, used to balls on his off stump 'just short of a good length by six inches to a foot'. Another Grace century seemed likely when Mason, strangely forgetting his partner's immobility between wickets, hit the ball to Walter Mead at wide mid-off and called for a single. W.G. was not amused to be run out by two yards.

Digby's most glorious moment occurred on the second day, after the Gentlemen were bowled out for 480. For a time, under a hot sun, the Players had advanced comfortably, with Tom Hayward looking commanding against the pace attack of Bradley and Jackson, and the score had reached 122 for 3 when Digby was given a bowl from the pavilion end. Bowling for an hour and three-quarters, Digby took 6 wickets for 21 runs. It was the best piece of sustained lob bowling seen at Lord's for a very long time and it made his reputation.

All his victims were caught! The first to go was Tom Hayward. If Tom had a weakness, it was against slow bowling, but he knew Digby's lobs well from the Surrey nets, and, at 77, his eye was well in. Receiving a half-volley on the leg stump, he drove it back fiercely. A feature of Digby's bowling was his swift follow-through down the wicket. His brave fielding to his own bowling was one of the reasons for its success. Now he hurled himself sideways and clung on to the speeding ball, which had never left the ground more then a few inches. Billy Brockwell, who came in next, likewise knew Digby's lobs well, but, with only 4 to his name, he hit across the spin of a leg-break, lofted his drive, and Stanley Jackson caught him safely at mid-on. Albert Trott, the crowd's favourite, arrived next. The Australian, who had come to England and settled with Middlesex after failing to make the 1896 touring party, was a renowned hitter. Only weeks previously he had hit the ball straight over the top of the Lord's pavilion. The crowd chattered merrily in anticipation. Who would want to be a lob bowler, when Albert Trott was at the wicket? Digby looked round his field, gesturing to them to spread deep and wide. Up came the first offering, one of Digby's best 'tices'. Down came Trott's bat in a mighty swing and away flew the ball, soon as miniscule as a golf-ball struck with a high iron. But the height had been gained at the expense of length, and when the ball began to descend, it was realized that it was not going to fall outside the ground. Indeed it was not going to fall beyond the boundary ropes. Archie MacLaren, at deep mid-wicket, started running in, veering to his left as he sped. The other deep fielders in his vicinity gratefully vacated the landing site. By the time MacLaren caught the ball (with an infuriating nonchalance) he was near the pavilion rails at deep mid-on. The crowd rose to their feet noisily, not quite sure whether they were cheering the batsman, bowler or fielder. Storer, meanwhile, had been watching things at the other end and decided on a different tactic, a policy of deep caution. As the balls turned from outside the off and leg stumps, he padded them away, bat held high. For some time there was a war of attrition. Eventually a full toss was properly dispatched to leg. It was the first and last boundary which Digby gave away that innings. George Hirst could play no such waiting game. Losing his patience, the sturdy Yorkshireman swung full-shouldered across the line, the ball finding the very centre of his bat. Archie MacLaren, down on the mid-wicket boundary, sensed early, before the ball was actually struck, that it might be coming his way. Twenty yards he covered in the direction of square leg, sprinting fiercely in front of the ropes before the old figure-board. With no deceleration, hands thrown forward, arms outstretched, he somehow intercepted the ball. Lord's had not seen a catch like it. An uninhibited frenzy of delight greeted it. The cheering had not stopped when George Hirst's retreating figure had vanished from sight. Walter Mead was the next victim. He might have learnt from the last hour's play. He might have heeded Storer's advice, but he didn't. He too lifted his head. Major Poore, on guard at the pavilion rails, in his last big match before leaving for South Africa, took the catch with military precision. As the wickets had been falling, Storer's defensive tactics had become even more exaggerated. The fielders closed in on him. If they felt some anxiety, they did not show it. Digby floated up another teasing leg-break. This time, Storer prodded forward and tamely lobbed the ball up to forward short leg, where W.G.'s large hands enfolded the ball. The Players had been bowled out for 196.

The reaction of the Press to the Players' discomfiture was purely one of derision. 'The failure of the leading professionals of the country against the lobs,' said the *Manchester Guardian*, 'was truly ludicrous.'

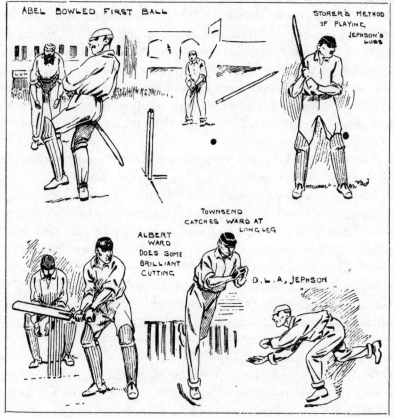

GENTLEMEN AND PLAYERS: THE CLOSING DAY OF THE MATCH AT LORD'S.

The Times gave a more balanced verdict: 'Lob bowling played a great part in yesterday's cricket at Lord's and led the professionals to having a very bad time, for last night, with 2 wickets down in the second innings, they were still 240 runs behind. But in these days, when a lob bowler's going on is a signal for a laugh from the crowd, it is a great rebuke to those who neglect the development of underhand slows that the only good lob bowler we have should get six of England's Players out for 21 runs. Deception in the flight of the ball and ill-timed hitting are the things sought for by the lob bowler and Mr Jephson certainly had them yesterday . . .'

In the Players' second innings Grace again gave Digby a long bowl, but this time the batsmen played him with more circumspection. He bowled 27 economical overs, taking a couple more wickets (including that of Hirst, stumped by MacGregor) as the Gentlemen gained a famous inning victory. It was long remembered as Digby Jephson's match.

No one on the Gentlemen's side, however, not even the underarm bowler or the elderly batsman, meant quite so much to the public of 1899 as Ranjitsinhji! Ranji was now England's favourite adopted son. Both Demon and Lobster considered him the best batsman of their age. Charles bracketed him with Tom Hayward, and Digby compared him to Jessop and Crawford. Digby not only had the privilege of close observation of Ranji but also the talent as a chronicler to do justice to his subject.

'One of the finest balls ever bowled,' wrote Digby, 'that failed to get a wicket was bowled by Lockwood to Ranjitsinhji at The Oval. I was standing at mid-off. Ranji had just come in to bat, and was, I think, still on the mark. It was very fast; it pitched three or four inches off the off stump, and came back like lightning. I listened for the pleasing rattle of the sticks, but at the eleventh hour – no, I had better say the last hundredth part of a second – Ranjitsinhji's right leg was bent across, and he received it full on the thigh. There was no other player living who, having failed to stop it with his bat, could have got his leg there in time. He certainly acquired a bruise, but the pain of this surely and swiftly dwindled in an innings of over 190!'

Ranji's strength lay in the back foot: 'The foundation of Ranji's marvellous success was laid when he first saw Arthur Shrewsbury watch the ball and not grope blindly forward.' Digby remembered bowling his lobs to both men: 'By their consummate placing Shrewsbury and Ranji could score off any ball I had the temerity to suggest to them. They played back or were up the pitch and smothered everything! I once hit Shrewsbury on the leg, and Ranji I hit on his pads! I was as pleased as if I had got them out, for, of all the men I have ever bowled at or seen bowled at, these two made the fewest mistakes. They so rarely missed a ball they played at.'

Until the change of law in 1910, it was necessary to hit the ball right out of the ground to score a six. 'At Hastings once in Hastings Week,' wrote Digby, 'Ranji was playing against the Australians, and he heard it said that he had never hit the ball out of the ground. "No, I have not," he said, "but let me stay in half an hour and I will put one through that round window in the church over there." Twenty minutes later there was the sound of glass and the umpire signalled six . . .'

Of a skilful Ranji innings on a rain-affected Oval wicket, Digby wrote: 'Sussex are in, and 7 are out for 107, but Ranjitsinhji is there. Playing at first with the feeling that he had not made runs – playing with the knowledge that he wanted practice – he was the acme of caution, a prototype of prudence. After 50 minutes he had made 14! – and then? Why, only those who were at The Oval on Tuesday could say how he played. There was every stroke that was known to *man*, and the variety of strokes that belong to *himself alone*! He never plays forward – he occasionally walks to the ball, and every one played back is met in the centre of the bat. And when he hits there is no wild motion of effort, no swinging the bat round the head; a short step, and Richardson is driven straight as a die on to the "first floor front" of the pavilion.'

Although Ranji scored his runs quickly, both Crawford and Jessop scored them quicker. The former applied to county cricket the hard-hitting technique which had made him such a successful schoolboy cricketer. He specialized in the lofted drive, the most exciting stroke in cricket, and his initials VFS were soon transmogrified. Very Fast Scoring Crawford became a great favourite. Digby was the witness of several remarkable Crawford innings: 'I remember when we were playing Gloucestershire at Bristol in 1901, sitting on the roof of the pavilion there. Everything tended to a close finish; we wanted 190 or so to win, and as the wicket was a bit on the soft side it was about a level money chance. Crawford was in; Paish was bowling; Champain, the old Oxford Blue, was in the outfield on the edge of the cinder track. I was watching the score with feverish interest. Suddenly the boy took the usual short step and the ball ballooned heavenwards. "Bother," I murmured, "caught in the country." Not a chance. The ball cleared Champain, it cleared the track, it sailed 20 yards over our heads on the top of the pavilion, to fall nearly 170 yards from the crease, in a strip of cottage garden behind us! It was the biggest hit I have ever seen, and by far the most wonderful in the face of the minute particle of effort that he appeared to put into the stroke. There was no dancing up the pitch, no swinging of the bat round the head, no crouching down. It seemed to us who were watching that he played forward – rather hard, perhaps, but in the manner, almost in the perfect style, of William Gunn. In reality, he "pushed" the ball into the longfield and out of it, not for one, but for six!'

Greatest of all the hitters of the Golden Age was Gilbert Jessop, off the field the most modest and retiring of men, on it the most feared of batsmen. To bowl underarm lobs to such a man would have required great nerve. Digby took his wicket several times. However, it was one near-miss which he recorded most graphically: 'We were playing at Bristol, that happy hunting ground of so many batsmen, when that most original of all cricketers, Gilbert Jessop, arrived on the scene, and with him as usual came his three pounds of willow. I waved my outfields back to the verge of the horizon and the outmost edge of their respective beats. The great hitter took guard and I started to bowl. Instinctively I felt that the ball had gone too high, that it was too far up; thoughts of six, lost ball, broken windows and a thousand similar fancies dashed into my head. I was prepared to dodge, to duck, to do anything to avoid the atrocity that must ensue, when, wonder of wonders, the great bat came down, the ball was resting at my feet, and I had tried to hold on the end of my thumbs the silliest catch it has ever been my lot to miss! It was my only chance, for the rest of the two overs that I had the foolhardiness to toss up produced as fine a pyrotechnic display of hitting as the Gloucestershire folk could hope to see.'

The public was in need of such brilliant diversions as those afforded by Ranji, Crawford and Jessop, for news from South Africa was not as expected in the first months of the war. The Boers, far from giving their wickets away, were taking wickets of their own, but these early Boer successes did not lessen morale. Arthur Balfour, Leader of the House, described the December defeats as simply 'incidents in a protracted campaign'. Alluding to minority pacifist views, he dismissively declaimed: 'We will neither sacrifice our empire to the Boers nor our constitution to the bores!' Such empty rhetoric was well received.

As the new season of 1900 started, the relief of Mafeking was reaching its final stages. It had been a long and costly procedure. In Plumer's unsuccessful attempt to retake the shanty town, Frank Milligan, the Yorkshire all-rounder, had been shot and killed. At last, on 17 May, Mafeking was finally relieved. Britain went mad with delight. There was double delight at Leyton. For on the same day the much-missed Kortright returned to the Essex XI.

Owen was still captain. The throwing controversy was still raging. Yet the Demon returned! The most likely explanation for this change of heart is that he was encouraged over the winter to return to the Essex fold, possibly with his neighbours Bunny Lucas and Freddie Fane acting as peacemakers.

He could not have chosen a more dramatic fixture for his return on Mafeking day than the needle match with Gloucester! Big crowds came to cheer the Demon. They watched anxiously as he bowled his first few overs. He was still fast, very fast. If he did not quite have the pace of 1898, it was not surprising after the long lay-off. Charles had to cope too with six balls an over instead of five, a change which found approval with few fast bowlers. He also expressed concern at the nature of Ted Freeman's wicket. Nonetheless it was a triumphant return and spirits at Leyton soared. The Demon had taken 10 for 98 in the match.

Some spectacular performances followed. On the placid Oval wicket Charles led Essex to their first ever victory beneath the gasometers. He took 7 Leicestershire wickets for 67 and destroyed a strong Yorkshire team too, taking 8 for 57 in one innings. His progress attracted much comment and it was noted that he was third in the national averages.

Then, mid-season, while he was playing against Lancashire, Charles learnt that his brother Mounteney had been dangerously wounded in South Africa, with injuries to chest and spine. Further news was tantalizingly slow in coming. In the meantime Charles played on throughout June: 'All who knew sympathized with him and admired him for the grit he showed in turning out to do battle for his county in such circumstances.' Finally, after weeks of anxiety, a communiqué from Lord Roberts in Pretoria announced that Mounteney had succumbed to his wounds. He was 28, married, with a baby son and daughter. Gradually the full picture emerged. Mounteney's unit had been involved in fighting close to Johannesburg in the big push through the Transvaal to capture Pretoria. Mounteney's death had been a brave one: 'With calm and heroic courage he gave his life to save the brigade from what could have been a terrible disaster.' So runs the tablet which his wife erected in Fryerning Church. 'Sans peur et sans rapproche.'

For the rest of the summer Charles bowled with only moderate success. Indeed he never again bowled really fast after the death of his younger brother. There were rumours about his failing health. 'I have reason to believe,' wrote one source close to him, 'that the Essex amateur is by no means a robust type of cricketer.' But Charles finished the season with an exciting century which quite altered the atmosphere of Walter Mead's benefit match against Middlesex. Striking balls from Albert Trott time and time again over the ropes, he aroused the crowd from docility to wild enthusiasm. 'Nothing is more refreshing to the jaded partisan,' wrote one observer, 'than an innings à la Kortright.'

Despite the disappointing final games, Charles' come-back season had been a considerable success. There was already talk of the composition of the next side to tour Australia and the names of both Demon and Lobster were on many people's lists. They had played together at Lord's in 1900 for the Gentlemen v. Players, a game which the latter won, quite dramatically, by scoring over 500 runs in the last innings. Exciting as the game was, it lacked the aura of previous encounters, for W.G. was missing, and Sammy Woods had been given the captaincy of the Gentlemen. W.G., though 52, was still making runs and keen to make more, but he had fallen foul of the authorities.

He had not enjoyed cordial relations with the Gloucestershire committee for some time. It had been noticeable at W.G.'s Jubilee match celebrations that his own county had sent little official representation. And when the Gloucestershire president proffered congratulations, W.G.'s curt reply was hardly indicative of a warm relationship: 'Mr Beloe and Gentlemen, I sincerely thank you. I hope you will excuse me saying more as I have a long afternoon before me.' The Committee had always found Grace a difficult man with whom to deal, very set in his autocratic ways. In addition, he had been planning to play some cricket in London, managing a team of his own at Crystal Palace, and would only be available for certain Gloucester matches. Not unreasonably, Gloucester wanted a full-time captain. W.G.'s parting remarks bear witness to sad acrimony: 'I have the greatest affection for the county of my birth, but, for the Committee as a body, the greatest contempt.'

Grace had been lured to London by the initial offer of £600 a year by the Crystal Palace Company to captain their new club. Grace's London County was to be part of the enormous leisure complex at Sydenham. This was centred on the glass exhibition hall, the 'crystal palace', which had been moved there, shortly after the Great Exhibition of 1851, in the days of W.G.'s infancy. The cricket field to be used had belonged to the now defunct Crystal Palace cricket club, for whom Digby had often played. There was a football ground adjacent to it, the scene of many F.A. Cup Finals, and a polo ground was now being created as an additional sporting facility. The Crystal Palace was said to have attracted over 91,000,000 visitors. It was hoped that the new cricket club, with Grace as the figure-head, would help attract many more. There would be a very full fixture list of both first- and second-class matches. Visiting teams would include the Wanderers as well as the Australians. Well-known amateurs and professionals from existing counties would be invited by W.G. to play for the London County on a match to match basis. In the meantime, before the cricket started, the management continued to offer to the public not only its permanent exhibition, but also firework displays, horse and dog shows, fêtes and festivals.

Cricket mixed uneasily with these other entertainments. The public, never convinced of its seriousness of purpose, was lukewarm towards it. No one was very sorry when the scheme ended in 1905. It was sad to see cricket's Champion enveloped in the commercialisation of the Crystal Palace complex. His motives of anger and financial gain were neither attractive nor concealed. Digby himself remained loyal. As captain of Surrey, he enjoyed revisiting one of the favourite grounds of his youth and tossing the coin with W.G. On one occasion he also enjoyed claiming the Doctor's wicket: 'It was indeed a pleased lobster who, in his third over, watched the heavy shoulders swing round at a slow half-volley just on his legs and saw the ball mount skywards, to drop into the safe hands of H. C. Pretty at deep square leg. And, as W.G. passed me smiling on his way back to the pavilion, out came the well-known phrase: "Sha-ant have it! Ought to have been six!" It was my lucky day, for I never got him out again.'

It was while Grace was playing at Crystal Palace that the Boer War finally came to an end. Its prolongation had caused much dismay; as the real facts and the real motives slowly began to emerge, disillusion grew. For Charles there must have been mixed feelings. The loss of his brother must have been hard to bear, however essentially right he may, as a conservative, have felt the war to have been. Ironically, the more liberal Digby may have been the less questioning, for he was uncomprehending when one of his young team-mates, E. M. Dowson, constantly queried the rightness of the cause and the loss of 25,000 British soldiers.

Disillusion with the war was complemented for many by disillusion at the spectacle of cricket's Champion playing out his final years for money at Crystal Palace. The national game, like national pride, was somehow no longer the same. There was much good cricket yet to be played in the next 12 years. But, by the end of the Boer War, the Golden Age had lost something of its sparkle. Even emerging talents like Hobbs, Woolley, Blythe, Strudwick and Barnes were no compensation for the loss of cricket's Champion.

12
Cares of
captaincy

Both Demon and Lobster only enjoyed the shortest of tenures of the captaincy of their county. Digby captained Surrey for three seasons, from 1900 to 1902, and Charles captained Essex for only one year, 1903. The truism that good cricketers do not necessarily make good captains is supported by many examples, ancient and modern. In the case of Demon and Lobster, there was much more to it than simply that. Various circumstances off the field played their part, and, to understand the years of their captaincy, one must also examine the period immediately preceding their election to office.

Kingsmill Key unexpectedly resigned as captain in 1899, a season when Surrey again won the Championship. That Surrey had won yet again was quite remarkable, for the Committee's new policy of including as many amateurs as possible was one likely to achieve neither success on the field nor harmony off it. Some of the new amateurs were not without ability. The Oxford Blue, Neville Miller, and Harold Pretty of the Wanderers had both scored centuries on their county débuts. Others were less effective. And the invitation to the Harrovian E. M. Dowson, while still at school, exemplified Surrey's obsession with youthful amateurs. Understandably, the professionals in the team felt insecure and those out of it, frustrated. They were not much mollified by the Committee's recent decision to pay half match fees to those professionals who 'stood down'. Resentment towards the intruding amateurs undermined team spirit. Key grew more and more unhappy about the situation, the implementation of which he sometimes found most embarrassing. For the match with Kent, for example, he was told to accommodate a young amateur, H. O. Dolbey, by dropping one of the six professionals (Abel, Hayward, Brockwell, Lockwood, Lees or Hayes). Dolbey was a useful club cricketer and later became a successful district judge in East Africa. The six Surrey professionals, on the other hand, all won England caps.

Matters came to a head in 1899 when Surrey were down at Cheltenham, playing Gloucester. Key and Digby debated the situation long into the night at the Queen's Hotel, where the amateurs always stayed. Digby urged patience, but Key believed the Committee should now be challenged and wrote forcefully, offering his resignation. Meanwhile he took his holidays early, leaving Digby to captain the side for the rest of the season. No compromise was reached during the winter and, in February, Key's resignation was confirmed.

Digby, as vice-captain and the only successful amateur, was the obvious replacement, but the Committee, with its strong Wykehamist leanings, offered the captaincy instead to Leveson Gower. He, tactfully, declined, pleading pressure of work. The Surrey president, Sir Richard Webster, determined that his policy should continue and suspicious of Digby's known familiarity with the professionals, summoned the Match Committee to his rooms in the House of Commons to read them a prepared statement of intent: 'I have long been anxious that the Surrey County XI should afford greater opportunities to first-class amateurs to play county cricket. Desirable as it is that the county should always be at the front in county cricket, I certainly do not believe that the Championship should be the only object and, while I always wish Surrey to win, I should be sorry if the County Championship remained with Surrey for a long series of years . . . I should like, if possible, to arrange matters for the future so that at least three places in the XI in all ordinary county matches should be filled by amateurs, and that other first-class amateurs who are eligible should play two or three times in the season, so that there should be more change in the XI . . .' He suggested that, to start things off, five or six amateurs should be approached and asked when it would be convenient for them to play.

Richard Webster was misguided but not deliberately perverse. His policy was merely one way of responding to the continuing worry that something was wrong with cricket. Webster, by championing the amateur cause, was deliberately turning his back on history, which could have told him that Surrey's past successes had depended largely upon professional skills. Few Surrey supporters would have agreed with their president's assertion that the Championship was not all-important. His premise was to be sorely tested, moreover, for it was partly responsible for the tremendous decline in Surrey's fortunes which now ensued. History took her revenge. Surrey, who had won the Championship nine times in the past 13 years, would enjoy but one success in the next fifty.

The captaincy was finally offered, therefore, to Digby, with Webster's strings firmly attached. When the appointment was announced, shortly before the beginning of the new season, Surrey's off-field problems must have been common knowledge. 'Mr Jephson has a difficult task,' wrote *Cricket* magazine, 'but he is just the sort of man to face difficulties with a stout heart and to overcome them.' It was hard to credit, from these ominous words, that Digby was taking over the reins of the Champion County!

Unfortunately, Digby inherited a team which was not only plagued by internal dissensions but was also growing old. He made a magnificent personal effort, as captain, to combat all the problems, raising his own game considerably in the process. 'Mr Jephson', said *Wisden*, 'was a far finer cricketer in 1900 than he had ever been before and it was certainly no fault of his that the team should have fallen so far below their recent standard.' Surrey had finished in seventh place.

As a batsman, Digby doubled both his previous season's aggregate and average. He scored four centuries for Surrey (and was presented with four bats). His highest innings was 213, when he and Bobby Abel put on 364 for the first wicket against Derbyshire. But Digby's best century was at Bramall Lane, achieved against the fine Yorkshire attack of Rhodes, Hirst and Haigh. As a bowler, he had never been more effective, his lobs winning high praise from *Wisden*: 'Mr Jephson bowled uncommonly well and might with advantage have put himself on more often and stayed on longer.' At The Oval he took 5 wickets for the Gentlemen against the Players, including that of Abel.

The Guv'nor had carried his bat for 153 in the first innings but, in the second, experienced that sudden reversal of fortune so characteristic of cricket: he was bowled second ball by a lob.

One thing which Digby tried particularly hard to remedy was the slack Surrey fielding. To him was attributed the saying, 'If a captain holds his catches, the team will.' The motto's validity was sorely tested during the season. So exasperated did Digby become about his team's poor fielding that he wrote on the subject, in general terms, for *Wisden* that year: 'Taken as a whole, fielding in 1900 has been bad, thoroughly bad. Men stand in the field today like so many "little mounds of earth" or waxen figures in a third-rate tailor's shop. The energy, the life, the ever-watchfulness of ten years ago is gone and in their place are lethargy, laziness and a wonderful yearning for rest . . .' There were a few outstanding fielders to be singled out for praise, none of them from his own county: Hirst and Denton of Yorkshire, MacLaren, Briggs and Tyldesley of Lancashire, Jessop, Trott, A. O. Jones and a Hampshire professional, Victor Barton, 'perhaps the finest cover point of the day'.

In Digby's second year of captaincy Surrey could only improve by one place in the Championship and were again reckoned to have done badly. Digby was sorely tried by the eccentricities of the Match Committee. The team was constantly changed. It became rare for the same side to take the field in two successive matches. 'As a natural consequence,' said *Wisden*, 'the eleven lacked cohesion and had far less energy and concentration of purpose than in former years.' There was a diplomatic rider: 'It really would have been better if there had been less variety of talent available.' The professionals, unsure of their places from match to match, became demoralized. Herbert Strudwick, who two years later was contesting the wicket-keeping place with Fred Stedman, claimed that they had to wait until ten minutes before the start of a match to learn which of them was playing. Sometimes, he said, the umpires would be on their way to the pitch before the team list went up.

Digby was subservient to the Match Committee. On being asked by the MCC for his views on the lbw rule, he at once sought the advice of the Committee. Frequently he did not attend selection meetings, happy, apparently, to implement the Match Committee's instructions. Often the most he was entrusted with was the choice of the final place: 'Same team to play v. Hants and Warwick, except Mr Knox

149

for Mr Leveson Gower, and last place to be between Brockwell, Lockwood and Lees.' Sometimes, even after the team had been selected, Digby was told to accommodate an amateur: 'It was decided to ask Mr H. C. McDonnell to play v. Hampshire, the captain to leave someone out for him.' On the odd occasion on which he took issue with Stein and Shuter, the most powerful members of the Committee, he lost the argument. In 1901 W. G. Grace had written to Surrey, suggesting that if their game with London County did not finish, the result should be decided on the first innings, with 1 point awarded instead of 2. This idea had merit and Shuter and Stein both approved. Digby did not. The matter was thereupon referred to the General Committee which overruled Digby's objection. Shuter himself as captain of Surrey had enjoyed a much easier relationship with his Committee than either of his two immediate successors: 'I was fortunate enough to have the complete confidence of the Committee,' he wrote, 'who practically left everything to me and never interfered. Undoubtedly it is best that a team should be left in the hands of one man.' Then, at the time of Digby's growing crisis, he wrote: 'I am strongly of the opinion that, provided the captain has the confidence of his Committee and XI, his opinions should carry great weight in the composition of the side.' Clearly Digby never enjoyed the Committee's confidence.

The most blatant undermining of his position occurred after the famous meeting at Lord's in 1900 in which the county captains had tried to do something about illegal bowling. Digby had voted with the majority of captains – weakly, and against his better judgment – that Bill Lockwood and others of doubtful action would not be put on to bowl next season. The Surrey Match Committee, chaired by Shuter with Digby an embarrassed member, agreed to write to the MCC to say that the directive of the captains, lacking the MCC's sanction, would be completely ignored by Surrey.

Quite why Digby so lacked the confidence of his Committee can only be a matter of surmise. To the more conservative of its members his lack of public school background would have told against him. His literary and musical interests made him an unusual figure, whilst much suspicion may have accrued from his familiarity with the professionals. In short, the Committee may have found him somewhat odd and compared him unfavourably with his two predecessors, Shuter and Key, whose social credentials were impeccable.

Even had he enjoyed the support of his Committee, however, Digby would not have found the team an easy one to handle. On away matches discipline was bad and the evenings spent in a manner not conducive to good fielding the next morning. Many players were experiencing problems. Holland, who should by now have been a leading batsman, was constantly being dropped and hopeful of following Len Braund to Somerset. Richardson was still bowling effectively but was unalterably overweight. He was trying, in vain, to persuade the Committee to take action against the *Daily Express* for defamatory remarks. Worst of all, Brockwell and Lockwood had lost form. Lockwood, in trouble with his bowling action and his washed-out benefit match, began drinking heavily again and was dropped from the side for the second half of 1901.

Surrey treated Lockwood firmly but well. He was not an easy man to deal with at the best of times. 'He was never likeable', wrote Home Gordon, 'and there was in his bowling a viciousness somewhat characteristic of the bad-tempered fellow he always showed himself.' Surrey might well have discarded him. Instead, they persuaded Yorkshire to come down again for an extra benefit match and safeguarded Lockwood's future by investing part of the proceeds for him, thereby ensuring him an income for the rest of his life. This idea, pioneered by Lord Hawke, was very worthwhile. The preceding year's beneficiary, Billy Brockwell, by contrast, was given all his benefit money to spend as he liked. He fell on very hard times and died a pauper. Digby was part of the small committee which debated Lockwood's drink problem. It was agreed that he would be re-engaged, provided that he again signed the pledge. But there would be instant dismissal if the pledge were broken. It was just the firm response which Lockwood needed. He pulled himself together and in 1902 he was again playing for England, enjoying his best-ever season.

In December 1901, George Lohmann died at the age of 36. He had not played for Surrey for five years and it was no great surprise when his tuberculosis killed him. Nonetheless his death unsettled the professionals still further and cast great gloom over The Oval. With business acumen to match his great cricket skill, Lohmann had been a father figure in the professional dressing room, full of wise financial advice for those who sought it. Digby too had lost a valued friend.

In 1902 Digby's fortunes plummeted. The previous year he had been full of runs, only Abel and Hayward scoring more. He also took

60 wickets for the county very cheaply. His 7 for 51 against Gloucestershire were the best figures of his career. He played on three occasions for the Gentlemen, under Grace at The Oval and Hastings and under MacGregor at Lord's. Then things went wrong. In 1902 his batting faltered and he took only 30 wickets. In August he dropped out of the Surrey XI.

The season began inauspiciously with the Committee complaining about poor results, yet expressing pleasure that 'an unusually large number of amateurs played for the county'. Amateurs were again encouraged in 1902. No less than 12 played during the season. Two newcomers, at least, were worthy of consideration. Captain Harry Bush, newly returned from India, was a fine off-driver, a batsman who might have repeated for Surrey his fine scores for the Army. 'Toddles' Dowson, an all-rounder up at Cambridge, was also useful, but the amateurs were generally poor substitutes for good professionals, and, with Tom Hayward taking against bowling and ceasing to be an all-rounder, Digby's resources were particularly stretched.

Faced with big problems on and off the pitch, the Surrey captain needed a resilience of character which he did not possess. He himself was only too aware of his own temperamental limitations: 'I myself am a curiously uneven player – one who in the dread hour of defeat is all too miserable, and in the hour of victory would change places with no man on earth.' Henry Leveson Gower, who very much admired Digby's qualities as a player, wrote perceptively: 'To my mind he was too sensitive and took to heart too much his occasional personal failures.' An example of Digby's inability to cope with personal failure occurred at Bristol in 1901. The Surrey captain had not made any big scores for a while and was therefore especially keen to do well against Gloucestershire: 'We had won the toss on the easiest wicket in England, slow-paced and close-cropped; the day was ideal and the bowling attack not one of the most formidable. I suggested I might go in first and the boys agreed. Bobby Abel and I started. I got three "gift" fours off Charlie Townsend and thought my bad luck had broken. "Splendid, now I'm off the mark!" and I smiled all over my face. Fatuous fool! The first ball of the next over Bobby Abel pushed one to Jessop at cover and shouted "Come on!" I went on, and was eight yards off the crease when the middle and off stumps rattled into Jack Board's ribs. What I said I am afraid no self-respecting editor would print. It was 12.30. I took a four-wheeler, a victoria, with an old friend and drove through the by-paths and hedgerows of Bristol, to return in the late afternoon and to find 400 for 4 wickets on the board. Abel had scored a century. Thank heaven I smiled as I heartily congratulated him . . .' Digby's self-deprecating narrative omitted to mention his own subsequent capture of 7 Gloucester wickets, and that a week later he scored 174 at The Oval.

In deserting his team at Bristol, an act of great despondency, Digby had shown a glimpse of his real, complex personality. He was much less self-assured than he tried to pretend as he played the role of the confident captain of Surrey. Another manifestation of his uneven temperament, even inner turmoil, was the regularity with which he suffered from nightmares. These often occurred before a difficult day's play. He could remember them vividly: 'I am next man in. To all intents and purposes I seem to be ready; gloves and bat handy; I am simply waiting for a wicket to fall. A man is bowled. I get up; I look down; I've got no pads on! I look again. My immaculate flannels have given place to a pair of grey "slacks"; my buckskin boots to a pair of ancient pumps! In a frenzy of excitement I shout for Reid (this nightmare invariably smites me at The Oval). "Reid! Reid! Get me dressed!" I snatch off the slacks, I plunge into clean trousers and a shirt; I thrust on my boots, first one lace breaks, then the other. My pads have no buckles – everything goes wrong. Outside I hear the angry crowd shout "Play! Play!" I snatch up my bat and charge down the pavilion steps. Every member is glaring at me. The "Play! Play!" of the enraged spectators gives place to ironical cheers. Once on the grass my spirits recover; courage comes to me again. Then, instead of the well-known gasometers and Clarke's hostelry, I see a park that stretches to the horizon, and as if looking through the wrong end of a pair of Zeiss I see the game miles and miles away. I start to run, but the faster I run the faster the game recedes. I run and run. At last, after hours, I arrive breathless. I look at the ground. "Great Scott! It's Blackheath!" Kent v. Lancashire! And I was playing at The Oval for Surrey v. Yorkshire! Still carrying my bat and gloves, I rush to the gate. "Taxi!" I yell. "Where to, sir?" "The Oval, like Hades!" Crash! Bump! Was it a bus or only a lamp-post? I wake to find Mary with my morning tea!'

Over-sensitive about his own performances, Digby suffered greatly at the hands of the critics. His writings frequently betray his injured feelings. In his column in the *Westminster Gazette* he talked of 'the ever

153

present pavilion critics', invariably ensconced behind the thickest plate-glass, their backs to the warmest of fires, while he and his team struggled in bitter conditions. Their hostility towards him, when Essex visited The Oval on a really wintry day, stung him enough to remark: 'It is not so easy a thing to stop a good length breaking ball from Mead on a sodden wicket with a full-sized snowflake in one's eye . . . Temper your rigid criticisms with a grain of mercy, my friends.'

His fellow cricket writers could be as unsympathetic as the pavilion critics. Digby was easily wounded by them. He complained, for example, of one occasion at Nottingham, where, on a far from easy wicket, he and a few other Surrey players had fought hard to make a few runs: 'At the "George" in the evening afterwards, we were discussing the day's play, every one of us agreeing that we had been lucky to do as well as we had, when a well-known writer on the game walked in and commenced the conversation by saying how easy the wicket had been and, in consequence, how dreadfully slow the scoring . . .'

Unluckily for Digby it was not until early June that Surrey won their first match of 1902. The critics were quick to point out that the last Surrey victory had been in the previous July! Digby made a very dignified reply in his own newspaper column, but was moved to observe that when a man was down it seemed now the practice to kick him. Digby could rebut these open criticisms. He could make no reply, however, to the dozens of anonymous hostile letters which he now received. Instead of throwing them away, he brooded on them: 'The anonymous letter writer is certainly of the same breed as men who scrawl on walls, of the same genus with individuals who, with a blunt knife, turn "seat" into "eat" in our railway carriages, to all of whom nuisance is too mild a word to apply. He is a difficult subject to handle, for we know not the lair of the beast; he works in the dark in secret places, and his methods of work are those of the dirty alien who stabs in the back with a rusty skewer. Come out, you reptile!'

Digby became more and more depressed as the season of 1902 progressed. He and the Match Committee were very much at odds. In June, the Committee picked Dowson and Leveson Gower for The Oval fixture of the Gentlemen v. Players, omitting Digby in the initial selection. It was a calculated slight. There were rumours in the Press of friction between captain and Committee. In vain the latter published an official denial. Digby opted out of the team in August, leaving Leveson Gower to captain the final games.

One other, personal factor influenced Digby's resignation. His closest friend during the years of his captaincy had been Frank Crawford, eight years Digby's junior known as 'the boy' to the team. Digby's admiration for Crawford's big hitting was boundless and he had published, in 1902, an article about Crawford entitled 'My Favourite Cricketer'. Together, they had travelled around England, wined and dined, played the part of stockbrokers, and always been the staunchest of comrades for Surrey, the Wanderers and many scratch XIs. Crawford had taken over Walter Read's old job as assistant secretary but, finding that working for the Surrey Committee had its problems, he applied for the post of secretary at Leicestershire, for whom he was also qualified to play. It was a great blow to Digby when Crawford got the job. Only a month afterwards, in February 1903, Digby resigned: 'Will you kindly inform the committee', he wrote to Alcock, 'that I am very sorry I shall be unable to take on the captaincy of this year's side owing to my business engagements. If I should be in good enough form, I shall only be too pleased to play occasionally . . .' The Surrey president replied formally to him, regretting his decision: 'The judgment and tact you have displayed during the very trying seasons of your captaincy merit the highest praise.' Digby mistook formality for warmth: 'Many thanks for your exceptionally kind letter. I need hardly tell you how much I feel resigning the captaincy of the XI, but your cordial expressions of regret are of no little help in relieving the sense of loss.'

The Committee duly invited Leveson Gower to become captain. He again declined. So an urgent telegram was sent to 'Toddles' Dowson, still an undergraduate, inviting him to take over the captaincy after the Varsity match. Only four words came back: 'Cannot possibly accept captaincy.' Finally, a delightful member of the 2nd XI, Livingstone Walker, became captain for a time, but Surrey fared abysmally. Lord Dalmeny, later the 6th Earl of Rosebery, took over soon afterwards (a significant event, in that it was he who persuaded the club's patron, the Prince of Wales, to allow the use of his feathers for the Surrey badge). But not even the Prince of Wales' feathers and the emergence of two promising players, Strudwick and Hobbs, proved compensation for the retirement of Abel, Richardson, Brockwell and Lockwood, and the premature departure of Digby.

Digby's years of captaincy are well documented. But there is much mystery about Charles' final years with Essex. It is not simply a question of why he enjoyed so short a period as captain. There is also the problem of what went wrong with his bowling. He had made, in 1900, a successful comeback as a fast bowler. But after that year he ceased to be anything but an occasional trundler. In 1901 he took just 25 wickets, in 1902 merely 2, and in 1903, the year of his captaincy, he took 28. Something clearly went amiss. There is no mention of a recurrence of the leg injury in these years. The throwing controversy, therefore, seems to offer the likeliest solution.

Some counties had immediately dissociated themselves from the county captains' list of proscribed throwers. Not so Essex! Charles Green's Committee convened a special club meeting, which heartily endorsed Hugh Owen's participation. A public statement of approval was made. This strong anti-throwing stance was in keeping with the summary dismissal of F. G. Bull. It is very likely, therefore, that Charles was told in 1901 that his present bowling action was unacceptable, moral pressure, as requested by the MCC, being brought to bear. Home Gordon, a writer with close Essex links, made an interesting comment on the brink of this season: 'Though it is not often suspected, Mr C. J. Kortright is a cricketer affected by his surroundings, and, if he would confidently believe in his own capacity, his bowling might be more destructive than ever.' Clearly *something* was bothering him; it is most likely that it was the legality of his bowling action.

Before the county campaign of 1901 began, Charles played for the Essex Club & Ground against Chelmsford. He was experimenting with alternative actions, for a report states: 'Kortright met with no success and was very firmly hit, change his delivery as he might.' The next week he was invited by Bunny Lucas to play for Chelmsford against the London club, Beaumont. This time he took 5 for 11, as Beaumont were bowled out for 18. He had reverted to his familiar, flat-out style: 'One of the players hit Mr Kortright for four, but the next ball, sent down with tremendous pace, smashed the bails!' The old style follow-through was also in evidence: 'The speedy bowler performed another smart thing by catching a player mid-way between the wickets after one of his deliveries.' Unusually, Hugh Owen also played for Chelmsford that day. He was probably there to scrutinize the Demon's action. A week later, in an early match for Essex, Charles took 6 for 107, opening the county's bowling with Mead and showing plenty of hostility. During the whole of May the Demon seemed back in his old form. Even the catches were going down with their wonted regularity. A terrible pun was made in consequence: 'When do Essex people Lucas if they were C. E. Green with anger?' 'When it's Owen to a man not being Kortright.' Charles was still at this time considered one of the fastest bowlers in England. Bob Carpenter said as much in an interview, but then, quite suddenly, the Demon ceased taking wickets and became only an occasional bowler. There can only be one reason. Charles Green, loyal to the MCC (whose president he was shortly to become) and loyal to the Fenner's philosophy of clean cricket, told the Demon that his action simply wouldn't do.

Charles does seem to have been the object of attention from the clean cricket lobby in other matters apart from throwing. He had a reputation for running down the wicket to create patches on which the spinners could bowl. F. G. Bull and Walter Mead may have benefited much from this piece of gamesmanship. Digby had come across it, when playing with Charles at Lord's in 1900. Charles had created a magnificent patch, just outside the line of a right-hander's leg stump, and had no doubt told the leg-break bowlers on the Gentlemen's side (Townsend and Digby) all about it. On this occasion the ploy back-fired, for Townsend later recalled what a terrible time he had, batting left-handed to Wilfred Rhodes, who exploited the patch unmercifully.

The extent of Charles' reputation for 'unclean' cricket can be seen from an extraordinary outburst by Digby in *Wisden* relating to the season of 1901: 'In connection with this subject of a bowler making a mark for his confrère to aim at, I may say that it occurred at Canterbury during the "Week". Essex were Kent's opponents. Kortright bowled from the end opposite to the pavilion, a broken patch was created, and McGahey bowled on to it with deadly effect. A. P. Lucas, who was captain on that particular occasion, as soon as he noticed it, thorough sportsman as he is, refrained from bowling Kortright in the second innings.' Digby was playing elsewhere at the time, so he is simply relating gossip of the day. But to do so in print, so openly, suggests that there was much hostility from within the game towards Charles in 1901.

By the end of 1901 Charles had made the drastic decision to develop leg-breaks. In April 1902 Home Gordon wrote: 'It may prove a sensational novelty if Mr C. J. Kortright begins to bowl what are termed "slow cock-a-doodle leg-breaks". He is practising in private, but is not likely to try in county cricket without reasonable prospect of success.' Charles may have been encouraged by the case of Fred Geeson, the Leicestershire medium-pacer, whose action had been condemned by the county captains. He had changed to leg-breaks and in 1901 took 125 wickets with them. Unfortunately for Charles, Essex already had a leg-break bowler in Charles McGahey. There were rumours too that Charles would return, bowling very fast indeed, with an 'improved' action. Charles Green subscribed to this, telling the members that 'Mr Kortright is going to bowl very fast this season and that is what we want, a very fast bowler.' A leg-break bowler would not bring the crowds back to Leyton like a demon, but, as it turned out, Charles bowled neither fast nor slow in 1902 and played purely as a batsman, albeit a conscientious, improving one. He also captained the side in the absence of Hugh Owen, who frequently stood down because of loss of form.

There was much to cheer about in 1902. The nation rejoiced at the ending of the Boer War and at the coronation of Edward VII. But for Essex cricket there was little rejoicing, as the county dropped down to an unprecedented thirteenth place. Spirits sank. In vain did their great supporter, Colonel Lockwood MP, joke that he would sell the county some of the willows from his Lambourne End estate, 'to make Essex better bats'. The members were not amused.

The professionals were as unsettled as the members. Bob Carpenter, who had not enjoyed a lucrative benefit, asked the Committee for a three-year contract. The Committee replied that it would consider his request only at the end of the season. The frustrated Carpenter threatened resignation. Charles Green angrily insisted on an apology. Carpenter submissively apologized. Green had got his own way too on the subject of bonus payments. Lord Hawke had pioneered a scheme whereby he awarded points for good play during the season to the Yorkshire professionals, which were converted to cash awards at the end of the season. This was a great improvement on the old system whereby certain achievements, such as fifties, were rewarded, regardless of their value to the side. Essex now adopted this points scheme; and Charles, as captain in 1903, was responsible for its introduction. But Essex still did not pay proper winter wages. Carpenter and Mead campaigned hard for these, both missing seasons whilst in dispute

158

SURREY -v- ESSEX
AT THE OVAL   LAST MONDAY.

M°GAHEY PLAYS A FINE INNINGS

TOM 'N GRAND FORM

HAYWARD GETS CARPENTER IN THE SLIPS

A SNAP SHOT OF C J KORTRIGHT ON THE TRAIL

APTED DOES NOT THINK MUCH OF THE WEATHER

with the county. With such distrust prevalent between Committee and professionals, Essex were unlikely to be successful.

Charles' assumption of the captaincy, however, seemed like the beginning of a new era. The comments of the Essex secretary, O. R. Borradaile, reflected the optimism: 'The general opinion amongst the players is that Mr Kortright will make a splendid successor to Mr Owen. He is thoroughly popular both with professionals and amateurs and is expected to put energy and go into the leadership of the team. He keenly appreciates the necessity for improvement in the fielding, which is the weakest spot in the Essex play, and means to pay special attention to this department.'

159

There were some newcomers in the Essex XI to support the optimism. Johnny Douglas, straight from Felsted School, was starting on his long career, while the curate of St Paul's Mission Church, Leyton, Frank Gillingham, at once proved himself a fine attacking batsman. There were two promising professional bowlers in Claude Buckenham and Bill Reeves.

The team started very well under its new captain. There was a much greater sense of purpose. Home Gordon wrote that Charles was proving an excellent captain, and E. H. D. Sewell, a regular member of Charles' team, was full of lavish, if uncritical, praise. The captain still flung the ball down fast in the nets and, on rare occasions in the middle, but in the main he now confined himself to his leg-breaks. By the end of July the county was challenging for the Championship, having its best season for six years. Then, in August, the side fell apart dramatically. Charles missed some matches because of 'rheumatism in the arm' and then dropped out altogether. The season ended with the 46-year-old Lucas as captain. That winter Charles resigned the captaincy, which he once had so coveted, and, for all serious purposes, his Essex career was ended.

Charles was only 32 and had many more years of cricket in him. It is not immediately obvious why he felt compelled to resign. His own form with the bat was not very good, but his limited leg-breaks had put him top of the Essex bowling averages and his fielding was as inspirational as ever. His experience and his leadership were, anyway, much more valuable than his batting average. The reason must lie in his frustration, as he watched matches from first slip, restrained by Charles Green from bowling anything but his 'cock-a-doodle leg-breaks'. He had tried the occasional fast foray and been severely reprimanded for it. He now longed to get away from the careful scrutiny of the first-class game, to feel free once more to indulge in his long run-up, to feel the wind in his hair and enjoy the pleasure of hurling the ball down at nervous opponents. If the batsmen were rabbits, all the better. Above all, no square-leg umpire on Witham Green or Navestock Common would dare to question the legality of his bowling action. So Charles retired from first-class cricket, to stay a demon bowler.

Both Demon and Lobster enjoyed their new-found freedom. Digby played very few more matches for Surrey. His last was in 1904, when he played, appropriately, against a Middlesex side captained by

Gregor MacGregor. It was thanks to his old Cambridge captain that Digby performed the hat-trick: 'Gregor MacGregor gave it to me. Bosanquet had been stumped by Strudwick, and Nicholl bowled, and then MacGregor arrived – he took guard and then he slowly scraped forward, a thing I very rarely saw him do – the ball pitched on the leg stump and did just enough to beat the bat.' Surrey gave Digby an inscribed silver cigarette case, to mark this achievement. It was a thoughtful gesture of reconciliation, but Digby never played for Surrey again.

There had been no real need for Digby to lose heart with his own performances. His first-class batting average was still over 30 (which compared honourably with Abel's of 35, while his predecessors as captain, Shuter and Key, averaged 21 and 26 respectively). He had scored 11 centuries. With his lobs he had taken nearly 300 wickets at only 25 runs each. His contribution in the field, also, had been an outstanding one. But, released from the aggravation of his dealings with the Surrey Committee, Digby was able to enjoy the Edwardian years with carefree cricket, often in the company of the Wanderers. Once again he was able to go on their summer tours. In 1903, as Surrey struggled under their new captain, Digby was enjoying a tour of Kent and Sussex, taking a great number of wickets and scoring heavily wherever he went. His centuries at Devonshire Park, Eastbourne and on the St Lawrence ground, Canterbury, were delights to watch. For several seasons he again became one of London's leading club cricketers, until in 1909, at the age of 38, his form suddenly left him.

Charles too enormously enjoyed the freedom from restraint. In 1904, as Freddie Fane took over the Essex captaincy from him, Charles terrorized the club cricketers of Essex, his 64 wickets for Brentwood costing only 9 runs each. 'Bowled Kortright' was once again the familiar means of dismissal. He cared not that the opposition was now the Shoeburyness School of Gunnery rather than Surrey County Cricket Club. He knocked the gunners' wickets down and enjoyed the experience hugely. He played too for the MCC, the Stoics and many times for the Free Foresters.

In 1904 Charles returned to Lord's, to play for the Gentlemen of England in a three-day match against I Zingari. Sir Kingsmill Key was on his side, Bunny Lucas and Captain Wynyard among the opposition. Keeping wicket for the Gentlemen of England was Cecil

Headlam (who, as an Oxford undergraduate, had first experienced Charles at Wallingford). Headlam wrote illuminatingly of the 33-year-old Demon: 'Kortright was upon this occasion bowling as fast as ever he did in his life. With that glorious action of his, he was rushing up to the wicket and hurling down the ball faster than any bowler before or since.' Teddy Wynyard took his stance outside the crease, to try to put Charles off his length. Seeing this, Headlam moved up to the wicket, as MacGregor had done 11 years before him. 'You had better go back, Cecil,' said Wynyard. 'Not if you go out of your crease', said Headlam, and he stayed. Presently Headlam nearly equalled the achievement of MacGregor in taking a catch, standing up to the Demon: 'Down came a ball which the batsman endeavoured to glide to leg. It touched the face of the bat held close to the hip, and lodged in my hands – the catch of a lifetime. But to our appeal the umpire said "not out". It was the most disappointing moment in my career. I shall never forget the sickening sound of that umpire's "not out".'

In 1904 Essex had disbanded its 2nd XI to help solve one of its many financial crises, but, when it was later re-formed, Charles often played, sometimes as captain. He played the occasional 1st XI match too. He toured with the Essex XI to Dublin and Scotland and against Forfarshire in 1911, at the age of 40, he took 8 wickets for 27. Playing for the Free Foresters he took all 10 wickets against Stanmore Masters (a feat which Digby also achieved, when playing for a scratch XI at Streatham). Sometimes, when the wicket suited or the mood took him, Charles bowled his slow leg-breaks. But usually he bowled the way which he enjoyed most. At Winchester College, in 1907, while playing for A. J. Webbe's XI, he bowled a ball so fast that it went for 6 leg-byes. One of the Winchester batsmen, John Leslie, wrote to *The Times* 45 years later: 'After making a 100, Kortright went on to bowl. His first ball hit me on the knee and went out of New Field and some way into Meads. We ran six leg-byes. Pawson, who batted the other end, caught me up, so I had to complete the sixth run alone.' Guy Pawson, some 79 years afterwards, remembered the incident differently, as byes, not leg-byes. There were no boundaries then and, despite the long grass, Pawson believed that 8 runs would have been possible, if his partner had been faster between the wickets. Most of the time, said Pawson, Charles contented himself with medium-fast deliveries, but from time to time let go a really fast one.

Whether it was 6 byes or 6 leg-byes matters little. The story is further proof that the ability to bowl really fast stayed with Charles long after his halcyon days with Essex. Throughout Edward's reign, both Demon and Lobster happily continued to ply their particular crafts in their own inimitable fashion.

Neither Essex nor Surrey benefited from the resignations of their captains. The machinations of the Surrey Committee seem especially deplorable. No modern Committee, not even that of Yorkshire, can rival it for folly. The Essex Committee was less culpable, but some gesture of support for its captain might well have gained it a longer use of his experience and lust for victory. Ranji, that most autocratic and short-tempered of captains, postulated seven qualities for captaincy: tact, resource, readiness, decision, an even temper, enthusiasm and the power of inspiring it in others. Perhaps the Lobster lacked decision. Certainly the Demon lacked tact and an even temper. But they both possessed enough of the other desirable qualities to have become good captains, had the problems of Golden Age cricket not counted so strongly against them.

13
The scent of summer

O marry, when we are old, dear heart,
What a woe of a world 'Twill be!
Never a tree but is ruff'd and dry,
Never a bird but the curlew's cry;
And I'm wondering will it come by-and-by,
O will it come by-and-by?

'O never and no,' my heart replies,
For the morn and eve are one,
And the bird that awoke with a merry lay
Has sweeter songs for the close of day,
And the scent of summer abides for aye
Tho' the flowers themselves are gone!

Lyric: Gunby Hadath
Music: A. H. Behrend

The Golden Age, if it survived the Boer War, certainly perished in that of 1914–18. Over a hundred first-class cricketers died in the fighting, and the socio–economic conditions were so altered afterwards that the game lost that delicate balance between Gentlemen and Players, which gave the cricket of the late Victorian and Edwardian era its very distinctive flavour.

Cricket's response to the Great War was swift. W.G. led the way with his famous letter to *The Sportsman*, urging all able-bodied cricketers to enlist. Archie MacLaren, from the columns of *The World of Cricket*, likewise urged sporting youth to rush to the colours. It was not just the young men that responded. Sammy Woods, now 47, saw the war as a piece of sport not to be missed. After unsuccessfully trying to enlist in several parts of the country, he finally pulled some strings and obtained a commission in the 6th Somersets. After a lurid time at Khartoum, he contracted malaria and had to watch the rest of the match from the grandstands. Another Cambridge captain, Stanley Jackson, became Lieutenant-Colonel of a West Yorkshire Regiment battalion. He raised the battalion himself and, among the many cricketers who joined him, was Essex's Freddie Fane, who later won the M.C.

Both Demon and Lobster, at 43 exempt from military service, made a less spectacular contribution to the war effort. Charles was sufficiently moved by the spirit of the times to enlist as a Special Constable with the local police force; such had been the rush of young policemen enlisting for the army that there was need for volunteers at home. With Charles wielding a truncheon around Ingatestone, no doubt all criminals despaired and enlisted. Digby contented himself with local journalism at Cambridge. Although there was now a period of four seasons with no first-class cricket, he believed that the game itself had a big contribution to make to the war effort: 'Cricket seems a puny, childish thing to many', he wrote in 1917, 'when the nations of the world are at each other's throats; but every man is a better soldier or sailor who has learnt its two great lessons – discipline and the sacrifice of self for the good of one's side, for the good of one's king, one's country, and for the sake of right.'

For both men the war brought personal losses. Charles' nephew, his brother William's only son, was killed in 1917. Named Mounteney, like the youngest of the Kortright brothers, Charles' nephew had shown promise as a cricketer, playing for Harrow at Lord's. As a 2nd Lieutenant he had survived the fighting at Gallipoli and the battle of the Somme, only to fall later near Arras.

165

For Digby the demise of Frank Crawford was particularly distressing. After leaving Leicestershire Crawford had become a tea planter in Ceylon, and, on the outbreak of war, enrolled in the Ceylon Planters' Rifle Corps. Sent to Gallipoli, he endured seven months in the same dug-out, contracting dysentery, from which he never fully recovered. He was afterwards gassed when serving with the East Surrey Regiment in France. Although he attempted after the war to return to Ceylon with his wife and son, poor health forced him back to England, where he spent much time in hospital. When he died, in 1922, he was given full military honours. 'Of all the cheery, merry-faced players – the men of an upstanding, fine physical culture, cheery heart, and the power, the courage to step into line where others failed, there are few that were his equal, and none his superior . . .' So Digby wrote, in tribute, in *The Sporting Life*. 'Well, friend, you have passed, but to those who knew and loved you, you have left many memories. You will live in our hearts as a clean-cut Englishman . . .'

During the second year of the War, Grace, Trumper and Stoddart all died. W.G.'s death, after a stroke, left the nation stunned. 'I remember the feeling of shock it gave me to read that W.G. had gone,' wrote one enthusiast. 'Though it came in the midst of the holocaust of war, the news of the passing of the Old Man seemed like the death of cricket itself.' Grace was 67 and had seemed indestructible. A huge gathering of cricketers assembled at Beckenham for his funeral, despite the War. Charles Green and Bunny Lucas represented Essex. (Kortright had been unable to take time off his special duties.) Jack Shuter and Henry Leveson Gower represented Surrey. Ranji, MacLaren and MacGregor were among the many familiar faces who paid their last respects to the Old Man in the autumn chill. Digby, like Charles, was not present, but his verses *in memoriam* expressed the sentiments of all:

> With what great zest through all your merry years
> Did you not cast into a million hearts
> The golden spirit of our England's game,
> To hearts that otherwise had passed it by!
> Dead – and from Death a myriad memories rise
> Deathless – we thank you, friend, that once you lived.

Victor Trumper's death in Australia, from peritonitis, caused similar shock, for he was only 37. Trumper epitomized Golden Age batsmanship at its most graceful and aggressive. He had toured

England four times and Digby had admired him from close range: 'Trumper is a batsman to watch,' he wrote in 1902, 'by which I mean that cricket enthusiasts should take a long journey and, if necessary, miss their breakfast to see him make a hundred. Of the many good strokes he made against us, two stand out by themselves. Richardson dropped the ball a bit short, not a long hop, and he was back on his off-stump and it was pushed with tremendous force between shortleg and mid-on – four. The other, a full-faced, slighty hooked punch off a half-volley of Brockwell's that must have pitched on the middle and off – it flashed away over mid-on's head and rattled against the rails of the football stand.'

Stoddart's death was in some ways the most shocking of all, however, for, when he shot himself in a fit of depression, it further emphasized the disturbing fact that many amateurs suffered hard times once their playing days were over. 'Drew' Stoddart had been many people's ideal of the all-round amateur athlete. His scintillating batting had drawn thousands to Lord's during the Boom years. But his background was similar to Digby's and his insecurity as deep-rooted. The boy who had gone to Olivers School, Acacia Road, St John's Wood, had as many concealed self-doubts as the boy from Manor House, Clapham.

Like Stoddart, Digby encountered financial problems on giving up his county captaincy. Support from the Surrey Committee for Digby's business career abruptly ceased, but he continued his association with the Stock Exchange for a while. The Jephsons continued to live with the Behrends in north Clapham, but a regular income eluded Digby. In 1907 he applied for the secretaryship of Surrey (on the death of Charles Alcock). The salary of £400 would have been useful. Together with 'Jerry' Weigall, he reached the short list of nine, but a committee, under Lord Alverstone, rejected him in favour of the Oxford wicket-keeper and Old Etonian, William Findlay.

Soon afterwards, probably in 1910 when he played no cricket, Digby suffered a severe financial setback. As a result, Digby and Lina were forced to move from London and to live with Digby's mother in her small house in Cambridge. That Arthur Behrend was unable to help suggests that the Behrends too lost money at this time, perhaps in a bad piece of stock-market speculation. For the rest of his life Digby endeavoured to earn a living solely from cricket journalism. It was a hard struggle. He himself talked of a period of 'vast vicissitudes'. His financial embarrassment probably determined his absence from the well-attended funerals of Grace, Frank Crawford and Tom Richardson (who had died abroad in strange circumstances, in 1912).

Union Road, Cambridge, where Digby lived his last years, was a narrow, residential side street. Many of its buildings have since been demolished, including Panton Cottage, Emily Jephson's home. It was situated at the end of a terrace of cottages, of modest size, containing just four main rooms with a tiny garden in front and a yard behind. It faced the side entrance to the Perse School for Girls, high-walled, black-doored, brass-plated. Union Road, when Digby knew it, was a lively, friendly place. Among its residents were a plumber, a builder, a baker, a blacksmith, a teacher of Swedish gymnastics and a grocer. The road contained two pubs. In this down-to-earth atmosphere 'Old Jeffer', as Digby came to be known, must have been something of a local celebrity. Many must have been the cricketing tales told in a smoke-filled bar. Socially, life in Union Road was far removed from the ambience of the Lord's and Oval pavilions. Although his past cricketing record allowed him to renew acquaintance with this world from time to time, it was no longer his natural habitat. One suspects that, despite the privations of Union Road, he enjoyed playing the role of 'Old Jeffer' in 'The Light Dragoon' much more than that of Gentleman Captain of Surrey.

During these years he formed a very strong friendship with the Haywards. Daniel Hayward, Tom's brother, the Fenner's groundsman, lived in an adjacent road and became a boon companion, while Tom, whose first-class career endured to the Great War, was frequently at home nearby. Theirs had been a mutually beneficial friendship. Tom's advice had helped Digby's cricket, and Digby had helped Tom exploit his great success. Several of Tom's letters, for example, negotiating with Surrey about financial matters, seem written in Digby's polished prose. When Tom Hayward achieved the distinction of scoring 100 hundreds – something which, hitherto, only the Grand Old Man had achieved, Digby delightedly celebrated the occasion:

> So now, instead of one, we gather two,
> That from the smiling face of willow wood
> Have drawn a hundred hundreds – sportsmen true
> In every sense, in every varying mood,
> The G.O.M. and Tom!

Digby took his cricket verse very seriously. It seems to have acted as a substitute for other, frustrated literary endeavours. Mixing with writers and artists at the Savage Club may have encouraged him to look beyond cricket. At all events, in 1904 he had published a short, illustrated story, entitled *A Fragment*. According to its prologue, Digby and an artist friend were moved to the creation of the work by witnessing one night the death of a young girl, who jumped off a bridge with her baby. Digby's brief text describes, poetically, 12 scenes in the imaginary journey to suicide of a girl, innocent at heart but driven by circumstances to become 'a woman of the night'. 'Who will judge her,' Digby asks in conclusion, 'laden with sin as they say she is?' Twelve highly stylized drawings by Will Mein form the nucleus of the book, each illustrating one stage in the girl's dream-like travels. They are done in the fashion of Aubrey Beardsley and the whole enterprise seems to have drawn its inspiration from the Art Nouveau movement. The book was expensively produced, with rich hide covers and elaborate bindings.

If it was intended that *A Fragment* should bring him some literary acclaim, it failed. There were rumours in the sporting world that Digby had, rather oddly, written a fairy story. Shortly afterwards, however, he was able to let off literary steam, by ghosting *The Spalding Book of Cricket* for Tom Hayward. The latter was already putting his name to Spalding cricket bats and, as in 1906 he was enjoying a superb season (in which he scored a record 3,518 runs), it seemed timely for him to put his name to a cricket manual too. Digby gives himself away as the ghost writer by the inclusion of a piece which occurs elsewhere under his own name. The nature of his writing is often elaborate and, as such, quite out of keeping with the essentially monosyllabic Hayward. Moreover, Digby's love of the arts pervades the book: 'It is only practice which makes perfect. Take the case of our great musicians and singers. Paderewski and Melba devote hours daily to practising simple scales . . .' On the need for a bowler to possess intelligence, he digressed: 'When Opie was asked with what he mixed his paints, his answer was "With brains".' Quite what Tom Hayward thought of it all, it is difficult to imagine. Perhaps he only looked at the illustrations, but many must have been the ironic congratulations on his new-found fluency of expression. *The Spalding Book of Cricket*'s final words of advice may well have made the pragmatic Hayward cringe. He would certainly have heard them all before: 'Cricket, in addition to being a pastime, is a creator of character. It teaches patience, perseverance and pluck, three Ps which will carry you well through the trials of life . . . One word more, my youthful master. Take for your motto "Play the Game!" Cricket is a game which, above all others that I know, generates gentlemanly characteristics. It is not wealth which makes a gentleman; it is conduct. So compose yourselves on the cricket field that, whether you win or lose, you will at any rate bring credit to yourself and to the game which you and I love so dearly.'

Shortly after their move to Cambridge, both Lina and Digby had volumes of verses published. In 1911 Lina's 'Songs For Sailormen' (volume 1) was issued. Perhaps at 2/6d a copy its 44 poems of the sea did not represent good value, for volume 2 never appeared. Lina's nautical lyrics seem to have been written essentially as pieces to be set to music, and no doubt her brother, Arthur Behrend, did indeed give many of them a musical setting. Perhaps Lina's imagination had been fired by her father's tales of adventures of Danzig merchants on the high seas. There seems no other explanation for her apparent obsession with the sea. Her sentiments reflect those of the times. They express an overwhelming confidence in the superiority of British sea power.

Lina's slim volume was shortly matched by one from Digby. Just before the War, Heffers of Cambridge published a small selection of his cricketing poems under the title *A Few Overs*, the cover in an appropriate shade of pale blue. Costing 6d, it was on sale for many years at The Oval bookstall. Charles Fry provided Digby with a short foreword. It is singularly lacking in any enthusiasm for, or endorsement of, the contents, for which Fry can hardly be blamed, for Digby's poetic muse is not always in evidence. Fry resorts to a foreword of stern defence: 'If ever a man has won a Gentlemen v. Players match by his own bowling, he is entitled to write a book of verse about cricket, so the author is absolved from his temerity beforehand, and may dare to expect that those who read him will look for what is good in his verse, even as he himself always looked for what is best in the game . . .' In some ways, Digby's unsatisfactory book of poems reflects the mixed fortunes which he himself experienced in the Edwardian era. He has moments of success in his verses, just as he had moments of success as Surrey captain, City stockbroker and imaginative author, but total success eludes him.

After the Great War Digby and Arthur Behrend combined on a

ballad to celebrate the resumption of county cricket. Entitled *A Song of Cricket*, it was published in 1919 and dedicated to Ranjitsinhji. But Digby's efforts to get a selection of his best prose and verse published were unsuccessful. For a time he was in contact with the writer F. S. Ashley-Cooper, who promised to edit material (including many of his articles from national newspapers) and to write a foreword. There was much optimism, at least on Digby's side. He wrote, in 1921, suggesting that the book might start with his poem *Fascination* and end with *Farewell*. However, Ashley-Cooper was unsuccessful in attracting a publisher and the project faltered. Digby himself was no longer well enough to persevere.

By the end of the Great War he was beginning to suffer from arteriosclerosis and slowly but steadily lost mobility. His mother's failing health preyed on his mind, as did his own financial difficulties. 'I have been seedy,' he confided to a friend. 'I have had a bad go of neuritis and I have been away a fortnight, nursing . . .' In 1921 he wrote: 'I have had a multitude of troubles, neuritis, extraneous illness, worries etc.'

It was in these early post-war years, when his health was failing, that Digby became the authoritative voice of Cambridge cricket. Forays to London were now special occasions, ones of physical and financial hardship. Fenner's became again the centre of his life. He scarcely missed a ball which was bowled there. It was the best possible medicine for his illness: 'Many people like to take their pleasures sadly', he wrote, 'and prefer to take them in sad, sombre places, but there are others, folk of wisdom, who revel in sunshine, in the waving of stately trees and all the glories of the baby days of summer. To these I would say "Come to Fenner's", for at this time of year it is one of the most beautiful, restful places to be found this side of eternity.'

At Fenner's, as Cambridge correspondent for Plum Warner's new magazine, *The Cricketer*, Digby watched, coached and admired the new generation of Blues. His writings of this period are aglow with love for the game. As he himself experienced ever further the darker side of life, so he came to appreciate ever more keenly the sunlit beauties of cricket. Illness added an extra poignancy to middle-aged regret for lost youth: 'What a splendid thing to watch is this youth – the vigour of the thoroughly fit. We in the sere and yellow cry in vain for even one short hour of what we too have been!' But he avoided bitterness.

There were some outstanding young cricketers at Cambridge in the early 1920s and Digby wrote so glowingly of them that Warner suspected exaggeration. 'I promised the editor', wrote Digby cheerfully, 'to be sparing in the use of purple in the pigments in which I was to portray the Cambridge side. If there should be too much colour splashed upon the following page, I think he will forgive me, for the subject surely warrants it!' The subject was Percy Chapman. Chapman had arrived at Cambridge with a big reputation from Uppingham, the school of Gregor MacGregor, and he played in the manner of the Golden Age. Digby became his devoted admirer and most vociferous supporter. He was behind the nets when Chapman first appeared at Fenner's: 'We have stood delighted with that most original young player, Chapman. It really is astonishing how late he can play, or rather, hit the ball.' Chapman got better and better. 'His batting bristles with surprises and stirs the imagination of those who delight in originality . . . Not for a long time have we old students of the game seen greater possibilities in a youngster.' Chapman's lithe fielding was Digby's pure joy. It probably made up for all those slow, fumbling Surrey sides which Digby had tried to enliven. He reckoned Chapman a better fielder than Sammy Woods and possibly as good as Jessop.

Then there were the three Ashton brothers, all from Winchester, who captained the Cambridge XI in successive years. Hubert Ashton's side was particularly good in the field. Digby watched with delight. Later he produced an extravagant metaphor in its honour: 'It is certainly true that Hubert Ashton had good material to work on – close to his hand was excellent straw, and his master touch turned it into excellent bricks, from which he was enabled to erect a very useful, substantial edifice, perhaps not so imposing or so decorative a cricket structure as has been built by other Cambridge captains, but one that more than answered its original purpose. It was a cricket house built on the best, the strongest, the most enduring foundations that can exist – for it stood on the SOLID ROCK OF FIELDING!'

Digby was quick to appreciate the worth of Gubby Allen, fresh from Eton: 'The caviare of the day's play was the bowling of Allen – he bowled an excellent length with that surplus of energy that is so exhilarating to watch . . .' There were many other fine players . . . Tom Lowry, who later captained New Zealand, Jack Bryan, who toured Australia with the MCC, and M. D. Lyon, in whose controversial style Digby took great pleasure.

Digby never managed to produce a Cambridge lob bowler, though he had hopes of the Harrovian Cecil Bennett: 'I often wonder', he wrote in 1923, 'why lob bowling has gone the way of the Dodo; it is amusing to watch and has been known in its day to remove many an obstreperous batsman besides being a really excellent tonic in the field. I should like to see how C. T. Bennett performs in the middle.'

Digby's greatest hour in his role as Cambridge sage came at the end of 1921. England had been soundly beaten by Australia. Late that Summer Archie MacLaren captained an England XI to play the unbeaten Australians at Eastbourne. Digby prevailed upon him to pick five members of his Cambridge side, the three Ashtons, Percy Chapman and the bowler C. H. Gibson. The Cambridge men played their part magnificently in a famous victory, the most heartening event in English cricket since the Great War. That winter MacLaren took Chapman and several other Cambridge Blues on his tour of Australia and New Zealand. Digby's enthusiasm for the venture was boundless, and he expressed it in a poem, 'Winter Cricket':

> Winter – a pipe, an easy chair,
> A fire for warmth; but you out there,
> O lucky men, will taste anew
> The joys that summer gave to you.
> You will have missed the miry ways,
> The leaden skies, the cold, dark days;
> Where heavens are blue, bright sun above,
> You still can serve the game you love
> With all the zest you showed when here
> In our brief 'playtime' of the year.
>
> Winter – I smoke and watch the flame,
> And sometimes, too, *I* play the game,
> For looking round my study walls
> Group after group its tale recalls
> Of clean-fought fight, or safe-held catch,
> Or glorious drive that won the match,
> And so the old game lives again
> Through winter's frosts and wind and rain.
> A game of ghosts down from their shelf! –
> You play the real live game itself!

Digby still played a little cricket around Cambridge, despite his physical limitations, sometimes appearing in charity matches and regularly playing for the MCC against The Leys School. In 1917 he took 5 of the boys' wickets, with Tom Russell and Jack Hearne among the professionals on his side. Two years later, aged 50, he again took some wickets (and so did an even older Walter Mead). One of the virtues of lob bowling, as its foremost exponent William Clarke had illustrated, was that it was one of the few cricketing skills which lasted into middle age. Ronnie Aird, a Cambridge Blue in 1923, remembered Digby as a very effective player: 'I cannot remember what the match was, but I think it was some sort of Cambridge scratch XI against a side from Newmarket. I think Digby Jephson took 6 wickets, bowling extremely well. My impression is that he bowled his lobs quite quickly and they were never very high off the ground.'

Digby's visits to Lord's now became treasured reunions, though not all the old faces could be found in the pavilion. Gregor MacGregor, for example, for many years a stockbroker, had died of heart trouble at the end of the Great War. 'Many were the faces I saw and recognized of long ago,' Digby wrote of one Varsity match. 'Many were the hands I shook I had not shaken for years. I saw Archie MacLaren with hair of the silver badger; I saw 'Jerry' Weigall also whitened (great instructor as he is!). And I saw Ranji, fit and fat and well and quite *sunburnt*!' On another occasion, while Gentlemen met Players, he sat in the pavilion with Fry, Ranji, MacLaren and Jack Mason, discussing how best to play Frank Woolley's bowling. He chatted with 'Toddles' Dowson (who had upset Lord Alverstone's calculations, by devoting himself entirely to business after leaving Cambridge) and Sir Timothy O'Brien. The subject under debate was the current fad for jumping back in front of the stumps. 'They wouldn't have done it 20 years ago,' said the Irishman. 'You only want one Richardson, one Lockwood or one Kortright on the kneecap, and you don't want any more!'

In 1923 Digby travelled down to London for a dinner, at the Connaught Rooms, celebrating the Wanderers' first 50 years. There were over 130 present, to witness the presentation to Stanley Colman. Arthur Behrend, now aged 70, sang 'Daddy' and Digby read the poem which he had composed for the occasion. There were many present who had played first-class cricket. It was quite like old times, except for the absence of Frank Crawford.

The death of Digby's mother, in 1924, seems to have hastened on his own final illness. Emily Jephson was a strong personality. Even when his cricketing friends visited him in Union Road, Emily never faded into the background. 'Do you remember coming to our cottage, George,' wrote Digby, in an affectionate article, celebrating George Hirst's fiftieth birthday, 'and the mother taking your cap off, year after year?' Emily had been both parents to Digby. Her home had become refuge for him and Lina in their worst hour and so it had stayed. Her death seems to have broken him. Shortly afterwards he made his own will. It was not that he had any money. He merely wanted to leave things in order.

In 1925 Digby was compelled to give up all his writing. Somehow he managed to turn out as usual for the MCC against The Leys, but by the autumn he was seriously ill. For eight weeks Digby battled for breath in Panton Cottage. He rallied slightly at Christmas, and wrote cheerfully to a friend: 'I hope to get to the next university match, even if I have to crawl there on two sticks!' It was even thought that, with the approach of spring, he might recover. Then haemorrhage set in and, a day later, on the evening of 19 January 1926, he sat up in bed, only to fall back dead from heart failure. Lina was beside him when he died.

Digby was buried in the churchyard of St Andrew's, Cherry Hinton. The Cambridge undergraduate, who had not read for a Tripos, was buried near a number of distinguished academics, including two former Masters of Peterhouse. Peterhouse connections always remained strong. A don conducted the funeral service. The Head Porter, who had greeted Digby when he first came up 37 years ago, was at the graveside, as was a former Dean. Their joint attendance symbolized Digby's wide social acceptability. Digby's 80-year-old father, living in Kent, was unable to attend. Lina was supported by her composer brother and other relatives on her side of the family. From the Jephson side there was none, but there was a very large gathering of friends. Tom Hayward and his wife were there. So too the old Surrey wicket-keeper, George Watts. Surrey sent a wreath. Plum Warner sent one on behalf of *The Cricketer*. There were wreaths from many Wanderers, including the Beldams and Gunby Hadath, and one which simply said 'From Mr and Mrs Dan from Fenner's'. There were some long tributes in the national Press. The *Daily Mail* was typical: 'Charming companion, loyal friend, fascinating writer, attractive batsman, clever bowler, gentle and lovable. Hundreds of cricketers – amateur and professional, University men and Club men – will mourn the death of "Dear Old Jeffer".' He had been buried in his mother's grave. He had not been able to afford a headstone for her, nor could Lina for him. He had left only £127. When Lina died, in 1944, and the three were reunited, she too could make no provision for a headstone. Together they lie in a known, but unmarked grave.

Whilst Digby had been experiencing ecstasy and anguish at Cambridge in the years after the Great War, Charles Kortright's life moved forward more gently among the placid Essex fields. After the War he turned his attention from cricket to golf. He had been a keen player for many years and the formation of a new club, outside Brentwood, in the former stately home of the Petre family, Thorndon Hall, was the catalyst needed for his enthusiasm. He became, in 1920, a founder member and golf at Thorndon Park became the centre of his life for the next 30 years.

Despite an eccentric putting technique, Charles was an excellent five-handicap golfer. He played the game the same way he played his cricket. He knew no other method. Caddies winced before his invective, if they had failed to locate his ball in the rough. Fellow players cringed into submissive silence on the greens, lest they put the Demon off his putt. He drove ferociously, but, before playing a shot, he would practise meticulously, often to the exasperation of his companions and the detriment of their game. Nobody dared to speak to him as he strode down the fairways, and, back in the clubhouse, nobody dared to sit in the arm-chair by the fireside, to which he had taken a particular fancy. Just as he had enjoyed to see fear playing at the mouth of an opposing batsman, so he delighted in the discomfiture of anxious new members. *Oderint, dum metuant* was his motto. Let them say unpleasant things behind my back, provided they never sit in my chair. There is one particularly telling anecdote, told by Frank Keating in *Punch*: 'Kortright remained venomous till death. Once, in his later years, he was playing golf with Douglas Jardine, another snooty patrician, who didn't give a fig. The players in the party behind drove into them without shouting "Fore!" Charles, furious, picked up their ball, teed it up precisely, took aim, and drove a howling beamer right back at them.'

Venomous? Yes, on the field of play. Whether it was golf, snooker, shooting, fishing or bridge, his competitive nature always brought out the worst in him. At the bridge table, he played like a demon, fixing his partner with steely stares, and no amount of pink gin was sufficient antidote to the venom of his tongue if he took exception to Dummy's cards. He hated losing tricks as much as he had loathed giving away boundaries. It took a brave player to make a successful finesse through Charles Kortright.

Off the field of play, he was becoming more mellow with age. He would never entirely lose his harsh exterior, but, underneath there lurked some warmth and fellow sportsmen were beginning to find it. He was, however, still an essentially solitary man. If there was no sport to be had, he would stride forth out of doors, to commune with the Essex countryside. He loved the trees and the bird life. It was a healthy existence. When Charles was 55, at the time of Digby's death, he had as trim a figure as 30 years before, as tall and straight-backed as ever.

His personal life was less carefree. One of his devoted sisters, Alice, died quite suddenly and quite young before the Great War. Moreover, just as he had lost one nephew in the First World War, he lost another in the second, his brother Mounteney's son, a serving officer, drowned at Dunkirk. Charles had continued to live at Fryerning until, in 1922, the death of his mother (who, by her marriage as Mary Jephson, had united the families of Demon and Lobster). For the first time in their lives Charles and his sister Caroline left Fryerning. They did not move far away, only to Warley, and, later, Navestock, but it was part of the dissolution of the Kortright empire. When Charles' elder brother, William, died in 1929, Charles sold off a number of assets including Furze Hall, the house of his birth. Death duties and the depreciation of invested capital had changed the family's circumstances. Charles and Caroline were able to live comfortably but the Kortrights were no longer rich.

The move to the village of Navestock resulted in the Demon's return to cricket! His fame had preceded him, for Freddie Fane lived nearby. It was not long before the 60-year-old Charles was persuaded to turn out for Navestock. He did so for four years, bowling at a good medium pace with a high arm, batting in typically rumbustious fashion, and fielding energetically in the slips. His attitude had not altered at all. He is remembered at Navestock as someone of volatile temperament, quick to anger, standing on his dignity and taking the games with deadly seriousness of purpose. The village had seen nothing like it. Off the field, he was a different person. He fraternized with his team-mates in the locals and enjoyed his celebrity. The years had certainly mellowed him, for he took it upon himself to oversee the re-laying of the Navestock square. The young Demon, who had been such a terror on bumpy Berkshire pitches, would never have dreamed of doing such a thing!

Charles finally retired from cricket when he and Caroline bought a bungalow in Brentwood, in 1934, when he was 63. 'Earleywood' in Hillside Walk was a very different proposition from the big houses which he had known at Fryerning but it suited his purposes well. It was a very easy drive to Thorndon Park and he was also nearer for the Essex cricket weeks at Brentwood in which he always took a keen interest. He was proud of being an Essex vice-president, like his old team-mate Brigadier-General A. J. Turner, and he watched the county keenly. He and Walter Mead were regular spectators at Brentwood. Visiting teams were invited down to 'Earleywood' for drinks.

In his seventies Charles began to be troubled by arthritis. He continued to go to the golf club most days, but in the latter years it was to talk rather than play. A plaque now denotes his favourite resting place in the clubhouse: 'Korty's Corner'. In his late seventies he was forced to give up his golf, but he remained as slim and straight as ever. 'It is easy to picture that live wiry figure bounding to the wicket 50 years ago,' wrote Charles Bray admiringly of the 77-year-old Demon.

Like Digby before him, Charles now became something of a sage. His opinion on past and present cricket was much sought and he was pleased to give it, in short, thrustful phrases. His views were expressed in an article in *Wisden* in 1948 and shortly afterwards John Arlott, through the medium of radio, brought him to an even wider sporting audience. Charles talked much as he had bowled, with no elaboration or superfluity, taxing the interviewer's skills to the limits. John Arlott and the Demon formed an immediate rapport, so much so that Arlott was invited to Charles' eightieth birthday celebration at 'Earleywood'. The writer and broadcaster was captivated by the Edwardian aura of the Kortright retreat, describing it as 'Utopia'. He was impressed by Charles' 'huge gaiety' and saw him as a fast bowler 'to the last gradation of mind, chuckle and story'. The Demon had mellowed much with age.

Charles died on 12 December 1952, in his eighty-second year, peacefully at 'Earleywood'. Although two walking sticks had perforce replaced the one, he had otherwise remained extremely active and had been wonderfully looked after by Caroline. His last years, unlike those of Digby, were not marred by financial worry, although he left less than £5000. He was buried at Fryerning Church, like most of the Kortrights. His grave lies close to that of Bunny Lucas, who predeceased him by nearly 30 years. A third cricketer lies in the remarkable Fryerning churchyard, for Claude Ashton, one of the three brothers whom Digby so admired at Cambridge, is also buried there, a casualty of World War Two. All three men scored centuries for Essex!

Although Charles was survived by many famous names, Charles Fry, Gilbert Jessop, George Hirst, Wilfred Rhodes and Walter Mead, most of his Essex contemporaries had died and, of the famous Gentlemen in W.G.'s Jubilee year, only Jack Mason and Charles Townsend lived on. It was now nearly 20 years since Ranji's ashes had been scattered over the Ganges. Charles' death, therefore, occasioned many tributes and many assessments of the Golden Age in which he bowled.

Charles never doubted that the cricket of his time transcended that played after the Great War. When asked his opinion in the 1940s about the current English batsmen, players like Hutton, Washbrook, Edrich and Compton, he replied with a shrug of the shoulders, 'I'd cut 'em in half!' He thought little better of the modern bowling. The fast ones were too preoccupied with swing to concentrate on the basics: 'They forget to keep a length and bowl at the stumps.' And he hated the sight of an off-spinner, like the young Jim Laker, bowling to a cluster of short legs. These 'would not have been allowed to stay in their suicidal positions by some of the old-time batsmen like Gilbert Jessop or Johnny Tyldesley'. The Demon's view of modern bowlers was all the lower because, in his opinion, they started with an advantage: 'They have a slightly smaller ball – easier to get the hand round – a wider crease, which helps in varying the angle of delivery, bigger stumps at which to aim. There is also the new lbw law by which it is possible to get a decision from a ball pitching on the off-side of the wicket, a boon to the modern bowler.' Charles was quite perplexed about the constant no-balls of modern times: 'I was always very careful about my line that I didn't go and bowl no-balls. You very seldom, in my day, unless you'd had a long slogging afternoon, found people bowling

179

no-balls . . . Now they seem to be very common . . .' He remained a harsh critic of modern times all his days. One day at Brentwood, the 80-year-old Demon was watching, with the writer A. A. Thomson, many runs being scored, and, eventually, some sympathy was expressed for the conditions under which the bowlers were labouring. 'What's that? What's that?' growled Charles. 'Haven't they got three stumps to aim at?'

Digby did not live long enough to look back on his own time from such a distance. His attitude in 1919, when cricket restarted, was that cricket was as good as ever. 'The schools are full, the universities are packed, the army plays, the navy plays – the pent-up love of the missed summer days rings in every heart. Yes, cricket still attracts. The spirit of the game is, if that were possible, whiter, cleaner, brighter than for many, many years.' However, as the 1920s advanced, Digby realized that the approach to the game had altered. Away from Fenner's, he did not like what he saw. In particular, he viewed with alarm the new approach to batting. When his own Cambridge protégé, M. D. Lyon, made a century for the Gentlemen, he was quick to point out the difference in styles, between old and new: 'Lyon's innings was a thing for the two-eyed, four-eyed stance artists to study, not only to study but to "mark, learn and inwardly digest". We saw the left leg swing across in perfect synchronization with the left shoulder, we saw the powerful wrists using the face of the bat to lash the ball by third man or second slip, we saw the full-shouldered punch on the on side, and we saw, *mirabile dictu*, a man unafraid as he left the cherished crease!' There is every indication that, had Digby lived longer, he would have been quite as strong in his criticisms of modernity as Charles. In one of Digby's more whimsical pieces, two stumps are holding a conversation. One is a young 1920s stump, the other had seen service in the Golden Age. The young stump has been moaning. The older one points out how much easier life is for modern stumps. 'I wonder how you youngsters would appreciate a yorker on the toe from Kortright,' he exclaims, by way of clinching the argument.

Despite the conversation of the stumps, one might still question the conclusions of Demon and Lobster about the cricket of their time. The days of one's early cricket, when viewed from an appreciable distance, tend to assume a golden hue. The bad moments get forgotten, the good undergo a certain magnification. They were days, after all, when prospects seemed more wide-ranging, vigour more boundless, intimations of mortality less obtrusive. So it is not altogether surprising to find that the ailing Digby of the 1920s and the elderly Charles of the 1940s were not wholly objective in their assessments of their Golden Age.

As we have seen, it was a far from perfect time in a number of ways. It was not a Golden Age, for example, in the way it treated its professionals. It was neither a particularly just nor compassionate age, and it was not a totally honest one, as the under-counter payments to amateurs bear witness. The players too, being only human, from time to time showed the less attractive side of their natures. Pride, loss of temper, envy, petty-mindedness, deceit were not unknown. Since the days of Adam, men have been fallible creatures and, even if given a game of such potential for perfection as cricket, will still do their human best to make a nonsense of it! The Golden Age was unexceptional in this respect. There was no superior species at play in those times, no paragons of an especial virtue. The standard of play was much improved on what had gone before, yet not entirely comparable with what came after. The Golden Age represented an important time of development, when enormous improvements occurred in many aspects of the game. Maybe because of this, too many claims are sometimes made for its standards.

In wicket-keeping, modernity arrived in the sequence which led from MacGregor, through Lilley and Storer, to Strudwick. In this process cheerful stoppers like Surrey's Harry Wood and Tom Russell of Essex were gradually eclipsed by more rounded skills. In contrast, the fielding remained at a very low level. The evidence of photography is most damning. More often than not, outfielders stand motionless; close fielders fail to arch their backs. They display no interest in the ball until it is well on its way to them. Digby's criticism of fielders as "little mounds of earth" was very justified.

In bowling, as roundarm faded, so the possibilities of overarm were more fully exploited, most notably in the development of swing, fast seam bowling and slow leg-breaks and googlies. Really fast bowling replaced much that was merely medium. Slow jacks-of-all-trades, tossing up an off-break here, a leg-break there, were gradually superseded by the specialist spinner. There was less emphasis in the Golden Age on the containment of the batsman than in later years. In such an atmosphere a lob bowler could still operate with some success and the overarm leg-spinners developed (although, ironically, it was the success of the latter which finally put paid to the former). Bowling tended to be less tight but more adventurous.

It is not so much in bowling, therefore, as in batting that the Golden Age compares less favourably with later times. Photographs (particularly the fine ones of George Beldam) give decisive proof to a certain lack of all-round proficiency. Of course there are the famous shots of Trumper driving and Ranji gliding. One has to admire the full face of Archie MacLaren's bat as he drives on the front foot, whilst the photographs of C. B. Fry, though a little studied in their elegance, reveal a complete mastery of back-foot play. Other photographs, however, are less impressive. R. E. Foster, one of the brightest amateur talents, who scored two famous centuries for the Gentlemen at Lord's in 1900 when playing alongside Demon and Lobster, looks very unsettled before Beldam's camera. His front-foot play is ponderous and fraught with peril. Johnny Tyldesley, one of the most exciting of professional batsmen, cuts dangerously close to the body and looks surprisingly stiff at other times. Essex's Bob Carpenter, playing on the offside off the back foot, displays a gap between bat and pad like the proverbial barn door . . . Examples abound. For every three photographs which would delight a modern coach there is one which would make him wince.

This very variable standard in the Golden Age did produce one big benefit for the spectators, in that both runs and wickets came more freely. The bat was swung with considerably fewer inhibitions. A Beldam shot of Grace is instructive in this respect. The ball has pitched on his off stump, a little short of a length. Down the pitch towards it has gone his giant front foot, across the line has gone his bat, and the ball is soaring to the mid-wicket boundary. Although this was probably a shot of his later years, developed to cope with physical limitations, Grace was equally uninhibited as a young man. His technique, he declared, was to play himself in for just one over or two, after which he 'placed' balls for runs, 'however straight and good the length'. What a marvellous limited-overs player Grace would have been!

Golden Age cricket, then, was eminently watchable and much of the batting, despite any technical limitations, was very free. It has been calculated that Gilbert Jessop, over his entire first-class career, scored at the extraordinary rate of 80 runs per hour. Beldam's photographs, showing him making some huge blows to leg and a savage swat into the covers off the front foot, encourage belief in the statistic. Most arresting of all is a view, from mid-off, of Jessop jumping out to drive. Such is his ferocity of expression, such the belligerent intent, that the comments of a mid-off who happened to face Jessop in a country house match spring readily to mind: 'I was in a state of nervous apprehension, watching those forearm muscles of his twitching with eager tension. Presently I heard a ball – I did not see it – whizz past my right ear and crash against the boundary.' Jessop's scoring rate was all his own, but there were several other remarkably swift scorers. Frank Crawford is said to have scored all his runs at 61 an hour, Trumper at 56, Ranji 50 and Maclaren 48. Charles Fry and Stanley Jackson had the less spectacular, but still impressive, rate of 40.

It is in the strength of its personalities, as well as in its scoring power, that the Golden Age compares most favourably with other times. In the professional ranks were all manner of men, whose homely virtues and human failings drew a very ready sympathy from the ring. Whatever the weather, whatever the state of play, there was the imperturbability of Tom Hayward and the sprightly optimism of Bobby Abel. There was the solid good humour of Tom Russell and the dour determination of Bob Carpenter. The impulsiveness of Billy Brockwell was matched by the dependability of Walter Mead, Tom Richardson's breezy serenity by Bill Lockwood's unpredictability, Albert Trott's sense of adventure by Dick Lilley's discretion.

Then there were the flamboyant amateurs, and, at their head, Grace, massively genial and intimidating, with Ranji, exotic and forgivably overbearing. Arrayed behind these was an impressive brotherhood, its scope of personality most wide. It stretched from the confident self-belief of F. S. Jackson to the enigmatic self-doubt of F. G. Bull, from the coolness of MacGregor to the extrovert bluntness of Woods, from Frederick Fane, the perfect English gentleman, to Sir Tim O'Brien, the not completely perfect Irishman. There was the singlemindedness of the not-very-talented Hawke and the engaging tactlessness of the multi-talented Fry. If one should be shocked by an over-boisterous Wynyard or an opinionated MacLaren, one could be reassured by the cheerful humility of a Lucas or a Jessop.

Demon and Lobster fitted easily into this colourful world. Eccentricity, in the form of exaggerated behaviour, was welcomed in the Golden Age. How else could W.G. have got away with things so long? How could Key have captained Surrey, or Owen Essex? And a man who by bowling underarm brought the past pulsating back to life showed as acceptable an eccentricity as the gentleman athlete who beat the professional fast bowlers at their own game. It is unlikely that Charles would have admitted to one grain of eccentricity. He simply got on with doing what he most enjoyed, bowling at the limits of his considerable physical resources. Even as the professionals trembled before him, he would have failed to see the funny side, the humour in the role reversal. Digby, however, as has been suggested, with his more acute perception of the ridiculous, accepted and even cultivated his eccentricities.

Apart from their shared status as Gentlemen, they had little else in common in their approach to the game. The one used brain, the other brawn. The one had a highly developed sense of responsibility towards his own side, the other tended to play for himself, in much the way that fast bowlers always have. Yet, conversely, the more selfish player was the truer amateur, someone who devoted his life to sport and who paid for all his pleasures, whereas the other, the champion of 'pure' cricket, was forced by circumstances to adopt the uncomfortable, hypocritical position of the paid amateur.

Both shared the same unlucky fate that they never played for England, yet both were, for a time, of the highest class. But opportunities for Test selection were very limited, with the Australians the only visitors, every three years. It was the Demon's bad luck that in his two best seasons of 1897 and 1898 England did not take the field. Digby was similarly unlucky in the seasons of 1900 and 1901. Both men fully justify their inclusion in Christopher Martin-Jenkins' recent selection of the best XI never to play for England.

Charles and Digby themselves remained perfectly happy to have achieved their ultimate distinction in representing the Gentlemen at Lord's, still, in their day, the highest of accolades. It was something on which they always looked back with great content. Indeed, as they looked back, so the less agreeable aspects of their careers receded . . . The throwing controversy, the accusations of unfair play, the bickering at The Oval, the impossibility of holding an ageing, demoralized team together . . . It was not long before both men were able to look back on their playing days as a truly Golden Age.

Succeeding generations haven't always agreed with them. The ages of Hobbs and Sutcliffe, of Edrich and Compton, of Trueman and

Statham have each had their advocates. Yet there has always been a nostalgic warmth for the era of walrus moustaches, gaily striped blazers, beribboned boaters and underarm bowlers. Secure and confident, it remains encapsulated in a more simple England, before World War destroyed much of its youth and challenged its values. Some of its spirit survives down the years, for the players of the Golden Age, amateur and professional, possessed one quality which quite transcended all the problems of their time and which speaks to us as powerfully today. It was their love of cricket, passionate, simple, almost child-like, which characterized their age and made it golden. Demon and Lobster, for all their differences, united in this love. With all his heart Charles echoed Digby's cry: 'For eight months I exist! For four I live!'

"On the Free List at the Oval."

Farewell

Farewell! this age that creepeth on apace,
Deadens the life within the once strong hands,
Deadens the grip, that then, as hardened bands
Of steel coerced the well-worn willow face
  Unto my needs; – old bat, farewell!

Farewell! this age that ever gaineth speed
Leadens the limbs, – no more the rhythmic run
Lightens the load, that in the blazing sun
I daily bore, bowling I gave no heed
  Unto the hour; – old ball, farewell!

Farewell! this age that creepeth on apace
Leaves me the memories of a former day,
Leaves me the love of the great game they play
Those younger men; I gladly yield them place
  A looker on; – old friends, farewell!

D.L.A.J.

Bibliography

Alcock, C. W., *Famous Cricketers & Cricket Grounds*, Hudson & Kearns, News Of The World, 1895

Allen, David Rayvern, *A Word From Arlott*, Pelham, 1983

Allen, David Rayvern, *Arlott on Cricket*, Collins, 1984

Allen, David Rayvern, *Another Word From Arlott*, Pelham, 1985

Altham, H. S., *A History of Cricket (Vol 1)*, Allen & Unwin, 1926

Alverstone & Alcock, *Surrey Cricket*, Longmans, 1902

Arlott, John, *Concerning Cricket*, Longmans, 1949

Ashley-Cooper, F. S., *Cricket Highways and Byways*, Allen & Unwin, 1927

Bailey, Thorn & Wynne-Thomas, *Who's Who of Cricketers*, Newnes, 1984

Bardswell, Emily, *Played On*, Horace Marshall, 1898

Barlow, R. G., *Batting and Bowling*, Bussey

Beldam & Fry, *Great Batsmen, Their Methods at a Glance*, Macmillan, 1905

Beldam & Fry, *Great Bowlers & Fielders*, Macmillan, 1906

Bettesworth W. A., *Chats On The Cricket Field*, Merritt & Hatcher, 1910

Bray, Charles, *Essex County Cricket*, Convoy Publications, 1950

Collings, T. C. (ed.), *Cricket*, Fisher Unwin, 1900

Darwin, Bernard, *W. G. Grace*, Duckworth, 1934

Deadman & Sheppard, *The Bardswells, Fact & Fiction*, Private, 1979

Ellis, Clive, *C. B. The Life of Charles Burgess Fry*, Dent, 1984

French, E. Gerald, *The Cornerstone of English Cricket*, Hutchinson, 1948

Frith, David, *The Golden Age of Cricket, 1890–1914*, Omega, 1983

Frith, David, *The Fast Men*, Van Nostrand Rheinhold, 1975

Frith, David, *The Slow Men*, Allen & Unwin, 1984

Bibliography

Fry, C. B., *The Book of Cricket*, Newnes, 1899
Fry, C. B., *Life Worth Living*, Eyre & Spottiswoode, 1939
Goldman, J. W., *Bibliography of Cricket*, Private, 1937
Gordon, Sir Home, *Background of Cricket*, Barker, 1939
Grace, W. G., *Cricket*, Arrowsmith, 1891
Grayson, Edward, *Corinthians & Cricketers*, Naldrett Press, 1955
Green, Benny (ed.), *Wisden Book of Obituaries*, Macdonald, 1986
Green, Benny (ed.), *Wisden Anthology, 1864–1900*, Macdonald, 1979
Hawke, Lord, *Recollections & Reminiscences*, Williams & Norgate, 1924
Hawke, Harris & Gordon, *W. G. Grace, The Memorial Biography*, Constable, 1919
Hayward, Tom, *Cricket*, Spalding, 1907
Hodgson, R. L., ('Country Vicar') *Cricket Memories*, Methuen, 1930
Hodgson, R. L., *Second Innings*, Hutchinson, 1933
Hutchinson, H. (ed.), *Cricket*, Country Life, 1903
Jennings, Grenville, *Cricket On Old Picture Postcards*, Reflections Of A Bygone Age, 1985
Jephson, Arthur W., *My Work In London*, Pitman, 1910
Jephson, Digby L. A., *A Few Overs*, Heffer, 1913
Jephson, Digby L. A., *A Fragment*, Everett 1903
Jephson, John Mounteney, *Shakspere, His Birthplace, Home & Grave*, (London), 1864
Jephson, Lina, *Songs For Sailormen*, A. L. Hants, 1911
Jephson, Maurice. D., *An Anglo-Irish Miscellany*, Allen Figgis, 1964
Jephson, R. Mounteney, *Through The Keyhole*, Routledge, 1877
Jessop, Gilbert, *A Cricketer's Log*, Hodder & Stoughton, 1922
Jessop, Gilbert, (ed.) *Cricket*, Pearson, 1903
Jessop, Gilbert, *Cricket*, Arrowsmith, 1903
Kent, William, *Fifty Years A Cricket Watcher*, Cricket Book Society, 1946
Kynaston, David, *Bobby Abel, Professional Batsman*, Secker & Warburg, 1982
Laver, Frank, *An Australian Cricketer On Tour*, Chapman & Hall, 1905
Lemmon, David, *Percy Chapman*, Macdonald, 1985
Lewis, R. R., *The History of Brentwood School*, Private, 1981
Leveson Gower, Henry, *Cricket Personalities*, Williamson, 1925
Leveson Gower, Henry, *Off & On The Field*, Stanley Paul, 1953
Lilley, A. A., *Twenty Four Years Of Cricket*, Mills & Boon, 1912
Martin-Jenkins & Morrell, *Cricket: A Way Of Life*, Century, 1984
Mason, Ronald, *Jack Hobbs*, Hollis & Carter, 1960
Midwinter, Eric, *W. G. Grace – His Life & Times*, Allen & Unwin, 1981
Morrah, Patrick, *The Golden Age Of Cricket*, Eyre & Spottiswoode, 1967
Peebles, Ian, *Straight From The Shoulder*, Hutchinson, 1968
Pridham, C. H. B., *The Charm Of Cricket Past & Present*, Jenkins, 1949
Pycroft, James, *The Cricket-Field* (7th edition), Cricket Press, 1882
Ranjitsinhji, K. S., *The Jubilee Book Of Cricket*, Blackwood, 1897
Read. W. W., *Annals of Cricket*, Sampson Low, 1896
Robertson Glasgow, R. C., *46 Not Out*, Hollis & Carter, 1948
Ross, Alan, *Ranji, Prince Of Cricketers*, Collins, 1983
Ross, Gordon, *The Surrey Story*, Stanley Paul, 1957

Rundell, Michael, *A Dictionary Of Cricket*, Allen & Unwin, 1985

Sale, Charles, *Korty*, Ian Henry, 1986

Sewell, E. H. D., *An Outdoor Wallah*, Stanley Paul, 1945

Sewell, E. H. D., *Cricket Under Fire*, Stanley Paul, 1941

Sewell, E. H. D., *Cricket Up-to-Date*, Murray, 1931

Sewell, E. H. D., *From A Window At Lord's*, Methuen, 1937

Sewell, E. H. D., *Overthrows*, Stanley Paul, 1946

Sewell, E. H. D., *Well Hit! Sir*, Stanley Paul, 1947

Sewell, E. H. D., *Who's Won The Toss?*, Stanley Paul, 1944

'Sportsman' (ed.), *British Sports & Sportsmen (vol 15)*, Sporting Life, 1917

Standing, Percy (ed.), *Cricket Of Today & Yesterday (Vols 1 & 2)*, Blackwood, 1902

Strudwick, Herbert, *Twenty-Five Years Behind The Stumps*, Hutchinson, 1926

Tassel, Bryan, *Band of Brothers 1858–1958*, Private, 1958

Thomson, A. A., *Cricket My Happiness*, Museum Press, 1954

Thomson, A. A., *The Great Cricketer*, Hale, 1957

Thomson, A. A., *Vintage Elevens*, Pelham, 1969

Thorpe, James, *A Cricket Bag*, Wells Gardner, 1929

Trevor, Philip, *The Problems Of Cricket*, Sampson Low, 1907

Trevor, Philip, *Cricket & Cricketers*, Chapman & Hall, 1921

Turner & Miall, *The Edwardian Song Book*, Methuen, 1982

Walker, T. A., *History of Peterhouse*, Heffer, 1935

Warner, P. F., *The Book Of Cricket*, Dent, 1911

Warner, P. F., *Gentlemen v Players, 1806–1949*, Harrap, 1950

Warner, P. F., *Lord's, 1787–1945*, Harrap, 1946

Weigall, Gerald, *Cricket, The art of 'playing the game'*, Cricket Press, 1922

Wilde, E. E., *Ingatestone & The Essex Great Road*, Milford, 1913

Wisden Cricketers' Almanack, Wisden, 1890–1953

Woods, S. M. J., *My Reminiscences*, Chapman & Hall, 1925

PERIODICALS AND NEWSPAPERS

Abingdon Herald
Athletic News
Badminton Magazine
Berks & Oxon Advertiser
Black & White
Blackwood's Magazine
Bristol Evening News
Cambridge Chronicle & University Journal
Cambridge Daily News
Cambridge Independent Press
Cambridge Weekly News
Cassell's Magazine
Clapham Observer
Cricket

Bibliography

The Cricketer
The Cricket Field
Daily Chronicle
Daily Graphic
Daily Mail
Daily Telegraph
Eltham & District Times
Essex County Chronicle
Essex County Cricket Club Annuals
Essex Weekly News
Folkestone Argus
Folkestone Chronicle
C. B. Fry's Magazine
Hastings & St Leonards Advertiser
Hastings & St Leonards News
The King
Leytonstone Express & Independent
Manchester Guardian
Morning Leader
Neath Gazette
Northern Daily Telegraph (now Lancashire Evening Telegraph)
Oxford Times
Richmond & Twickenham Times
Richmond, Twickenham & Barnes Herald
Sporting Life
Sportsman
Star
Surrey Mirror
Taunton Echo
The Times
Walthamstow Express
Walthamstow & Leyton Guardian
West Ham & Stratford Express
Westminster Gazette
Wimbledon Boro News
Yorkshire Post

Index

191

Index